TABLE OF CONTENTS

DEDICATION

To Philip and Ann Callanan

PREFACE

Company law is a vast area and students are often confused by the complex web of rules and legal principles which govern the area. If the reasoning behind those principles are understood, the technical rules can be easier to understand. This book is designed to help students recognise and understand the basic rules and principles which govern company law.

Nearly all the rules relating to company law are intended to protect the investor or the creditor. The reason why these categories need protection is simple. First, companies are managed on a day-to-day basis by directors, and while the directors of small private companies are often the shareholders this is not always the case and there is no legal requirement that this should be the case. Therefore investors are placing their resources in a company that is often run by someone else, and while the members are the ultimate decision makers in a company, for practical reasons they cannot make all the decisions. The decision-making power is delegated to a board of directors who make decisions on their behalf. To prevent arbitrary use of the decision-making powers rules are provided which attempt to curb any potential abuses.

Secondly, limited liability companies, with which this book concerns itself, enjoy a privilege granted by the state which no other form of business enjoys viz, the liability of their members is limited. In the event that the underlying business and ultimately the company fails there is generally no recourse to the owners of the company. Bearing this in mind, along with the potential for abuse, legislation has attempted to protect creditors by imposing obligations on those natural personalities which are the face of the company and whose decisions can ultimately affect those who deal with the company.

Company law also takes into account the requirements of other players in a company's existence viz., the promoters, the directors, the employees, and those who may become involved with a company only when it is in financial difficulty such as examiners, liquidators and receivers. Since the last edition there have been many developments in the area of Corporate Governance and Enforcement. These developments have culminated in the passing of the Company Law Enforcement Act 2001. This Act is designed to create a new era of company law compliance and enforcement which was perceived as so lacking in our previous system of company law.

The text is aimed at students who are studying company law at certificate and diploma level in Institutes of Technology and other third-level colleges in Ireland. These students are invariably required to have a thorough, though not overly academic, knowledge of the subject. It is also written for students who have no legal training, but who are required to study company law either as part of a business degree or as a component of the professional accountancy examination. Law undergraduates who wish to obtain a sound knowledge of the first principles of company law before engaging in the more advanced works by

Keane, Courtney, Forde and Ellis should also benefit from the book.

I wish to express my gratitude to a number of people without whose advice and support this text would not have been completed: Dr John Ennis, Dr Michael Howlett, Dr Albert Keating, Dr Shane Kilcommins, Mr Jason O'Riordan, Mr Wil O'Leary, Mr Jim Nestor, Mr Ian Walsh, Ms Deirdre Byrne, Ms Caroline Larrissey, Mr Philip F. Callanan. Mrs Ann Callanan, Mr Michael Brennan-Roe, Ms Ailbhe O'Reilly, Ms Deirdre Greenan, Mr John Wolfe, Ms Monica Mernagh, Ms Sinead Callanan, Mr Mark Weston. Finally, all authors usually clog some area of office space with paper, coffee mugs and some more paper. In my case it seemed to be my entire home. My husband, Bertie Weston Jnr, never seemed to complain and for that and all his support a special word of thanks ... I promise one of these days!

Grainne Callanan
10 November 2002

Table of Cases

Table of Cases

Table of Statutes

Table of Articles of the Constitution of Ireland 1937

Table of Statutory Instruments

Table of EU Legislation

CHAPTER ONE

THE DEVELOPMENT OF COMPANY LAW

Introduction

Prior to 1844, persons who associated for the purpose of carrying on business generally did so by way of a partnership arrangement. Although companies existed, they were rare and enjoyed only by the privileged. This was because incorporation was possible only by obtaining a charter from the Crown or by the authority of a special Act of Parliament. In the 17th century joint stock companies emerged,[1] possessing some of the characteristics of the modern company, in that the shares were transferable, the assets and liabilities of the company were separate from those of the members and the company could sue in its own name. However, the main advantage of the modern company — the limited liability of the members — was not enjoyed by these companies, even where they were incorporated by charter, because some charters expressly conferred a power on the company to make calls or 'leviations' on the members to meet the company's liabilities. If the company failed to make such calls, creditors could step in and recover the amounts due from the members.[2]

In the early 17th century, persons with common business objectives began associating together by forming companies based on contract. The contract would determine the rules regarding membership and share transfers. Rather than applying for a charter, which was an expensive and tedious procedure, some of these companies purchased charters from defunct companies. Representing themselves as having charter status, many of these 'companies' succeeded in raising funds from the public. One of the more noted schemes was that of the South Sea Company. Formed in 1711, the company proposed a scheme whereby it would purchase the entire national debt (of £31 million) by either buying out the holders of the debt or offering them company shares in return for their holdings. On the basis of having an interest-bearing loan from the state, the company hoped to raise further monies to expand its trade. The company experienced difficulties for two reasons. First, it had paid an excessive price for the privilege of buying the national debt, and second, it was unable to expand its trade. However, it was the institution of legal proceedings against the company's bankers, the Sword Blade Company, which had been operating under an obsolete charter, that caused a panic among the South Sea investors. As a result, the value of the company's shares plummeted. Because of the government's heavy

---

1 The term 'stock' referred to 'stock-in-trade', and not to 'stocks and shares'.
2 *Salmon v. The Hamborough Co.* (1671) 1 Ch Cas 204.

involvement in the South Sea Company and the growing public disquiet about the fraudulent and speculative activities of company promoters in general, Parliament intervened with the passing of the Bubble Act 1720.

The Bubble Act 1720

The Bubble Act sought to check the rise in company promotions by prohibiting the formation of joint stock companies, except those incorporated by statute or charter. In an attempt to divert investment from other schemes into the South Sea Company, that company was granted an exemption under the Act. If the Act's principal objective was to save the South Sea Company, it failed. The loss of public confidence in joint stock companies caused by the Act, together with the events which had led to its introduction, caused a further downward spiral in the fortunes of the South Sea Company, which never fully recovered.

The Act did, however, exempt most partnerships from its effect, with the result that a new form of company emerged based on a combination of the partnership and trust concept. Using this device, the subscribers to these 'deed of settlement' companies would agree by deed to associate in an enterprise with a predetermined joint stock divided into shares. The deed usually provided for the vesting of the company's property in a board of trustees and the delegation of the management functions to a committee of directors. Like the joint stock company, the deed of settlement company was still treated as a partnership before the law and the liability of the members remained unlimited.

Nineteenth-Century Developments

In 1825 the Bubble Act was repealed and the Crown was given the power to grant charters which declared the extent of members' liability rather than exempting them totally from liability. Because applications for charters were still dealt with strictly, and as the statutory procedure remained expensive, most promoters continued to rely on the unincorporated association. In 1834 the Trading Companies Act was introduced which gave the Crown the power to grant — by way of letters patent — the privileges of incorporation. This Act did not, however, make provision for limiting the liability of members. In fact, it specifically provided that members were liable to the extent of a judgment against the company for up to three years after they had ceased to become members. This obvious disincentive to investors was rectified by the Chartered Companies Act 1837, which provided that limited liability could be conferred by letters patent to a specified amount per share.

In 1844 the Joint Stock Companies Act[3] introduced some of the features of modern company law. In particular, it provided for the following:

---

3 William Gladstone, who had become the President of the Board of Trade, chaired the Parliamentary Committee on Joint Stock Companies, whose Report led to the introduction of the Act.

(a) the incorporation of companies by registration, which obviated the need for incorporation by Royal Charter, letters of patent or an authorising Act of Parliament;
(b) the registration as companies of all associations with more than twenty-five members or with freely transferable shares;
(c) the introduction of publicity requirements; and
(d) the establishment of the office of the Registrar of Companies in England and Ireland.

Despite these developments, it was not until the passing of the Limited Liability Act 1855 that members of companies could enjoy limited liability, upon compliance with certain conditions, including the use of the word 'limited' at the end of the company's name. The Joint Stock Companies Act 1856 relaxed many of the conditions for registration and introduced for the first time the requirement that registered companies provide a memorandum and articles of association.

Ireland's Independence

By the early 20th century, several further pieces of legislation had been introduced which sought to amend, repeal or consolidate the legal framework governing companies. The Companies Acts of 1900 and 1907 were significant in that they not only recognised the small private company, but also exempted it from many of the statutory requirements regarding publicity. Following Ireland's Independence in 1921, little was done to amend the Companies (Consolidation) Act 1908, which remained the principal legislation governing companies in Ireland until 1963.[4] In 1951 a Committee was established with the remit of investigating the entire area of company law. Its findings were reported in 1958 and although some of its recommendations were given legal effect in the Companies Act 1959, it was the Companies Act of 1963 ('the Principal Act') that embodied many of the Committee's recommendations.[5]

The Principal Act

The most significant changes effected by the Principal Act relate to the following:

(a) the requirement to maintain proper books of account by all companies;
(b) the imposition of an obligation on all companies to present annual accounts to shareholders;
(c) the introduction of measures designed to protect oppressed shareholders;

---

4 Although a Committee was appointed in 1927 to investigate the law relating to bankruptcy and the winding up of companies, no legislation was introduced following its Report.
5 The draftsmen of the Principal Act also embodied some of the recommendations of the 1962 Report of the Jenkins Committee in the UK.

(d) the imposition of penalties for fraudulent trading;

(e) a relaxation of the common law doctrine of *ultra vires*, whereby third parties could now enforce transactions against the company which were outside its stated objects;[6]

(f) the requirement that auditors be professionally qualified; and

(g) the requirement to maintain a register of directors' shareholdings.

The Principal Act remains the cornerstone of modern Irish company law. However, given the number of amendments that have been made to it by successive pieces of legislation and statutory instruments, there is now an obvious need for consolidating legislation.

Subsequent Legislation

Between 1963 and 2001 successive Companies Legislation was introduced as follows:

1. The Companies (Amendment) Act 1977 simplified procedures in relation to share transfers in public companies.

2. The Companies (Amendment) Act 1982 introduced relatively minor changes in respect of company registration and other miscellaneous matters.

3. The Companies (Amendment) Act 1983 gave effect to the Second EU Directive on Company Law which was mostly concerned with rules governing the formation and capital requirements of public companies.

4. The Companies (Amendment) Act 1986 gave effect to the Fourth EU Directive on Company Law which primarily concerned publicity, disclosure and the accounts requirements of all companies.

5. The Companies (Amendment) Act 1990 was introduced in response to the impending collapse of the Goodman Group of Companies (such an occurrence would have had a disastrous effect on the Irish beef industry and the economy as a whole). The Act introduced into Irish law, for the first time, the concept of 'court protection' for companies which, although in financial difficulties, have a chance of survival if a rescue package can be organised. Under the Act the court, by appointing an examiner to formulate rescue proposals, can give the company a temporary reprieve from actions by creditors whose rights against the company are effectively 'frozen' for the duration of the court protection. This Act is considered in detail in Chapter 27.

6. The Companies Act 1990.

7. The Companies (Amendment) Act 1999.

8. The Companies (Amendment) (No.2) Act 1999.

9. The Company Law Enforcement Act 2001.

---

6 See Chapter 7.

4

The Companies Act 1990

The Companies Act 1990 is the most comprehensive piece of legislation introduced since the Principal Act. It was not hurried into law in the same manner as the Amendment Act of the same year. Rather, its passage was prolonged as successive governments between 1987 and 1990 exerted their influence upon its content by way of amendments before it finally became law on the 22 December 1990. The Act, containing thirteen parts, introduced substantial changes to company law including *inter alia* the following:

(a) the transfer of the power to appoint company inspectors from the Minister to the court;[7]
(b) the imposition of further restrictions on transactions between companies and their directors;[8]
(c) the introduction of disclosure requirements in relation to certain persons' interests in shares held in companies;[9]
(d) the prohibition of insider dealing;[10]
(e) the introduction of further legislative provisions in relation to liquidations and receivers;[11]
(f) the imposition of restrictions and disqualifications on company directors;[12]
(g) the implementation of the European Union's Eighth Directive which requires a minimum standard for persons who can be company auditors.

The Companies (Amendment) Act 1999

This act was introduced to amend and extend Part IV (relating to disclosure of interests in shares) and Part V (relating to insider dealing) of the Companies Act 1990, in order to permit stabilising activities in relation to the issue or sale of securities and other related matters.

The Companies (Amendment) (No. 2) Act 1999

The Companies (Amendment) (No. 2) Act 1999 makes provisions for the following:

(a) to exempt certain companies and partnerships from the requirement to have accounts audited;
(b) to impose a requirement on Irish companies that they carry on an activity within the State;

---

7 Part II of the Act.
8 Part III of the Act.
9 Part IV of the Act.
10 Part V of the Act.
11 Parts VI and VIII of the Act.
12 Part VII of the Act.

(c) to require, subject to certain exceptions, that one director of an Irish incorporated company be resident in the State;

(d) to limit the number of directorships any person can have to 25;

(e) to provide increased powers to the Registrar of Companies in relation to the striking off of companies; and

(f) to amend aspects of legislation relating to the court protection procedure.

The Company Law Enforcement Act 2001 (CLEA)

This Act was introduced following the recommendations of the Working Group on Company Law Compliance and Enforcement, which were published in March 1999. The Working Group found that Irish company law was characterised by a culture of non-compliance, with many companies and officers failing to fulfil their obligations under the Companies Acts. The Group also found that, in overall terms, very few of the offences under the Companies Act were ever prosecuted. The primary recommendation of the Group was the establishment of an independent statutory officer who would have general responsibility for the enforcement of company law. This recommendation and several others made by the Working Group were given a legislative footing in the Company Law Enforcement Act. The main provisions of this Act relate to the following:

(a) the establishment of the office of Director of Corporate Enforcement ('Director') — discussed later in this chapter;

(b) the transfer of many of the functions of the Minister relating to the investigation and enforcement of the Companies Acts to the Director;

(c) the introduction of additional measures to improve compliance with company law and filing obligations;

(d) the establishment of the Company Law Review Group as a statutory body;

(e) the amendment of existing legislative provisions relating to accounts and audit;

(f) the amendment of existing legislative provisions governing financial transactions between companies and their directors.

While the Companies Acts 1963–2001 are the primary legislation governing companies in Ireland, a number of other statutes also impinge upon companies including, *inter alia,* the Bankruptcy Acts, Stock Transfer Act, the Competition Acts, successive Finance Acts, Takeover and Merger legislation and Employment, Health and Safety legislation.

Other Sources of Law

While legislation is clearly the principle source of company law, it is not the only one. Indeed, the legal framework governing companies in Ireland is derived from several different sources including the following:

1. Common Law and Equity;
2. The Law of the European Union.

1. Common Law and Equity

Since the nineteenth Century, the courts have played an important role in the development of company law. Where legislation ends, case-law begins; and this is as true of company law as it is with any other branch of the law. In interpreting legislative provisions and adjudicating disputes, judges have developed key principles which are still regarded as central to company law today. While the courts of equity were the main influence, the common law has also made its own unique contribution. The influence of judges on company law is abundantly clear from the landmark decisions which are frequently cited in modern litigation. The speeches of Lord Macnaghten and his fellow Lords in the case of *Salomon v Salomon*[13] are regularly cited in modern cases concerning the issue of a company's separate personality. The principle, in *Ashbury Railway Carriage Co. v Riche*[14], that contracts entered into by a company for purposes other than those set out in its object clause are *ultra vires* void and unenforceable remains intact today despite subsequent legislative provisions to temper the effect of this principle. The rule in *Foss v Harbottle*, which states that when a wrong is done to the company it is the company who is the proper plaintiff, is a fundamental rule of company law. The fiduciary duty of directors towards the company, originating in the courts of equity, remains the yardstick against which a director's action will be judged.

2. The Law of the European Union

Accession to the European Union in 1973 created new legal obligations for the Irish State and its people. As part of the European Union's objective of creating a single market, a harmonisation process began which included *inter alia* the area of company law. To effect the harmonisation of company law a number of Directives have been adopted by the European Council, some of which have been implemented in Ireland by way of the statutory reforms mentioned earlier. Other directives have been given the force of law by Ministerial Regulations and Statutory Instruments.

The implementation of these directives has contributed in no small way to the existing body of Irish company law. The First Directive introduced measures aimed at protecting creditors who are dealing with companies that have not been properly registered or with companies that are acting outside their capacity.[15] The

---

13 [1897] AC 22.
14 (1875) LR 7 HL 653.
15 Council Directive (68/151/EEC) [1968] OJ 68, which was implemented in Ireland by SI 163/1973.

Second Directive imposes minimum capital requirements for public limited companies.[16] The Fourth Directive introduced disclosure requirements on most companies.[17] The Seventh Directive introduced requirements that all companies with subsidiary undertakings prepare group accounts.[18] The harmonisation of the qualifications of auditors through the introduction of a minimum standard throughout all member states was achieved by the Eight Directive on company law.[19] The Twelfth Directive introduced for the first time the concept of the single-member private company.[20]

Other Directives have also been introduced which, though not falling within the company law numbered series, have a significant impact on companies. These include Directives relating to the listing of company securities[21] and the issuing of prospectuses in connection with the public offering of securities.[22]

Of further relevance to companies is the convention negotiated by the Member States that deals with the mutual recognition of companies' and the enforcement of judgments on cross-border insolvency.

A Council Regulation of 1985[23] provides for the establishment of European Economic Interest Grouping (or EEIG). This is designed to enable existing business undertakings that have common interests, but are situated in different Member States, to form an independent body to provide common services. The members are jointly and severally liable for the liabilities of this entity. The regulation sets out the requirements for the formation and registration of an EEIG. Although EEIGs have full legal capacity, it is a matter of national law as to whether or not they will be afforded corporate personality in each member state of the European Union.

As part of the EU Financial Services Action Plan (FSAP), a number of further initiatives in relation to company law have been taken. In 2001, the Council

---

16 Council Directive (77/91/EEC) [1977] OJ L26/1, which was implemented in Ireland by the Companies (Amendment) Act 1983.
17 Council Directive (78/660/EEC) [1978] OJ L222/11, which was implemented in Ireland by the Companies (Amendment) Act 1986.
18 Council Directive (83/349/EEC) [1983] OJ L193/1, which was implemented in Ireland by SI 201/1992.
19 Council Directive (84/253/EEC) [1984] OJ L126/20, the substantive aspects of which have been implemented in Ireland by the Companies Act 1990.
20 Council Directive (89/667/EEC) [1989] OJ L395/40, which was implemented in Ireland by SI 275/1994 and which came into force in October 1994.
21 Council Directive (79/279/EEC) [1979] OJ L66/21, which governs the admission of securities to listing on official stock exchanges, Council Directive (80/390/EEC) [1980] OJ L100/1, which relates to listing particulars, and Council Directive (82/121/EEC) [1982] OJ L48/26, which introduced reporting requirements for companies once they are listed.
22 Council Directive (89/298/EEC) [1989] OJ L124/8.
23 2137/85 [1985] OJ L199/1.

adopted a regulation to establish a European Company Statute to make it easier for business to operate across the EU. The Commission has also published proposals for Directives on Prospectuses, Insider Dealing and Market Manipulation. The European Union is also in the process of introducing legislation to regulate International Accounting Standards.

Company Law Enforcement and Review

1. *The Director of Corporate Enforcement*

Part 2 of the CLEA 2001 makes provision for the creation of a Director of Corporate Enforcement. By virtue of Section 7, the Director shall be appointed by the Minister. A person cannot be appointed a Director, nor can a Director continue in office if he is nominated or appointed as a member of either House of the Oireachtas, the European Parliament or a Local Authority. The person appointed as the Director shall hold office for a period not exceeding five years, renewable for a further period of five years, and on such terms and conditions as the Minister, with the consent of the Minister for Finance, thinks fit. The Director shall not hold any other office or employment.

Acting Director

The Minister may appoint a person to be Acting Director where the Director is absent from duty or from the State, is unable to perform the functions of Director, is suspended from office or where a vacancy arises in the office of Director. The Acting Director can only be appointed for a maximum of six months during the vacancy in the office of Director.

Functions and Powers of Director

The Director must perform the functions and duties conferred by the CLEA 2001 and any other legislation, and shall be assisted in the performance of those functions by the officers of the Director. Officers include an officer of the Minister assigned to the Director, any member of An Gárda Síochána seconded to the Director and any person employed by the Minister or the Director under a contract for service or otherwise.

Section 12 (1) specifies the functions of the Director as follows:

(a) to enforce the Companies Acts, including by the prosecution of offences by way of summary proceedings;

(b) to encourage compliance with the Companies Acts;

(c) to investigate instances of suspected offences under the Companies Acts;

(d) at his or her discretion, to refer cases to the Director of Public Prosecutions where he has reasonable grounds for believing that an indictable offence under the Companies Acts has been committed;

(e) to exercise, in so far as the Director feels it necessary or appropriate, a supervisory role over the activity of liquidators and receivers in the discharge of their functions under the Companies Acts;

(f) for the purpose of ensuring the effective application and enforcement of obligations, standards and procedures to which companies and their officers are subject, to perform such other functions in respect of any matters to which the Companies Acts relate as the Minister considers appropriate and may, by order, confer on the Director; and

(g) to perform such other functions as may be assigned to him by, or under, the Companies Acts or any other Act.

In performing his functions, the Director must be independent and may delegate them to one of his officers. Any of the Director's powers may be delegated by the Director except the power of delegation itself. Any such delegation is revocable at will by the Director.

Section 109 provides that where the Director has reasonable grounds for believing that a person has committed an offence, he may, without instituting court proceedings, levy fines in respect of summary offences, under the Companies Acts.

The Director has the power to apply to the High Court for orders to restrict or disqualify company directors and other officers. (See Chapter 16, Restriction and Disqualification of Directors.)

The Director is also given supervisory and intervention powers in certain receivership and liquidation procedures.

Transfer of Minister's functions and powers to Director

In addition to the above, Parts 1 and 2 of the Schedule of the CLEA 2001 lists the functions and powers of the Minister which are to be transferred to the Director. These include the power to direct the calling of an AGM, the power to apply to court for the production and inspection of books where the Minister believes an offence has been committed, powers in respect of appointing inspectors to investigate certain matters and the power to investigate share dealings.

Indemnification

Section 15 relieves the Director, or office of the Director, from liability in damage for anything done in good faith by him in the performance of a statutory function.

Director's Report

Under section 16, the Director shall present a report to the Minister, within three months after the end of each year, about the performance of the Director's functions and other activities of the Director in that year. The Minister shall cause a copy of the report to be laid before the Dáil and Seanad within two months of receipt of the report. The Director's report shall include information about matters as the Minister may direct. In addition to this annual report, the Director must give any information about the performance of the Director's functions as the Minister may from time to time request. Where such a request is made, the Director must account to an appropriately established committee of either House of the Oireachtas.

It should be noted, that where the Director is presenting his report or complying with a Ministerial request to supply information, the Director is not required to furnish any information or answer any questions which would, in the opinion of the Director, prejudice the performance by the Director of his functions.

Information obtained by virtue of the performance by the Director, an advisor to the Director, or officer or former officer of Director, or any other person, must not be disclosed except in accordance with the law, unless it is necessary to do so, as part of the Director's investigative and enforcement functions.

Removal of Director

The Minister may at any time, for stated reasons, remove the Director from office. Where this occurs, the Minister must cause to be laid before the Dáil and the Seanad, a statement of the reasons for the removal.

2. The Companies Registration Office

The Companies Registration Office is the authority for the incorporation of new companies and the registration of business names in the Republic of Ireland. The Office is also responsible for the receipt and registration of post incorporation documents, for enforcement of the filing requirements of companies and for the provision of information to the public. Where necessary the Registrar can impose fines for late filing of certain returns and bring non-compliant officers to court. The Registrar of Companies co-operates closely with the Director of Corporate Enforcement.

3. The Company Law Review Group

The Company Law Review Group is an expert body with the responsibility for advising the Minister for Enterprise, Trade and Employment on the review and development of company law in Ireland. The Group was established in 2000 but was not given statutory recognition until the enactment of the Company Law Enforcement Act 2001. This Act sets out the functions and authority of the Group. The Group operates on a two-yearly cycle and its first report was published in February 2001. The report is substantial and makes recommendations with respect to the following:

(a) simplification of company law for all companies, in particular for small and medium-sized private companies;

(b) clarification of the law regarding *ultra vires* transactions;

(c) codification of directors' obligations which have to date existed in common law rather than in legislation;

(d) corporate litigation;

(e) the regulation of insolvency practitioners;

(f) the implementation of recommendations made by the Review Group on Auditing which reported to the Minister in November 2000;

(g) mitigating the effects of strike-off for creditors;

(h) consolidation of the companies code.

In its second two-yearly work programme, the Review Group is focusing on the following matters:

(a) a new Companies Bill which is to replace the existing companies code, and which will be composed of ten Acts of the Oireachtas and other secondary legislation;

(b) the requirement to simplify transactions involving stocks and shares with particular emphasis on how tradeable paper is offered to the public;

(c) the duties and rights applicable to shareholders and company officers in share dealings;

(d) the law relating to the winding-up of companies;

(e) the law related to charges and securities;

(f) the Regulations in Table A (First Schedule to the 1963 Companies Act) which were not dealt with in the First Report of the Company Law Review Group;

(g) the development of EU proposals which impinge upon company law, by ensuring that any recommendations it makes dovetail with EU developments.

CHAPTER TWO

COMPANIES IN GENERAL

Introduction

A company is probably more of a concept than a thing. This concept defines both the relationship between the persons who associate for a common purpose under a specific business form and the relationship between that business form and others.

Several theories, which often overlap, have been proposed to describe these relationships including *inter alia* the following:

1. the entity theory;
2. the concession theory; and
3. the contract theory.

1. The Entity Theory

A company is an artificial entity created for the purpose of conducting business. The basic elements of this theory are as follows.

(a) The company has the power to conduct business in its own name. It can sue and be sued. It may enter into contracts. It must pay taxes.
(b) The company is formed by a grant of authority from the state evidenced by a 'certificate of incorporation' which signifies that the company is a legal person.
(c) The company is regarded as a separate legal person by those who deal with it. However, in certain circumstances the court and indeed company legislation may refuse to allow the 'separate entity' analysis to develop to its logical conclusion.[1]
(d) As an artificial entity, with no mind or body of its own, a company requires a natural person to act on its behalf. Accordingly, management is vested in a board of directors which, as agent for the company, can bind the company by making and effecting decisions on its behalf.

2. The Concession Theory

The Concession theory, which dates back to the late Roman empire, is based on the role of the State in the formation of companies. The idea behind the theory is that the privileges of incorporation are conferred by way of concession from the

---

1 See Chapter 6 for those circumstances whereby the courts and the legislature have pierced this 'corporate veil'.

State, which can in turn impose restrictions on company behaviour or revoke the privileges in certain circumstances. Although the theory was more popular during the times when company charters were subject to restrictions and limitations, it is still relevant for the modern company, which owes its existence to the State. Although the process of incorporation has become largely procedural, with very little direct State action, responsibility for company law rests firmly with the Minister for Enterprise, Trade and Employment. The Registrar of Companies has also been conferred with significant supervisory and, indeed, decision-making powers in company law matters.

3. The Contract Theory

Another theory is that the constitutional documentation of the company represents a contract between the company and its shareholders, and between the shareholders themselves. This contract determines the business activities permissible for the company, together with the means by which those activities can be achieved. It also determines many of the internal rules and procedures which must be followed by the agents of the company. Section 25 of the Principal Act gives legislative recognition to this contractual relationship. Directors, as agents for the company, may have the power to bind the company by entering into contracts on its behalf. However, this power is subject to an important principle of agency law, namely that directors must act within the scope of their actual or apparent authority.

Types of Companies

There are three basic types of company, which can be classified according to the manner in which they are formed.

1. Chartered Corporations

Chartered corporations were created by the assent of the British Crown, which by the grant of a charter or letters patent conferred the privileges of incorporation. Many chartered bodies still exist in Ireland, including the Law Society of Ireland, the Honourable Society of Kings Inns, Trinity College Dublin and the Bank of Ireland.[2] Since Ireland's Independence, the Executive has assumed the power to grant charters although it has never done so.[3]

---

2 See *Geoghegan v. Institute of Chartered Accountants in Ireland* [1995] 3 IR 86, where the Supreme Court rejected the plaintiff's contention that the charter of the defendant body had not survived the enactment and coming into operation of the Irish Free State and Bunreacht na hÉireann.

3 By virtue of Article 49.1.2 and 28 of Bunreacht na hÉireann and section 377(4) of the Principal Act.

2. Statutory Companies

Statutory companies were granted their status by the authority of an Act of Parliament, and were usually conferred with special powers and monopolistic rights. Since Independence, most of these companies have been dissolved and their business undertakings transferred to new state bodies. However, several statutory companies have been established since 1921 whose objectives are considered to be of national importance, e.g. Aer Lingus, Aer Rianta, the Industrial Credit Company and the Agricultural Credit Company.

3. Registered Companies

The most common method of incorporation is by registration under the Companies Acts 1963–1990. The Acts set out the prescribed procedure which must be followed before registration can be effected by the Registrar of Companies. This procedure is considered further in Chapter 3.

Alternative Classification

Companies formed by any of the above methods may also be categorised according to the potential liability of their members. In this regard the liability of the members of the company may be limited or unlimited.

1. Companies Limited by Shares

Where companies are formed to carry on a profit-making activity, it is usual that such companies will have shares. Accordingly, profits can be divided among members on the basis of their percentage holdings. In such companies the liability of the members to contribute to the assets of the company is limited to the amount, if any, unpaid on their shares.

2. Companies Limited by Guarantee

The liability of the members to contribute to the assets of the company in a winding up is limited to the amount specified in the guarantee. This form of company is usually used by charitable companies because, as there is no sharing of profits, the division of the undertaking into shares is not necessary.

3. Unlimited Companies

The liability of the members is unlimited and, in the event that the company is wound up, they shall be liable to contribute to the assets of the company an amount sufficient for the payment of the company's debts and liabilities. It is for this reason that trading companies are rarely incorporated with unlimited liability. It is usual, although not necessary, for unlimited companies to have a share capital.

Public and Private Companies

Company law has always been based on the view that while the public company is the norm, the private company is the exception. This of course does not reflect the reality of modern business — far more private than public companies exist in Ireland. A private company is one with a share capital whose articles of association restrict the right to transfer its shares, limit the number of members to fifty (excluding employees and ex-employees), and prohibit any invitation to the public to subscribe for its shares or debentures.[4] Where default is made in complying with any of these provisions, a private limited company does not lose its corporate existence but it may forfeit many of the privileges and exemptions available to private companies.[5] It was not until the Companies (Amendment) Act 1983 that a public limited company was defined as one which is not a private company and whose memorandum states that the company is a public limited company.[6]

However, the differences between private and public companies are more significant than these definitions would seem to suggest. Certain requirements of the Companies Acts vary depending on whether a company is private or public. The most important of these relate to the following.

1. Membership

Section 5 of the Principal Act fixes the minimum number of members for a private company at two, and at seven for all other companies. If the number of members in a company falls below the legal minimum and that company carries on business for more than six months while the number is so reduced, members, who knew that it was carrying on business after the expiration of the six-month period, may be severally liable for the debts of the company contracted during that time.

It should be noted that since the introduction of the European Communities (Single-Member Private Limited Companies) Regulations 1994[7] it is now possible to incorporate a single-member private limited company. Therefore, private companies limited by shares or by guarantee can be converted into single-member companies, thus avoiding any potential difficulties that might arise should their membership fall below two.

Although the maximum number of members for a private company is limited to fifty, no such limit exists for public companies.

2. Capital

There is no minimum capital requirement for private companies. Public companies, on the other hand, are required to have a minimum share capital of

---

4 Section 33(1) of the Principal Act.
5 Section 34 of the Principal Act.
6 Section 2 of the Companies (Amendment) Act 1983.
7 SI 275/1994.

£30,000 (€38,092), at least 25 per cent of which must be paid up.[8] However, if a company appoints a person who is restricted under Part VII of the 1990 Companies Act, that company must have a minimum share capital of £50,000 (€63,487) in the case of a private company and £250,000 (€317,435) in the case of a public company.[9]

The ability of a private company to raise finance by way of capital is restricted somewhat because it is prohibited from offering its shares or debentures to the public. A public company, on the other hand, may raise capital in this way but is subject to the rules set out in the Companies Acts and, where appropriate, the European Communities (Stock Exchange) Regulations 1984[10] and the European Communities (Transferable Securities and Stock Exchange Regulations) 1992.[11]

Where new shares are being issued for cash consideration, companies must, as a general rule, offer them first to existing members. However, a private company may permanently exclude this rule by its articles of association. A public company can only do so for a period not exceeding five years, although this period can be extended for a further five years. Where shares are being issued for non-cash consideration, public limited companies are also subject to more stringent rules than private companies. These requirements are considered in Chapter 9.

3. Accounts and Annual Returns

Small and medium-sized private companies are exempt from many of the provisions of the Companies Acts relating to the filing of accounts and annual returns. Furthermore, certain small private limited companies are exempt from the requirements to have their accounts audited. (See Chapter 19, Accounts and Returns.)

4. Commencement of Business

A private company can commence trading once the certificate of incorporation has been issued by the Registrar of Companies. Even where the certificate of incorporation has been issued to a public company, it can only trade if it obtains a 'trading certificate' from the Registrar.[12] The certificate of trading will only be issued if the Registrar is satisfied that the company has allotted at least £30,000 (€38,092) in share capital and that 25 per cent of it has been paid up. The promotion and formation of all companies is considered further in Chapter 3.

---

8 Section 5(2) of the Companies (Amendment) Act 1983: see Chapter 16.
9 Section 150(3) of the Companies Act 1990.
10 SI 282/1984.
11 SI 202/1992.
12 Section 6 of the Companies (Amendment) Act 1983.

Other Types of Companies

1. Holding and Subsidiary Companies

The importance of the holding and subsidiary company relationship is recognised by a number of statutory provisions, including inter alia the following:

(a) a holding company must ordinarily prepare group accounts in which financial information pertaining to it and its subsidiaries is included; [13]

(b) at the end of each financial year, a holding company must generally include in its accounts, which are annexed to the annual return, information relating to the name and registered office of each subsidiary and various details relating to its shareholding in the subsidiary; and

(c) a subsidiary company is only permitted to hold shares in its holding company in limited circumstances.[14]

A company is a holding company of another company if any of the following situations prescribed by section 155 of the Principal Act exist:

(a) it is a member of that company and controls the composition of its board of directors; or

(b) it holds more than half in nominal value of that company's equity share capital; or

(c) it holds more that half in nominal value of the shares which carry voting rights; or

(d) the other company is a subsidiary of a subsidiary of the holding company.

Where a parent undertaking[15] is required to prepare and present group accounts under Regulation 5 of the European Communities (Companies: Group Accounts) Regulations 1992, an undertaking shall be deemed to be a subsidiary of another if, but only if:

   (a) that other —
       (i) holds a majority of the shareholders' or members' voting rights in the undertaking, or
       (ii) is a shareholder or member of it and controls the composition of its board of directors, or
       (iii) is a shareholder or member of it and controls alone, pursuant to an agreement with other shareholders or members, a majority of the shareholders' or members' voting rights; or
   (b) that other has the right to exercise a dominant influence over it —
       (i) by virtue of provisions contained in its memorandum or articles, or
       (ii) by virtue of a control contract; or

---

13 Section 150 of the Principal Act and Regulation 5 of the European Communities (Companies: Group Accounts) Regulations 1992: SI 201/1992.

14 Section 224 of the Companies Act 1990.

15 Undertaking includes a body corporate.

(c) that other has a participating interest in it and —
    (i) that other actually exercises a dominant influence over it, or
    (ii) that other and the subsidiary undertaking are managed on a unified basis; or
(d) the undertaking is a subsidiary of any undertaking which is that other's undertaking.[16]

2. Associated Companies

An associated company is one in which a company is beneficially entitled to more than 20 per cent in nominal value of the following:

(a) the voting shares of the company; or
(b) the allotted share capital of the company.

If a company is a subsidiary, it will not be an associated company.[17] Where a company has an interest in another company to the extent that the other company is an associated company, a note must be included in the annual accounts of the company, which is annexed to the annual return, specifying the registered office of the associated company, and the details of the interest held in that company.

3. Related Companies

The 1990 Companies Act introduced the concept of a related company. A company is related to another company if:

(a) that other company is its holding company or subsidiary; or
(b) more than half in nominal value of its equity share capital (as defined in section 155(5) of the Principal Act) is held by the other company and companies related to that other company (whether directly or indirectly, but other than in a fiduciary capacity); or
(c) more than half in nominal value of the equity share capital (as defined in section 155(5) of the Principal Act) of each of them is held by members of the other company (whether directly or indirectly, but other than in a fiduciary capacity); or
(d) that other company or a company or companies related to that other company together with a company or companies related to it are entitled to exercise or control the exercise of more than one half of the voting power at any general meeting of the company; or
(e) the businesses of the companies have been so carried on that the separate business of each company, or a substantial part thereof, is not readily identifiable; or
(f) if there is another company to which both companies are related.[18]

This definition of a related company clearly extends beyond the traditional view of group companies. Its relevance can be seen in various company law provisions.

---

16 Regulation 4(1) of the European Communities (Companies: Group Accounts) Regulations 1992: SI 201/1992.
17 Section 16(1)(b) of the Companies (Amendment) Act 1986.
18 Section 140(5) of the Companies Act 1990.

Under section 140 of the Companies Act 1990, companies may be liable to contribute to the assets of a related company in an insolvent winding up. Furthermore, the assets of related companies may be pooled in a winding-up situation.[19]

4. Single-Member Companies

Until October 1994 all companies had to have at least two members. Since the introduction of the European Communities (Single-Member Private Limited Companies) Regulations 1994[20] it has been possible to form a company with only one member. These regulations were introduced to give effect to the Twelfth EU Directive on single-member companies. The regulations alter the law relating to the affairs of private companies in the following manner:

(a) any enactment or rule of law ordinarily applicable to private companies shall apply to single-member companies;

(b) notwithstanding section 5 of the Principal Act, a private company with one member can now be formed;

(c) the sole member of a single-member company may dispense with the holding of an annual general meeting;

(d) instead of passing resolutions, sole members of single-member companies can make most decisions regarding the company by recording that decision in writing;

(e) the quorum for a sole member's meeting shall be one person. The sole member of a single-member company is deemed to be a person connected with the director for the purposes of section 26 of the 1990 Act;

(f) contracts entered into by sole members with their companies must be in writing except where such contracts are entered into in the ordinary course of business.

---

19 Section 141 of the Companies Act 1990.
20 SI 275/1994.

CHAPTER THREE

COMPANY FORMATION

Promoters

Although the Companies Acts refer to 'promoters', no express definition is contained therein.[1] For the purposes of liability in respect of mis-statements in a prospectus, section 49(8)(a) of the Principal Act defines a promoter as:

> ... a promoter who was a party to the preparation of the prospectus ... but does not include any person by reason of his acting in a professional capacity for persons engaged in procuring the formation of the company.

This particular definition is limited to actions under section 49 and, as many companies do not issue a prospectus, the definition is not appropriate in a general context. The apparent inadvertence by the legislature to provide a general definition may stem from a reluctance to limit the range of persons to whom the law applies. The judiciary has not, however, shown the same reluctance, and the most noted definition is that of Cockburn C.J. who described a promoter as:

> ... one who undertakes to form a company with reference to a given project and to set it going and who takes the necessary steps to accomplish that purpose.[2]

Applying this description, promoters are said to be those persons who associate together to bring about the formation of a new company. This may involve the conversion of an existing business into a corporate form or the development of an entirely new business through the vehicle of a registered company. In either case, the promoters will usually arrange for some or all of the following:

1. the necessary business assets and personnel to enable the new business to function effectively;
2. the necessary capital, in the form of equity or loans, to finance the venture; and
3. completion of the statutory formalities necessary to form a company.

Although a promoter is a person who is engaged in the formation of a company, it should be noted that those who assist the promoter, by acting in a professional capacity, are not themselves promoters. Accordingly, neither the accountant who values the assets to be purchased by the company, nor indeed, the solicitor who drafts the proposed constitutional documentation, is automatically deemed to be a promoter of the company. However, should they

---

1 See section 44(1) of the Principal Act for an implied definition.
2 *Re Twycross v Grant* [1877] 2 CPD 469 at 541.

negotiate on behalf of the proposed company, or actively arrange the placement of the company's shares, or indeed, arrange for somebody to become a director, they may be treated as promoters.

1. Fiduciary Duties of Promoters

While it may be difficult to identify precisely those persons who are considered company promoters, the same cannot be said of their duties. Promoters owe a fiduciary duty to the company, essentially a duty of good faith. The extent of the duty owed will depend on the part played by the promoter in bringing about the company's formation. If the promoter stands to make a personal gain from his position, he must make a full and proper disclosure to an independent board of directors or to all existing members.[3] If he does not so disclose, and makes a secret profit, he must account to the company for this gain.

In *Erlanger v. New Sombrero Phosphate Co.*,[4] Erlanger, a banker, formed a company and arranged for the appointment of five directors. Prior to its incorporation he had acquired a lease of phosphate deposits in the West Indies, which was held for him in the name of a nominee. A subsequent board meeting of the company, the majority of which was 'controlled' by Erlanger, approved the purchase of the lease for a considerably greater sum. Shares in the company were then offered to the public but the offer made no disclosure of the promoter's profit. It was held that the contract should be rescinded on the grounds that there was no disclosure to an independent board of directors. As Lord Cairns stated:

> I do not say that the owner of property may not promote and form a joint stock company, and then sell his property to it, but I do say that if he does he is bound to take care that he sells it to a company through the medium of a board of directors who can and do exercise an independent and intelligent judgment on the transaction.[5]

This insistence that a promoter is under a duty to ensure the existence of an independent board has since been relaxed, and it is now accepted that disclosure to all the members and potential members, if any, will be adequate.[6]

It is not the profit made by the promoter that the law forbids; rather, it is the non-disclosure of it. Thus in the *Salomon* case[7] the sale of the assets to the company at an over-valued price was not struck down because all the members had agreed to it. However, if Salomon had promoted a public company which later invited offers for its shares to the public, disclosure to the existing members may

---

3 In certain instances disclosure must also be made to potential members: see *Gluckstein v. Barnes* [1900] AC 240.

4 (1878) 3 App Cas 1218.

5 Ibid. at 1236.

6 *Salomon v. Salomon* [1897] AC 22 HL, *Lagunas Nitrate Co. v Lagunas Syndicate* [1899] 2 Ch 392.

7 [1897] AC 22 HL. See Chapter 6.

not have been sufficient, as the case of *Gluckstein v. Barnes*[8] demonstrates. There, a syndicate had purchased the freehold of the Olympia Exhibition Hall in London for £140,000 from a company in financial difficulties. The hall was also the subject matter of a secured debenture issued by that company which was purchased by the syndicate at a price below par. The company's liquidator subsequently repaid the debenture at its par value, giving the promoters a profit of £20,000. The syndicate then promoted a new company to which it agreed to sell the Olympia for £180,000. The profit from the sale of the freehold was disclosed to the public, which was invited to subscribe for shares. However, the profit made on the debenture was only disclosed to the existing members of the company, who all happened to be members of the syndicate. It was held that the promoters were liable to account for the secret profit they had made on the undisclosed transaction.

In addition to the equitable duties of promoters, civil liability and criminal liability may be imposed on them for any mis-statements in prospectuses by virtue of section 49 of the Principal Act[9] or at common law (e.g. fraud or negligence).

2. *Remedies for Breach of Promoters' Duties*

When a promoter breaches his fiduciary duty, the remedy available to the company will depend on the nature of the breach. Where the breach is caused by the non-disclosure of the promoter's interest in a property contract, which is prejudicial to the company, as in the *Erlanger* case, the primary remedy is rescission of the contract. In *Hopkins v. Shannon Transport Systems Ltd*,[10] the plaintiff and a business associate promoted a company for the purpose of operating a ferry service across the River Shannon. They hoped to raise capital for their venture from share subscriptions and government grants. The promoters had also formed a partnership which, using some of the proceeds of the company's share subscription, purchased vessels which were subsequently sold to the company. Some of the investors were unaware of the promoters' interest in the contract. Later, when the government grants were not forthcoming, the plaintiff pulled out of the project. He then issued proceedings against the company for his share of the sums due to the partnership. The High Court held that the plaintiff as a promoter of the company was under a duty to disclose his gain to the subscribers, and, having breached this duty, the contract was voidable at the instance of the company.

The effect of an order for rescission is to restore the parties to their original position, thus eliminating the promoter's secret profit. However, restitution may not be granted if it is impossible to restore the parties to this position or where innocent third parties have acquired rights. In those circumstances the more suitable remedy would be for the company to retain the benefit of the contract and sue the promoter for breach of his duty to disclose.

---

8 [1900] AC 240.
9 See Chapter 9.
10 Unreported, High Court, 10 January 1972, noted in O'Dowd (1989) DULJ 120.

3. Statutory Duties and Liabilities Relating to Promoters.

In addition to the fiduciary duties imposed on promoters, there are a number of statutory provisions which regulate aspects of public companies' dealings in non-cash assets. Where a promoter is selling property to the company as consideration for its shares, the property must be valued by an independent expert.[11] Breach of this provision renders the promoter as the allottee liable to pay the company an amount equal to the face value of the shares.[12] Where a public company within two years of commencing business acquires an asset from a subscriber to its memorandum — in many cases the original subscribers will be company promoters — and the consideration for that acquisition amounts to one tenth or more of the nominal value of the company's issued capital, then that asset must also be independently valued, the terms of the sale must be approved by the company in general meeting and a copy of the agreement delivered to the registrar of companies.[13] Failure to comply with this obligation entitles the company to recover its consideration and the agreement, in so far as it has not been carried out, shall be void.

Where shares in a company are being offered to the public, the information contained in the prospectus must include various details relating to: the promoters' preliminary expenses, the promoters' interests in any transactions with the company within the previous five years, any other amounts or benefits given to any promoter within the previous five years, or intended to be given, and the details of considerations for such payments or benefits.[14] The Prospectus rules are considered further in Chapter 9.

4. Pre-Incorporation Contracts

The exigencies of business may require promoters to grasp opportunities and enter into contracts on behalf of the venture being promoted. These contracts may be made either before or after the formalities for incorporation have been completed. If the company has already been incorporated, the normal rules of agency apply, and the promoter will act as the agent for the company. The difficulty arises when the proposed venture has not yet been incorporated. This is because the law of agency prevents a person from acting for a principal, if the principal does not exist. Neither could the company, once formed, ratify retrospectively the agent's agreement because ratification is only permitted if the principal itself could have entered into the contract at that time. Where a company has no legal existence, it has no capacity to contract. The difficulties facing promoters of 'yet to be formed' companies were clearly illustrated in *Kelner v.*

---

11 Section 30 Companies (Amendment) Act 1983.
12 Section 30(10) ibid.
13 Section 32 ibid.
14 Third Schedule of the Principal Act.

Baxter.[15] In that case three promoters entered into a contract for the purchase of wine, which was signed by them 'on behalf of' a company which was not yet in existence. The company was subsequently formed but it went into liquidation before payment for the wine was made. It was held that as the contract was signed by persons who represented themselves as being agents for a principal that did not exist, the signatories were personally bound by the terms of the contract.

Section 37(1) of the Principal Act alleviates these difficulties by empowering a company to ratify pre-incorporation transactions and contracts entered into by the unincorporated company itself or by persons acting on its behalf. Although the section does not specify the manner in which the ratification may be authorised, it will usually be effected by the board of directors, which will normally be vested with the powers of managing the company under the articles of association. Where the articles do not so provide, ratification will be authorised by the company in general meeting. In the event that the company is wound up before the pre-incorporation contracts have been ratified, it has been held that a liquidator can ratify these contracts.[16]

Once the contract has been ratified by the company, section 37(1) further provides that the company shall be bound by the contract or transaction, and entitled to any benefits accruing thereon, in the same manner as if the company had been in existence at the date of and was a party to the contract or transaction. In the event that ratification does not occur, section 37(2) provides that any person who purported to act on behalf of, or in the name of, the company shall, in the absence of an express provision to the contrary, be personally bound by the contract or transaction. This is so even where the other party knew that the company was not yet formed.

In *Phonogram Ltd v. Lane*,[17] the defendant intended to form a company, Fragile Management, to manage a new pop group. Before the company was formed he entered into a contract with the plaintiff recording company whereby an advance payment would be made, but which was repayable if a recording contract was not agreed within one month. The contract was signed 'for and on behalf of Fragile Management Ltd'. The company was never formed, the recording contract was never made and the plaintiff sued for the return of the advance payment. Lane argued that the equivalent English provision only applied where the outsider did not know that the company had yet to be formed, and as the plaintiff knew that the company was not yet in existence he could not rely on the statutory protection. The Court of Appeal rejected this argument and held Lane liable.

One way of avoiding these difficulties is to include a disclaimer of liability on the part of the promoter. However, while the contract may disclaim liability on the part of the promoter, it is unlikely that such a position would be acceptable

---

15 (1866) LR 2 CP 174.
16 *HKN Invest OY v. Incotrade PVT Ltd & Others* [1993] 3 IR 152 at 161.
17 [1981] 3 All ER 182.

to a third party. Furthermore, any disclaimer must be expressed in clear and unambiguous terms.[18]

If a promoter obtains payments under a pre-incorporation contract which is capable of being ratified by the company, those payments are held by the promoter as a trustee for the company. In *HKN Invest OY v. Incotrade PVT Ltd & Others*,[19] two foreign nationals set up a loan brokerage business in Ireland which defrauded a number of investors. In fleeing the jurisdiction, they left behind a sum of money in the personal account of one of the promoters. These monies represented commissions payable to the company, which were mostly in pursuant to pre-incorporation contracts. No monies were paid from this account to the company after incorporation. The High Court held that the liquidator of the company was entitled to the commissions as they were being held by the promoters for the company under a constructive trust.

5. *Preliminary Expenses of Promoters*

Promoters' remuneration and preliminary expenses are only payable if the company, once formed, ratifies the relevant contract. Any such contract must have been entered into before the promoter rendered the services, otherwise the contract will be invalid under principles of contract law. Where the promoter 'controls' the company he can cause it to ratify the contract, by ensuring that the memorandum and articles gives the directors the power to ratify pre-incorporation contracts, and that they do, in fact, ratify them. It is usual to include such provisions in the company's articles of association. Article 80 of Table A stipulates that the directors may pay all expenses incurred in promoting and registering the company.

6. *Disqualification of Promoters*

The provisions of the 1990 Companies Act, relating to the restriction and disqualification of persons from acting as a director of a company, extend also to a prohibition on their acting as a promoter. (See Chapter 16, Restriction and Disqualification of Directors.)

Registration of New Companies

Before a company can be registered, the following documents must be delivered to the Registrar of Companies:

1. a memorandum of association in the prescribed form, signed by the subscribers, dated and witnessed;

---

18 *Phonogram Ltd v. Lane* [1981] 3 All ER 182 at 188.
19 [1993] 3 IR 152.

2. articles of association in the prescribed form, signed by the same subscribers, dated and witnessed (unless Table A is adopted);
3. form A1, which is a statement giving the following details:
   (a) the name of the company;
   (b) the registered office of the company;
   (c) the name, address and signature of the secretary;
   (d) particulars of the directors including their signatures;
   (e) a statutory declaration, by a solicitor engaged in the formation of the company or by a person named as a director or secretary of the company, that all the requirements of the Companies Acts in respect of registration have been complied with;
   (f) a statutory declaration that the company will carry on an activity within the State, the nature of that activity, the place within the State where it is proposed to carry on the activity, and the place, whether in the State or not, where the central administration of the company will normally be carried on; this declaration must be made by either a solicitor engaged in the formation of the company or by a person named as a director or secretary of the company;
   (g) a statement of capital, where the company is to have a share capital;
4. the appropriate registration fees and stamp duty.

Section 43(1) Companies (Amendment) (No.2) Act 1999 requires that one director of a company shall be resident in the State. This requirement will not apply if:

(a) the company holds a bond to the value of £20,000 (€25,395) to satisfy any failure by the company to pay fines or penalties under the Companies Acts and certain Taxes Acts; or
(b) the Registrar has issued a certificate that the proposed company has a real and continuous link with one or more economic activities that are being carried on in the State.[20]

If the registrar is satisfied with the documentation, its contents, the company's name, the legality of the company's objects, and that the residency requirement is satisfied, he must register the company and issue a certificate of incorporation. The certificate of incorporation is analogous to a birth certificate and it will state the name of the company, the date it was incorporated and its registration number. The registration number is particularly important when identifying a company which has a similar name to another company. This will often be the case with companies in the same group. The company must publish a notice in *Iris Oifigiúil* that a certificate of incorporation has been issued.[21]

---

20 Section 44 Companies (Amendment) Act (No.2)1999.
21 Section 19 of the Principal Act.

Effect of Registration

From the date of incorporation the company exists with perpetual succession, and is capable of exercising all the functions of an incorporated company.[22] It is also subject to all the statutory obligations which pertain to a company. The certificate of incorporation is conclusive evidence of the following:

(a) that the registration requirements of the Companies Acts have been complied with;

(b) that the association is a company authorised to be registered and is duly registered; and

(c) if the certificate contains a statement that a company is a public company, that the company is such a company.[23]

Commencement of Business

Once the certificate is issued, a private company can commence trading immediately. However, section 6(1) of the Companies (Amendment) Act 1983 prohibits a public company from trading until it has been issued with an additional certificate of trading.[24] In order to obtain this trading certificate the company must apply in the prescribed form. The application must be supported by a statutory declaration signed by a director or secretary of the company. This declaration must state:

(a) that the nominal share capital is not less than the authorised minimum;

(b) that the amount paid up on the allotted share capital is at least one-quarter of the nominal value and the entire premium, if any;

(c) details of the preliminary expenses involved in promoting the company, to whom they were paid, together with any other payments or benefits to the company's promoters.[25]

The Registrar may accept the statutory declaration as sufficient evidence of the matters stated therein.[26] If a public company fails to obtain the trading certificate or does not re-register as a private company within twelve months, it may be struck off the register.[27] If a public company commences to trade without the appropriate certificate, the company and every officer in default is guilty of an offence and is liable to a fine.[28] Where a public limited company enters into a

---

22 Section 18(2) of the Principal Act.
23 Section 5(4) of the Companies (Amendment) Act 1983.
24 Section 115 of the Principal Act imposes additional restrictions on certain public companies, not being a public limited company or one which has no share capital, before they can commence business or exercise their borrowing powers.
25 Section 6(3) of the Companies (Amendment) Act 1983.
26 Section 6(5) of the Companies (Amendment) Act 1983.
27 Section 8 of the Companies (Amendment) Act 1983.
28 Section 6(7) of the Companies (Amendment) Act 1983.

transaction without having obtained the appropriate trading certificate, the transaction is still enforceable by any other party. However, if the company fails to comply with its obligations within twenty-one days of being called upon to do so, the directors of the company shall be jointly and severally liable to indemnify any other party to the transaction who suffered any loss or damage by reason of the company's failure to comply with its obligations.[29] A private company converting to a public limited company is not required to cease trading pending receipt of a certificate of trading.

Notification in *Iris Oifigiúil*

Regulation 4(1) of the European Communities (Companies) Regulations 1973[30] requires all companies with limited liability to publish in *Iris Oifigiúil* notice of the delivery to, or the issue by, the Registrar of Companies the following documents and particulars:

(a) any certificate of incorporation of the company;
(b) the memorandum and articles of association, or the equivalent documents which constitute or define the constitution of the company, any amendments thereto and the text of the amended documents;
(c) any return relating to the company's register of directors or any notification of a change among its directors;
(d) any return relating to the persons, other than the board of directors, authorised to enter into transactions binding the company, or notification of a change among such persons;
(e) the annual return of the company;
(f) any notice of the situation of its registered office, or of any change therein;
(g) any copy of a winding-up order in respect of the company;
(h) any order for the dissolution of the company on a winding up; and
(i) any return by a liquidator of the final meeting of the company on a winding up.

All notices must be published within six weeks of the relevant delivery or issue.[31] Section 55 of the Companies (Amendment) Act 1983 obliges public limited companies to publish in *Iris Oifigiúil* notice of delivery to the Registrar of certain additional documents, including inter alia certain special resolutions, various experts' valuation reports, statutory declarations and other miscellaneous matters.

---

29 Section 6(8) of the Companies (Amendment) Act 1983.
30 SI 163/1973.
31 Regulation 4(2) of the European Communities (Companies) Regulations 1973.

Other Methods of Corporate Formation

The process of registering companies in the manner described above can take a number of months to complete. The alternative means of acquiring corporate status are to register under the Company Incorporation Scheme or to acquire a shelf company. The Company Incorporation Scheme guarantees that incorporation will be effected within ten working days of the documentation being lodged in the Companies Registration Office. Only private limited companies can be incorporated using this method and even then the availability of the scheme is subject to the following conditions:

(a) the scheme is only available to companies required for immediate use;
(b) the memorandum and articles of association must be printed in clear black type on durable paper;
(c) the standard preprinted model articles and memorandum must be used which can only be varied in respect of the name, main objects, liability and share capital clauses;
(d) in the event that errors cause the application to be resubmitted, this will be treated as a new application.

Certain enterprises specialise in registering companies, which are then 'sold' to promoters who wish to acquire corporate status for a proposed business undertaking. As these 'off the shelf' companies are already formed, the original subscribers and directors will usually be the managers of these founding enterprises. Once acquired, the nominal shares will be transferred, and the new members can appoint their own directors.

Registration of Foreign Companies

Companies may be incorporated outside the State but establish a place of business within the State. Within one month of the establishment of the place of business, the company must deliver to the Registrar of Companies the following documents:

(a) a certified copy of the company's constitutional documents which have been translated into English or Irish, where necessary;
(b a certified list of the directors and secretary and the particulars relating to them;
(c) the names of at least one person who is resident in the State and is authorised to accept on behalf of the company service of process and any notices required to be served on the company; and
(d) the certified address of the company's principal place of business in the State.[32]

Companies incorporated outside the State but which only establish a branch within the State are subject to the requirements imposed by Regulation 14 of the

---

32 Section 352(1) of the Principal Act.

European Communities (Branch Disclosures) Regulation 1993.[33] These provisions impose similar registration requirements on foreign companies establishing a branch within the State. However, the requirements are more stringent for companies incorporated outside the European Union.

Re-registration of Companies

A company may convert from its original form during the course of its existence. Where the statutory requirements relating to re-registration have been satisfied, the Registrar of companies will issue a new certificate of incorporation. The procedural requirements for re-registration vary depending on the existing form of the company and the proposed new form.

1. Private to Public Company

Sections 9 and 10 of the Companies (Amendment) Act 1983 set out the prerequisites for converting from a private company to a public limited company. The first step is the passing of a special resolution to give effect to the change and to alter the memorandum and articles of association to reflect the form appropriate to a public company. An application is then made to the Registrar of companies, in the prescribed form, together with the following:

(a) a printed copy of the altered memorandum and articles;
(b) a copy of the balance sheet and an unqualified report by the auditors in relation to the balance sheet;
(c) an auditors' statement to the effect that the company's net assets are not less than the aggregate of its called-up share capital and undistributable reserves;
(d) a statutory declaration by the directors or secretary;
(e) a valuation report on any assets acquired for shares since the balance sheet date.

Assuming the Registrar is satisfied that the application form and the ancillary documents are in order, he will issue a certificate of re-registration of the company as a public limited company. The certificate is conclusive evidence that all the statutory requirements have been complied with. A private company will not be re-registered as a public limited company unless, at the time the special resolution for its conversion was passed, it had satisfied the capital requirements imposed on such companies.

2. Public to Private Company

Sections 14–15 of the Companies (Amendment) Act 1983 set out the procedure to be followed in order to re-register a public limited company as a private company. This procedure is similar to that mentioned above, but obviously the

---

33 SI 395/1993.

alterations to the company's memorandum and articles must reflect the proposed change in status. However, in this case dissenting members[34] may apply to the court to cancel the resolution purporting to make the alteration.[35] Where such an application is made, the company must notify the Registrar, and the re-registration cannot be completed until confirmed by the court. The court, in considering such an application, may approve or cancel the resolution or may make such order as it sees fit, including an order that the company purchase the dissenting shareholders' shares in the company.

In certain circumstances, a public limited company may have no alternative but to re-register as a private company. Where a lawful reduction in capital brings the company's capital below the authorised minimum, the court will not confirm the reduction until the company has been re-registered as a private company.

3. Unlimited to Limited Company

An unlimited private company may convert to a limited company where the members agree by special resolution to a change in status and the resolution also sets out the necessary changes in the memorandum and articles of association.[36] The resolution must be delivered together with the prescribed application form to the Registrar of companies.

4. Limited to Unlimited Company

A company formed with limited liability may re-register as an unlimited company.[37] The application in the prescribed form must be sent to the Registrar together with evidence of the written consent of every member. The requirement to have the unanimous consent of the members is necessary because members of an unlimited company will be assuming full responsibility for the debts of the company.

5. Private to Single-Member Company

A company may convert from a private limited company to a single-member company by reducing its members to one and by vesting all the company's shares in that sole member.[38] The conversion is then automatic, occurring by operation of the law. The company must however notify the Registrar of the fact and date of conversion and the identity of the single member within twenty-eight days from the date of conversion. A private unlimited company may not convert to a single-member company in this manner. It is first required to convert to limited status.

---

34 Dissenting members must hold at least 5 per cent of the issued share capital or of any class of share capital; or in the case of a company with no share capital 5 per cent of its members.

35 Section 15(2) of the Companies (Amendment) Act 1983.

36 Section 53 of the Companies (Amendment) Act 1983.

37 Section 52 of the Companies Amendment Act 1983.

38 Regulation 5(1) of the European Communities (Single-Member Private Limited Companies) Regulations 1994 SI 275/1994.

6. *Single-Member to Private Company*

Where the members of a single-member company increase to more than one, it is automatically deemed to have converted to a private limited company. The company is obliged to notify the Registrar within twenty-eight days of the conversion.

Company Dissolution

A company continues to exist until the grant of corporate status has been revoked and the company is dissolved. Dissolution brings the separate personality of a company to an end. The section 25 contract (see Chapter 4, The Memorandum of Association) between the members and the company is terminated. The assets of the dissolved company are vested in the Minister for Finance.[39] A company will be dissolved when one of the following events occur:

1) the court has made an order of dissolution following a compulsory liquidation;
2) three months, or such longer period as the court may direct, from the date of the submission of the liquidator's final report in a voluntary liquidation; and
3) where the Registrar has struck the company off the Companies Register for the following reasons:
   (i) failure to carry on business; or
   (ii) failure to submit the annual return; or
   (iii) where the company is being wound up and the Registrar believes that no liquidator is acting or the affairs of the company are fully wound up and the returns to be made by the liquidator have not been made for a period of six consecutive months; or
   (iv) the Registrar is satisfied that the company is in breach of the requirement that one director be resident in Ireland; or
   (v) where the Registrar believes the company has no directors; or
   (vi) where the Revenue has given a notice to the Registrar that a company has failed to deliver certain statements containing various particulars, as required by section 882 (3) of the Taxes Consolidation Act 1997.

Restoration to the Registrar

Where a company has been dissolved following a liquidation, the court may, within two years from the date of dissolution, on an application by a liquidator or any other interested party, declare the dissolution void.[40] Where a company is struck off without being wound up, the court may, on an application before it, order that the name of the company be restored to the register. The company will thereafter be deemed to have continued in existence as if its name had not been

---

39 Section 28 of the State Property Act 1954.
40 Section 310 of the Principal Act.

struck off and the court may make such an order and issue such directions as seem just for the placing of the company, and any other persons in the same position as nearly may be, as if the name of the company had not been struck off.[41] In *Re Amantiss Enterprises*[42] the High Court held that an order under section 311(8) had the effect of automatically validating retrospectively all acts done in the name or on behalf of the company while it was struck off the register.

---

41 Section 311(8) of the Principal Act.
42 [2000] 2 ILRM 177.

CHAPTER FOUR

THE MEMORANDUM OF ASSOCIATION

Introduction

The memorandum and articles of association together form the constitution of the company. The memorandum contains provisions regulating the external activities of the company and the articles regulate its internal affairs. Together, they determine both the legal parameters within which the company and its agents must operate and the basis for the relationship between the company and its members and the members *inter se*.

The Memorandum of Association

The incorporation of a company cannot be effected without the registration of the memorandum.[1] The form of the memorandum for a private limited company must be in accordance with, or as near thereto as the circumstances permit, the forms set out in Tables B, C and D of the First Schedule to the Principal Act. In the case of public limited companies the forms are set out in the Second Schedule to the Companies (Amendment) Act 1983. The memorandum must be printed, or in a form pursuant to section 80 of the Company Law Enforcement Act, 2001, signed and attested.[2] Once the format of the memorandum meets the statutory requirements, its contents are largely a matter for the company's promoters. However, section 6 of the Principal Act provides that the memorandum of all companies limited by shares must contain the following 'compulsory' clauses:

1. the name clause;
2. the objects clause;
3. the limited liability clause;
4. the authorised share capital clause; and
5. the association clause.[3]

The memorandum of a company limited by guarantee is not required to have an authorised share capital clause. However, it must include a statement of the amount which each member agrees to contribute in the winding up of the

---

1 Registration of the articles is not required because a company can adopt the model articles set out in the First Schedule of the Principal Act, as amended: section 13 of the Principal Act.

2 The requirement to have the memorandum stamped has been repealed by section 112 of the Finance Act 1996.

3 Although section 6 of the Principal Act does not specifically mention an association clause, every memorandum is required to have such a clause, often referred to as the un-numbered compulsory clause.

company. An unlimited company is only required to include the names and objects clauses in its memorandum.

1. The Name Clause

Every company must have a name with which it may be identified. The name is necessary to enable proceedings to be taken on behalf of, or against, the company and to distinguish it from other companies and business entities.

A private company, limited by shares or by guarantee, must end its name with the word 'limited', 'teoranta' or their respective abbreviations. In the case of a public limited company, the name must end with the words 'public limited company', 'cuideachta phoiblí theoranta' or their respective abbreviations. In certain cases, a limited company may obtain a dispensation from the Registrar of Companies to omit the word 'limited' from its name. Such a dispensation may only be granted to a private company that is limited by shares and which satisfies the following conditions:

(a) the company is formed for the purpose of promoting commerce, art, science, religion, charity or any other useful object; and
(b) its memorandum or articles of association require its profits or other income to be applied to the promotion of its objects, prohibit the payment of dividends to its members, and require all the assets which would otherwise be available to its members to be transferred to another company who can satisfy these requirements.

The memorandum and articles of association of a company seeking a dispensation shall not be altered where such an alteration would cause the company to cease to comply with the statutory requirements for dispensation.

A statutory declaration that the company has complied with the requirements for dispensation must be made by a director or secretary of the company and delivered to the registrar of companies.

Prohibition on the Use of Certain Names

As well as the above mentioned requirements, there are a number of statutory provisions which restrict the choice of company name. Section 56 of the Companies (Amendment) Act 1983 makes it an offence to use the words 'public limited company' in a business name unless the company is in fact registered as a public limited company. More importantly, section 21 of the Principal Act provides that no name shall be registered which in the opinion of the Registrar is undesirable. However, where the Registrar refuses to register a name, an appeal may be made to the court.

The Registrar of Companies has issued informal guidelines as to the names that may be refused registration. These include:

(a) a name identical to one already on the register;

(b) a name which is offensive;

(c) a name that would suggest State sponsorship;

(d) a name which includes 'bank' or cognate words where a licence has not been obtained from the Central Bank;

(e) a name which includes 'insurance' or cognate words unless an appropriate licence has been granted by the Minister;

(f) a name which includes the words 'society' or 'co-op' or 'co-operative'; and

(g) a name which includes the word 'university' unless the Department of Education has granted permission for such usage.

Even if a name is registered, the Registrar may, within six months after registration, compel a company to change its name if it is very similar to one already registered.[4] If the Registrar so directs, the name must be changed within 6 weeks or such longer period as the Registrar may allow. Even if the Registrar makes no direction in this regard, the company may be directed by the court to change its name if it is found liable for the tort of passing off. Passing off involves the use of a business name or brand which is so similar to that of another business or brand that it creates confusion among the public. In *Ewing v. Buttercup Margarine Co. Ltd*,[5] the plaintiff, whose business was called 'The Buttercup Dairy Company', was successful in his attempt to prevent the defendant company from continuing to use its name because the public might think that the two businesses were connected.

A company may trade under a name that is different to its registered name. In such circumstances the trading name must be registered under the Registration of Business Names Act 1963.[6]

Display of Company Name

The company's name must be painted up or affixed to the outside of every office or place in which the business of the company is carried on, in a conspicuous position and in easily legible letters. The name must be engraved on the company's seal and must be mentioned on all the company's business letters, notices and official publications.[7] Failure to comply with these requirements may result in the company, and any person acting on its behalf, being liable to a fine. The company's name must also be placed on bills of exchange, cheques, orders for money and goods and receipts issued by the company. Where this does not occur, the company will be liable to a fine and the company officer who signed on its behalf shall be personally liable to the holder of a bill of exchange,

---

4 Section 23(2) of the Principal Act.

5 [1917] 2 Ch 1.

6 Section 22 of the Principal Act.

7 Section 114(1) of the Principal Act.

promissory note or cheque or order for money or goods issued.[8]

In *Penrose v. Martyr*,[9] a bill was drawn on a private limited company which was described on the bill without the word 'limited' being mentioned. The bill was accepted by the company secretary. When it was later dishonoured, the company secretary was held personally liable for the amount of the bill because of the incorrect description of the company's name. Even if the error is caused by the holder of the instrument, the company's officers may still be liable as they ought to have ensured the accuracy of the name before signing it.[10] However, in certain circumstances the holder will be prevented from suing the officer who fails to correct the mistake. In *Durham Fancy Goods Ltd v. Michael Jackson (Fancy Goods) Ltd*,[11] a bill of exchange was drawn by the plaintiffs on the defendant company. The plaintiffs, in prescribing the form of words for the acceptance of the bill, had incorrectly described the defendant company's name. As the plaintiff had prepared both the bill and the form of acceptance, he was estopped from invoking the statutory liability of the signatory.

Change of Company Name

A company may change its name by passing a special resolution and obtaining the approval in writing of the Registrar.[12] A new certificate of incorporation on change of name will be issued and the change comes into effect from the date the certificate is issued. The registered number of the company, which appears on the original certificate of incorporation, will be included on all subsequent certificates of incorporation issued on change of name. Where the company is changing from a public to a private company, or *vice versa*, the procedures for re-registering must be followed.[13]

2. The Objects Clause

Section 6(1) of the Principal Act requires every company to state its objects in the memorandum of association. As the objects clause will prescribe the permissible activities of the company, the promoters should carefully consider the anticipated activities. As persons can only associate to form a company with a lawful purpose, the objects cannot be illegal.[14] If a company cannot achieve the objects for which it was established, it may be wound up under section 213(f) of the Principal Act. In *Re German Date Coffee Co.*,[15] the company was formed for the sole purpose of

---

8 Section 114(3) and (4) of the Principal Act.
9 (1858) EB & E 499.
10 *Lindholst & Co. A/S v. Fowler* [1988] BCLC 166.
11 [1968] 2 QB 839.
12 Section 23(1) of the Principal Act.
13 See Chapter 3.
14 Section 5 of the Principal Act.
15 [1882] 20 Ch 169.

acquiring a German patent under which to manufacture coffee from dates. The patent was not granted but the company continued to work the process by acquiring a Swedish patent. The members petitioned to have the company wound up on the grounds that it was no longer possible for the company to achieve its purpose. The court, in holding that the substratum of the company had failed, accepted the petition and ordered the company to be wound up. The inclusion of the objects clause in the memorandum is necessary for the following reasons:

(a) prospective investors will know what business the company is in;
(b) existing members can be assured that any plans to diversify into other activities will require an alteration of the objects clause which must be approved by the general meeting;
(c) creditors will be aware of what contracts are authorised and therefore enforceable against the company; and
(d) directors, as agents of the company, can be clear as to the type of transactions to which they can bind the company.

Where a company acts outside its objects, it is said to be acting *ultra vires*. An *ultra vires* transaction is void and can only be enforced by an outsider who either acted in good faith or was unaware of the *ultra vires* nature of the transaction. The doctrine of ultra vires and its effect on outsiders is considered in Chapter 7.

The objects clause may be altered by a special resolution of the company in general meeting. Holders of debentures secured by floating charges must be given notice of the meeting at which the proposed change is to be presented.[16] Any alteration must be made bona fide and in the best interests of the company. An application may be made to the court to have the alteration cancelled by the following:

(a) dissentient holders of at least 15 per cent in nominal value of the company's issued share capital or any class thereof; or
(b) in the case of a company with no share capital at least 15 per cent of the members; or
(c) holders of at least 15 per cent of the company's debentures secured by floating charges.[17]

The application must be made within twenty-one days from the date of the resolution purporting to alter the object. Where an application is made, the court may make an order cancelling the alteration or confirming it either wholly or in part, on such terms and conditions as it sees fit. It may also order the purchase of the interests of dissentient members. Where an application is made to the court, the alteration shall not take effect unless confirmed by the court. An alteration in the objects clause cannot have retrospective effect. Therefore, an *ultra vires* act

---

16 Section 10 of the Principal Act.
17 Section 10(3) of the Principal Act.

cannot be subsequently ratified by the general meeting agreeing to alter the company's objects.

3. The Liability Clause

In the case of a company limited by shares or by guarantee, the memorandum must contain a statement that the liability of the members is limited.[18] The liability clause can only be altered to increase the members' liability to the company if every member agrees.[19] Where it is proposed to change a company's status from limited to unlimited liability, the consent of all members must also be obtained.[20] However, if an unlimited company is proposing to become a limited liability company, a special resolution will suffice.[21]

4. The Authorised Share Capital Clause

The capital clause must set out the total amount of the company's authorised share capital and the division thereof into shares of a fixed amount. It is important to remember that the authorised share capital will usually be far in excess of the amount of issued share capital. The authorised share capital clause may be altered, where the articles of association so provide, by an ordinary resolution of the company in general meeting. Where the alteration will have the effect of reducing the share capital of the company the procedure set out in section 72 of the Principal Act must be followed. (See Chapter 11, Loan Capital.)

5. The Association Clause

Every memorandum ends with a statement whereby the subscribers indicate their wish to form the company and their agreement to take the number of shares in the capital of the company which is set out opposite their names. Each subscriber must take at least one share. This statement is followed by the names, addresses and descriptions of the subscribers, the number of shares to be taken by each, and the signature of the subscriber and of a witness.

Additional Compulsory Clause in the Case of a PLC

In the case of a public limited company the memorandum must contain a statement that the company is a public company.[22]

---

18 Section 6(2) of the Principal Act.
19 Section 27 of the Principal Act.
20 Section 52 of the Companies (Amendment) Act 1983.
21 Section 53 of the Companies (Amendment) Act 1983.
22 Second Schedule to the Companies (Amendment) Act 1983.

The Non-Compulsory Clauses

It is rare in practice to include clauses other than the compulsory clauses in the memorandum of association. However, usually to protect the balance of power, the promoters and original subscribers may decide to 'entrench' certain provisions in the memorandum by declaring that they are unalterable. This has the same legal effect as an irrevocable agreement by the first and all future members that these provisions will always remain unalterable.[23] Therefore privileges bestowed on the first members, such as weighted voting rights or lifetime directorships, can be safeguarded from any future changes by new members or a new majority.

There is a general power to alter all other non-compulsory or non-entrenched clauses by special resolution,[24] subject to the following restrictions:

(a) dissentient shareholders may apply to the court to have any alteration cancelled;
(b) where a specific alteration procedure is prescribed by the articles it must be complied with;
(c) where the court has ordered the alteration of a clause in the memorandum, it cannot thereafter be altered by the company without the consent of the court;
(d) no alteration can increase the liability of a member in respect of shares already held, nor can a member be compelled to subscribe for additional shares without the member's consent in writing;
(e) any alteration which affects the rights attached to a class of shareholders will not be valid unless the correct variation procedure has been followed. (See Chapter 8, Company Securities.)

The company is required to deliver to the Registrar a copy of the altered memorandum, together with a signed copy of the authorising resolution, within fifteen days of making the alteration.[25] Notice of the delivery of these particulars to the Registrar must be made in *Iris Oifigiúl*.

---

23 Section 28(3) of the Principal Act.
24 Section 28(3) of the Principal Act.
25 Section 10(9) of the Principal Act.

CHAPTER FIVE

THE ARTICLES OF ASSOCIATION

Introduction

While the memorandum determines the relationship between the company and outsiders, the articles govern the internal dealings of the company, including *inter alia* the issue and transfer of shares, directors' powers, remuneration and removal, procedures at board meetings and general meetings, and the payment of dividends. Where there is a conflict between the articles and the memorandum of association, the latter prevails.[1]

Every company must have articles of association. However, private companies limited by shares are not required to register articles.[2] Where they do not do so, the model articles (Table A), set out in the First Schedule to the Principal Act, will be deemed to be the articles of association of that company, in the same manner as if they had been duly registered.[3] Where a private company limited by shares voluntarily registers its own articles, the provisions of Table A will still apply unless they have been expressly excluded or modified by the company's own articles.

The form of the articles is determined by section 14 of the Principal Act. It provides that the articles must be printed or in a form pursuant to section 80 of the Company Law Enforcement Act, 2001, divided into paragraphs which are numbered consecutively, and signed by each subscriber to the memorandum in the presence of a witness who must attest the signature.[4] While the Companies Acts do not stipulate what the articles must contain,[5] Table A gives a clear impression of the particulars which would normally be provided in the articles. In any case, there are a number of provisions in the Companies Acts that will only permit certain changes to the company if the articles so permit. Furthermore, where a company is listed on the Stock Exchange, the 'Listing Rules' regime dictates that such a company's articles contain provisions on such matters as transfer of securities, share certificates, dividends, accounts, notices, voting entitlements and proxies.

---

1 *Ashbury Railway Carriage & Iron Co. v Riche* (1875) LR 7 HL 653.
2 Section 11 of the Principal Act.
3 Section 13(2) of the Principal Act.
4 The requirement that the articles bear the stamp as if they were contained in a deed has been repealed by section 112 of the Finance Act 1996.
5 Certain information must be provided in the case of private companies limited by guarantee and unlimited companies — section 12 of the Principal Act.

Alteration of the Articles

Section 15 of the Principal Act provides that a company may alter or add to its articles of association by passing a special resolution to that effect. Any attempt to deprive the company of this power, either by the articles themselves or by a shareholders' agreement, is void.[6]

However, it is possible to circumvent this rule by the use of certain devices. First, the articles may give additional or 'weighted' votes to a member where resolutions to alter the articles are proposed. In *Bushell v. Faith*,[7] the company was owned by three family members who were the company's only directors and who held equal shares. Each share carried one vote but the articles provided that in the event of a resolution being proposed for the removal of a director from office, the shares of that director would carry three votes per share. When it was proposed to remove one of the directors from office, he used his weighted votes to block the resolution. The House of Lords upheld the validity of the provision in the articles. A second method of preventing the alteration of the articles is to provide that, in the event of certain resolutions being proposed at a meeting, the quorum for that meeting must include a particular member. The member can then, by absenting himself, deny the meeting a quorum and prevent the resolution from being passed. Finally, the clause may be inserted and 'entrenched' in the memorandum by declaring it to be unalterable.

When an alteration is made to the articles, a copy of the altered articles together with a signed copy of the authorising resolution must be delivered to the Registrar within fifteen days.[8]

Informal Alteration of the Articles

An alteration may be effected without following the formalities of a special resolution. Both common law and statute recognise that informal agreements may have the same effect as a special resolution. In *Cane v. Jones*,[9] the shareholders entered into an oral agreement whereby the chairman was deprived of his casting vote at general meetings, a power which had been conferred on him by the articles. Later, when a dispute arose, one body of shareholders contended that the articles had not been altered, because a special resolution to that effect had not been passed. It was held that the 'assent principle', recognised by the common law, applied. The essence of this principle is that all members of a

---

6 However, the shareholders may enter into an agreement among themselves as to how they will exercise their voting rights: see *Russell v. Northern Bank Development Corporation* [1992] 3 All ER 161. However, shareholder agreements are not binding on future members in the same way as the articles are.
7 [1969] 1 All ER 1002.
8 Section 143 of the Principal Act.
9 [1981] 1 All ER 533.

company can, by unanimous agreement, whether orally or in writing, whether formally or informally, take a binding decision on any matter which is *intra vires* the company. Accordingly, the alteration was held to be effective.[10]

Restrictions on the Right to Alter the Articles

Whatever the form of agreement, a company does not have an unfettered right to alter the articles. This is because any alteration must be made *bona fide* and in the best interests of the company. It would appear from case-law on this particular point that once this test is satisfied the alteration is valid, despite any consequential detriment suffered by a minority of shareholders. This position was accepted by the Court of Appeal in *Allen v. Gold Reefs of West Africa Ltd.*[11] There, the articles provided that in the event that monies were owing to the company on unpaid or partly paid shares, a lien would attach to those particular shares. Following the death of a member, who owed the company certain amounts in relation to unpaid shares, the articles were altered. The effect of the alteration was such that the lien would extend to all shares, including fully paid shares, held by a member who owed monies on unpaid shares. The deceased member was the only holder of fully paid shares to which the lien would now apply. His executors argued that the alteration was discriminatory as it adversely affected only one member. The court, in rejecting this argument, held that as the alteration was for the benefit of the company as a whole it was valid. The court noted that the alteration applied to all members although in this particular instance only one happened to be affected.

1. The Bona Fide Test

The *bona fide* test is usually applied in terms of whether or not the alteration will benefit the general body of shareholders. Thus in *Greenhalgh v. Arderne Cinemas Ltd,*[12] the articles included a pre-emption right which gave existing members the right of first refusal when shares were being sold. The majority of shareholders, who wished to sell their shares to an outsider, proposed a resolution to remove the pre-emption right from the articles. Greenhalgh, a minority shareholder, objected to the alteration on the grounds that it was sacrificing the rights of the minority against those of the majority. The court was not swayed by this argument and held the alteration was valid because all members, including Greenhalgh, would now be free to sell their shares. Evershed MR stated that as long as the majority honestly believed that the alteration would benefit the company as a whole, the court would not interfere with its decision.

When considering cases of this type, the courts must balance two conflicting

---

10 See Chapter 14 for a fuller discussion of the 'assent principle'.
11 [1900] 1 Ch 656.
12 [1950] 2 All ER 1120.

claims. First, the majority is entitled to use its position to effect change, despite objections from the minority. Second, the minority must be protected from actions by the majority which are unfairly prejudicial to it. In *Shuttleworth v. Cox Brothers & Co. (Maidenhead) Ltd,*[13] the articles provided that five directors should be appointed for life unless one of six specified events occurred. One director failed on a number of occasions to account to the company for monies spent. This behaviour did not warrant his removal under the articles, so the company altered the articles to the effect that the other directors could resolve that a director be removed. The court held that the alteration was valid as it was *bona fide* and in the interests of the company as a whole. Similarly, in *Sidebottom v. Keeshaw, Leese & Co.*[14] the articles were altered to allow the directors to purchase the shares of any member who was competing with the company. A minority shareholder, who was in competition with the company, objected to the alteration on the grounds that it was an attempt by the majority to expel a minority. With no evidence of *male fides* on the part of the majority shareholders, the court accepted that the alteration was justifiable in the interests of the company.

However, in *Brown v. British Abrasive Wheel Co.,*[15] the majority did not persuade the court that the alteration was for the company's benefit. The company in question was in need of a capital injection. The majority agreed to provide the additional funds on condition that they could buy out the 2 per cent minority. The minority refused to sell and the majority caused the articles to be altered to enable them to acquire the minority shares compulsorily at a fair price. The minority's objection succeeded as the court held that the alteration was not an essential prerequisite to a capital injection, and was not therefore for the benefit of the company. A majority decision met with the same fate in *Dafen Tinplate Co. Ltd v. Llanelly Steel Co. (1907) Ltd.*[16] There, a minority shareholder had transferred his custom from the company to a competitor. The majority altered the articles to provide for the compulsory acquisition of the minority's shares without specifying any grounds. The court accepted the plaintiff's contention that this new power had too wide a scope, and that the alteration was designed only to compel him to transfer his shares. Accordingly, the court refused to confirm the alteration.

2. Other Limitations

The power to alter the articles is subject to further limitations:

(a) the articles cannot be altered where the alteration is contrary to the memorandum of association, the Companies Acts or the general law;

---

13 [1927] 2 KB 9.
14 [1920] 1 Ch 154.
15 [1919] 1 Ch 291.
16 [1920] 2 Ch 124.

(b) an alteration which requires a member to subscribe for additional shares or accept increased liability in respect of his shares will not be valid unless that member has given his consent;[17]

(c) where an alteration purports to vary the rights attached to a class of shares, it may only be made if the consent of that class has been obtained;

(d) where the court has altered the articles the company may not thereafter purport to make an inconsistent alteration without the court's consent.

The Effect of an Alteration on Outsiders

An alteration of the articles is valid even if it causes a breach of a contract with an outsider. Although the outsider cannot obtain an injunction to prevent the alteration, the company may be liable in damages for breach of contract. In *Southern Foundries (1926) Ltd v. Shirlaw*,[18] the respondent had been appointed managing director for a period of ten years. The articles provided that the managing director's appointment would automatically cease if he should cease to be a director. As part of a merger agreement with the Federated Industries Group, the members of the company agreed to alter the articles to the effect that Federated Industries would have the power to remove directors of group companies. This power was invoked to remove Shirlaw. As a result he ceased to be managing director even though the ten year period had not expired. Shirlaw's claim for breach of contract succeeded because it was held that his service contract included an implied condition that the company would not do anything that would make it impossible for him to continue as managing director.

The Contractual Nature of the Memorandum and Articles

By virtue of section 25 of the Principal Act, the memorandum and articles of association, once registered, bind the company and the members to the provisions thereof, in the same manner as if they had been respectively signed and sealed by each member. The legal effect of this section is therefore as follows:

(a) the company is bound to the members;

(b) the members are bound to the company; and

(c) the members are bound to each other.

Although the 'Section 25' contract applies to both the memorandum and articles most of the litigation in this area relates to the articles of association. In *Hickman v. Kent or Romney Marsh Sheepbreeders Association*,[19] the plaintiff was in dispute with the company which had threatened to expel him from its membership. The articles provided that disputes between the company and its

---

17 Section 27 of the Principal Act.
18 [1940] AC 701.
19 [1915] 1 Ch D 881.

members should be submitted to arbitration. The plaintiff, in breach of the articles, began an action in court against the company. The court held that the plaintiff was bound by the provisions of the articles and the proceedings were stayed pending the outcome of arbitration.

It is important to note that the 'section 25' contract applies only to rights and obligations affecting members in their capacity as members. As Steyn L J., in the case of *Bratton Seymour Service Co. Ltd v. Oxborough*,[20] observed:

> It is binding only in so far as it affects the rights and obligations between the company and the members acting in their capacity as members. If it contains provisions conferring rights and obligations on outsiders, then those provisions do not bite as part of the contract between the company and the members, even if the outsider is coincidentally a member.

Accordingly, directors and creditors who are enforcing their rights against the company cannot rely on the articles just because they also happen to be members. This position was clearly illustrated in *Beattie v. Beattie*,[21] which also concerned an arbitration clause in the articles. The company had commenced proceedings against the managing director, who was also a member, to recover monies improperly paid to him. The managing director applied to have the action stayed on the grounds that the dispute should first be put to arbitration as provided for by the articles. The court rejected this claim because the dispute related to obligations of the managing director in his position as managing director and did not concern his rights as a member. Similarly, in *Eley v. Positive Government Life Assurance Co.*,[22] the plaintiff — a solicitor — had, when drafting the original articles of association, included a provision that the company would always employ him as a solicitor. He subsequently became a member of the company. When his services as a solicitor were no longer retained by the company, he sued it for breach of the 'section 25 contract'. It was held that Eley's claim under the articles could not succeed as it was asserted as an outsider (i.e. a solicitor) and not as a member of the company. On this basis, it is clear that the memorandum and articles define the position of the shareholder as shareholder and do not bind him in his capacity as an individual. Similarly, the provisions of the memorandum and articles that do not concern membership of the company are not contractually enforceable as part of the contract formed between the member of the company and the company as a separate person.

In certain circumstances an outsider may rely on the articles to infer a term or condition into a contract with the company. In *Re New British Iron Co.*,[23] the articles provided for directors' remuneration of £1,000 and the directors had

---

20 [1992] BCLC 693.
21 [1938] Ch 708.
22 (1876) 1 Ex D 21.
23 [1989] 1 Ch 324.

accepted office on this basis. The company went into liquidation before any remuneration had been paid. It was held that the relevant provisions in the articles were also implied terms of the service contract between the directors and the company. The directors were therefore entitled to recover the arrears of remuneration. So even though the directors could not rely on Section 25, they were permitted to rely on some of the articles as implied terms of their own separate contracts with the company. Where provisions of the articles are incorporated whether expressly or impliedly in the terms and conditions of a contract, those provisions may still be altered but not so as to affect an accrued right by an outsider. In *Swabey v. Port Darwin Gold Mining Co.*,[24] the articles provided for directors' fees of £200 per annum. This provision was incorporated into a service contract with a director. An alteration was made to reduce the amount retrospectively to £60 per annum. It was held that the articles could not be altered retrospectively to deprive a director of his right to fees already owed, and the alteration could only take effect prospectively. Lord Esher declared that 'the articles do not themselves form a contract, but from them you get the terms upon which the directors are serving.' Directors who are relying on the articles as an implied term of their own contracts should be conscious of the fact that the articles may be altered, which could affect their future rights.

Although section 25 does not specifically refer to a contractual relationship between the members *inter se*, this is in fact the legal position. In *Rayfield v. Hands*,[25] the articles provided that every member who wished to transfer shares should inform the directors who would take them at a fair value. The directors refused to buy the shares of the plaintiff and denied that the members could enforce the obligation under the articles. The court accepted the plaintiff's contention that there was a contract between the members and the member-directors to which the directors were bound. Vaissey J. interpreted the reference to 'directors' in the articles as a reference to a class of members who were directors and that, accordingly, the article had contractual effect. He granted the plaintiff an order requiring the directors to take the shares.The outcome of this case is arguably inconsistent with the *Eley* case as the articles imposed the obligation to buy the shares on the directors, who are not party to the section 25 contract. However, it can probably be reconciled with *Eley* on the basis that the court held the contract to be enforceable against the directors in their capacity as members. Of course, the question remains whether or not such a provision could be enforceable against a director who was not a member of the company. In any case the principle is that the memorandum and articles of association bind the members *inter se* and this has long been the accepted position in Ireland.[26]

---

24 (1889) 1 Meg 385.
25 [1960] 1 Ch 1.
26 *Clark v. Workman* [1920] 1 IR 107 per Ross J. and *Lee & Co. (Dublin) Ltd v. Egan (Wholesale) Ltd*, unreported, High Court 27/4/1978, per Kenny J.

CHAPTER SIX

THE CONSEQUENCES OF INCORPORATION

Introduction

Once registered, and the 'certificate of incorporation' issued, a company has a legal existence separate and distinct from its members. As a separate legal entity the company is conferred with rights and is subject to duties and obligations. It can sue to have these rights enforced, and similarly it can be sued. It can own property in its own right and its existence will continue perpetually, irrespective of a change in its ownership, until the grant of incorporation has been revoked. The implications of the company's separate legal status were demonstrated in the case of *Salomon v. Salomon & Co. Ltd*.[1]

Salomon's Case

Salomon, a sole trader, sold his boot manufacturing business to a newly incorporated company. The business was sold to the company for £39,000 of which it was agreed that Salomon would be given cash, £10,000 in secured debentures issued by the company and 20,000 £1 shares in the company. To satisfy the statutory requirements that private companies could only be incorporated with seven members,[2] six members of Salomon's family were each given one share. These shares were held on trust for Salomon himself. Soon after incorporation the company suffered financial difficulties. In an attempt to keep the company going, Salomon sold his debenture, at a discount, for £5,000 and put this amount together with his other cash into the company. His rescue attempt proved futile and the company ultimately collapsed. The new debenture holder, a Mr Broderip, sought to realise his security by claiming against the company's assets. If his claim succeeded there would be nothing left over for the unsecured creditors. The liquidator of the company contended that the debenture, which had been issued to Salomon, was invalid because Salomon and the company were in fact the same entity and a person could not owe money to himself. The fact that there were other shareholders was irrelevant, as they were merely 'puppets' acting on Salomon's instructions. It was further argued that even if the company and Salomon were technically separate entities, the company was acting as the agent of Salomon who was the real owner of the business. These arguments persuaded the Court of Appeal, which held that Salomon was still effectively a

---

1 [1897] AC 22.

2 It was not until 1907 that the requirement to have two members for a private company was introduced.

sole trader because the other shareholders were not independent of his control. He could not therefore enjoy the privileges of incorporation just because he had satisfied the machinery of incorporation.

However, the House of Lords reversed the decision of the Court of Appeal and held in favour of Salomon. Its opinion centred on the fact that once a company is registered it acquires a legal personality of its own which is separate from that of its owner. Furthermore, as the Companies Acts did not require shareholders to be independent of each other, the court would not read such a requirement into them. Accordingly, the company's liabilities were its own and not the responsibility of the company's principal shareholder. It followed that the secured debenture holder had a prior claim to the company's assets. In the famous speech of Lord Macnaghten it was observed that:

> . . . the company is at law a different person altogether from the subscribers to the Memorandum; and, although it may be that after incorporation the business is precisely the same as it was before, and the same persons are managers, and the same hands receive the profits, the company is not in law the agent of the subscribers or a trustee for them. Nor are the subscribers, as members, liable in any shape or form, except to the extent and in the manner provided by the Act.[3]

The Separate Legal Personality Applied

The decision in the *Salomon* case established beyond doubt that once the statutory formalities have been complied with, a 'veil of incorporation' is placed over the company. This veil distinguishes the company from its members and in doing so separates their respective obligations. The effect of the decision in *Salomon*'s case can be seen in *Lee v. Lee's Air Farming Ltd*.[4] Lee, who held the beneficial interest in the shares of the defendant company, was also its governing director and employed by the company as a pilot. When he was killed, while in the course of carrying on the company's business, his wife claimed compensation under the Worker's Compensation Act. The Court of Appeal of New Zealand held that the widow was not entitled to compensation since Lee as owner and governing director of the company could not also be its worker. The Privy Council rejected this decision and held that by law, Lee and his company were separate persons and having been hired by the company as a pilot, he had become a worker within the meaning of the Act. Similarly, in *Tunstall v. Steigman*[5] a landlord attempted to avoid granting a statutory tenancy to the plaintiff on the grounds that the tenant wished to use the premises for extending her business practice. The landlord's claim failed on the basis that the business was in fact being carried out by a company in which the plaintiff was the principal shareholder.

---

3 [1897] AC 22 at 51.
4 [1961] AC 12.
5 [1962] 2 All ER 417.

The principles laid down in the *Salomon* case have been applied on numerous occasions by the Irish courts. In *Roundabout Ltd v. Beirne*[6] the employees of a public house, in a dispute with the owners, placed a picket at the owners' premises. The owners later transferred the pub to a company and the court ordered the picket to be lifted since there was no trade dispute between the workers and the new owner, despite the fact that ownership of the company was vested in the original owners of the pub. In the recent case of *Sweeney v. Duggan*[7] the plaintiff was employed by a company and was injured at work. The company went into liquidation before any compensation could be paid. The plaintiff sued the defendant, who owned and managed the company, on the grounds *inter alia* that he should have made sure that the company was insured. The Supreme Court held that the defendant was not liable to pay the company's obligations to the plaintiff.

It does not always work to the member's benefit to be treated as a separate entity from the company. Sometimes the 'veil of incorporation' will have a 'boomerang' effect on the member, as the following case illustrates. In *Macaura v. Northern Assurance Co. Ltd*,[8] the plaintiff sold his timber business to a company which he owned. The timber was subsequently destroyed and the plaintiff claimed under his own personal insurance policy. The insurers refused to pay on the grounds that the plaintiff had no insurable interest in the timber, as it belonged to the company. The House of Lords, applying the principle laid down in the *Salomon* case, held that the company and the plaintiff were two separate persons and as the company owned the timber, the plaintiff had no insurable interest in it. Accordingly, the insurance company was not liable. Similarly, in *O'Neill v. Ryan & Ryan Air Ltd*,[9] the plaintiff alleged that breaches of competition law by the first defendant had diminished the value of his shares in the second defendant. The Supreme Court rejected his claim on the basis that if the alleged actions caused a loss to the company, a claim for compensation was payable to the company and not to an individual shareholder.

Segregation of Ownership

One of the consequences of a company having a separate legal personality, which went to the core of *Salomon*'s case, is that a company owns its property, assets and undertaking and does not hold them as agent or trustee for the members. Accordingly, the rights and obligations incidental to that property are the company's alone and not those of the company's owners. In the *Macaura* case it was held that only the company could have an insurable interest in its own

6 [1959] IR 423.
7 [1997] 1 ILRM 211.
8 [1925] AC 619.
9 [1993] ILRM 557.

property. Similarly, in *Stewarts Supermarkets Ltd v. Secretary of State*,[10] it was held that a parent company was not entitled to compensation under a statutory compensation scheme because damage was caused to the property of its subsidiary company which was a separate legal entity.

Suing and Being Sued

Another consequence of a company's separate legal personality is that it is conferred with rights which are enforceable by way of litigation. A company's contractual capacity is determined by the objects clause of the memorandum of association and providing it acts within its capacity and satisfies the legal requirements for a valid contract, it can sue to have its contractual rights enforced. Similarly, a company can sue for torts committed against it, although certain torts, such as trespass to the person, cannot be committed against a corporation. What is less certain is whether or not a company has rights which are protected by the Constitution. It would seem that many of the personal rights afforded to citizens under Article 40 of Bunreacht na hÉireann do not ordinarily apply to companies.[11] However, it has been suggested that companies may be considered as citizens for the purpose of protecting their property rights.[12] Furthermore, a company is entitled to access to the courts in the same manner as natural persons.[13]

As well as having rights, a company has corresponding legal obligations which must be fulfilled. It must comply with its contractual and tortious obligations in the same manner as a legal person. However, a company's liability in crime is not as straightforward. First, companies have no physical manifestation and cannot therefore be prosecuted for crimes such as rape and assault which require a physical act. Second, a company has no mind of its own and is merely 'invisible, immortal and rests only in intendment and consideration of the law'.[14] Therefore, proving intent or *mens rea* on the part of a company is usually not possible, although in certain circumstances the intent or *mens rea* of the perpetrator may be attributed to the company.[15] There is no such difficulty in prosecuting a company for crimes which do not require a physical act or a *mens rea* on the part of the offender. When it comes to the matter of punishment, the most appropriate form for a company is the imposition of a fine or an order of sequestration because, naturally, a company cannot be imprisoned.

In order to commence any action against a company, it is necessary to serve it with the proceedings. The appropriate documents may be served at either the

---

10 [1982] NI 286.
11 *Quinn's Supermarket Ltd v. Attorney General* [1972] IR 1.
12 *Irish Rail Ltd v. Ireland and Others* [1995] 2 ILRM 161.
13 *Bula Ltd v. Tara Mines Ltd* [1987] IR 85.
14 Case of Sutton's Hospital (1612) 10 Co. Rep. 7a.
15 *HL Bolton (Engineering) Ltd v. TJ Gratham & Sons Ltd* [1957] 1QB 159.

registered office of the company[16] or with an agent who has agreed to be served on the company's behalf.

Piercing the Corporate Veil

In the *Salomon* case it was argued that as the business had been over-valued, the company should have a right to rescind the sale. Although the court recognised that the value of the business was extravagant, the House of Lords suggested that the amount merely represented the 'sanguine expectations of a fond owner' rather that an attempt to perpetrate a fraud. However, Lord Halsbury did suggest that the privilege of incorporation could only be availed of as long as 'there was no fraud and no agency and if the company was a real one and not a fiction or a myth'.[17] Where any of these circumstances occur the court will strip away the veil of incorporation surrounding the company. In doing so, the corporate personality remains intact but the members, and in extreme cases the directors, are held responsible for obligations which would ordinarily be the responsibility of the company. The courts have not defined the circumstances which will cause it to disregard the separate legal personality of the company. However, in *Re a Company*[18] it was suggested that the court 'will use its power to pierce the corporate veil if it is necessary to achieve justice irrespective of the legal efficacy of the corporate structure'. In any case the courts have identified a company by its members in the following circumstances:

(a) where an agency relationship existed between the company and its members;
(b) where the relationship between companies in the same group is so intertwined that they should be treated as a single economic entity;
(c) where the company is being used to avoid existing legal obligations;
(d) where the company is being used to perpetrate a fraud or an injustice;
(e) to establish the true residency of the company; and
(f) where the company is in reality a 'quasi-partnership'.

Agency

The court has shown a willingness to lift the veil when the company is acting as the agent of another party, particularly when that party is the parent company. This is clearly illustrated by the case of *Smith, Stone and Knight Ltd v. Birmingham Corporation*.[19] There, the plaintiff's subsidiary carried out waste business on land owned by the plaintiff. The land was subject to a compulsory acquisition order by the corporation, and the plaintiff claimed for losses suffered. The defendants argued that the plaintiff as a separate company was not carrying out any business and was not entitled to compensation. In determining whether

---

16 Section 379(1) of the Principal Act.
17 [1897] AC 22 and 23.
18 [1985] 1 BCC 99.
19 [1939] 4 All ER 116.

an agency relationship existed, the court considered that the following questions should be addressed.

(a) Were the profits of the subsidiary treated as the profits of the parent company?
(b) Was the management of the subsidiary appointed by the parent company?
(c) Was the parent company the 'heads and brains' of the subsidiary?
(d) Did the parent company govern the operation of the subsidiary?
(e) Were the profits of the subsidiaries the result of the skill and direction of the parent company?
(f) Was the parent company in 'effectual and constant' control?

Having answered these questions in the affirmative, the court held that the subsidiary was acting as an agent for the parent company. Accordingly, the plaintiff company was entitled to the compensation claim. An agency relationship was also found to have existed in *Firestone Tyre and Rubber Co. v. Llewellin*.[20] There, an American company formed a subsidiary in the United Kingdom for the purpose of manufacturing tyres and distributing them to the company's customers in the European market. The American company obtained the orders, and the agreement with the UK company was such that the latter, having received its costs and a 5 per cent commission, the UK company would transfer the balance of the selling price to the American company. When the American company was assessed for UK tax on its profits, it claimed that it was a separate entity from the UK company. The court held that the subsidiary had acted as the agent of the American company, which was liable for UK tax.

However, the mere fact that companies are part of the same group will not automatically create an inference that an agency relationship exists between them. This is so even where the corporate structures are established purely to enable one company to avoid any prospective liabilities. In *Adams v. Cape Industries*[21] the English-based defendant was a large multinational company engaged in the asbestos business. One of its former subsidiaries had been liquidated following a settlement for injuries suffered by its workers and its operations transferred to a company named CPC. CPC, though not a subsidiary of Cape Industries, was set up with the latter's financial assistance and received instructions from it through an agent. The workers at CPC's plant obtained judgment against Cape in the US and sought to have that judgment enforced in the English courts. In order to succeed they had to demonstrate that Cape had been carrying on business in the US either by itself or through an agent. The court accepted that CPC had been set up as part of an overall group arrangement to reduce the appearance of Cape's involvement in the US, while at the same time enabling Cape asbestos to continue to be sold there. Despite this, the Court

---

20 [1957] 1 WLR 464.
21 [1990] Ch 433.

of Appeal held that Cape had no presence in the US, with the deciding factor being that CPC was independently owned and was not a subsidiary of Cape.

Single Economic Entity

In certain circumstances the courts will ignore the separate legal personality of one or more group companies where the relationship between these companies justifies treating them as a 'single economic entity'. *DHN Food Distributors Ltd v. Tower Hamlet Borough Council* [22] involved a similar claim for compensation as in the *Smith* case mentioned above. Here the plaintiff had two subsidiaries, one of which owned the landed property interests of the group. The plaintiff was the trading company and occupied the subsidiary's land for its business activities. When the land was compulsorily acquired, the Lands Tribunal claimed that the subsidiary was not entitled to compensation as it had no business to lose. Furthermore, the plaintiff was only entitled to a negligible amount of compensation for the loss of a revocable licence. Lord Denning advocated the view that where subsidiaries are bound hand and foot to the parent company, they should not be treated as separate entities where this would deprive them of compensation which is justly payable. The court rejected the Land Tribunal's claim and treated the companies as a single economic unit. Accordingly, the plaintiff's compensation claim succeeded.

The 'single economic entity' test was approved in Ireland in the case of *Power Supermarkets Ltd v. Crumlin Investments Ltd and Dunnes Stores (Crumlin) Ltd.* [23] The first defendant developed a shopping centre and leased a unit to the plaintiff. One of the terms of the lease included a covenant by the lessor that no other lease would be granted to another tenant in the grocery or food business. The shopping centre was not a great success and the first defendant was acquired by Cornelscourt Shopping Centre Ltd, a company owned by the Dunnes Stores Group. The purchaser then caused the first defendant to convey a freehold unit to the second defendant, Dunnes Stores (Crumlin) Ltd, which would enable the Dunnes Group to operate a supermarket in the centre. The plaintiff objected to the introduction of a trading rival. In treating the defendants as a 'single entity', Costello J. observed:

> that a court may, if the justice of the case so requires, treat two or more related companies as a single entity so that the business notionally carried on by one will be regarded as the business of the group or another member of the group if this conforms to the economic and commercial realities of the situation. It would, in my view, be very hard to find a clearer case than the present one for the application of this principle.

Accordingly, the court held that the second defendant was bound by the restrictive covenant even though it was not a contractual party to it. However, it

---

22 [1976] 1 WLR 852.
23 High Court, 22 June 1981 (Costello J.).

is only in exceptional circumstances that the courts will ignore the strict veil that surrounds a company, even when it is part of a group of companies. In *Adams v. Cape Industries*,[24] it was suggested that in the context of group companies the court did not accept that:

> . . . as a matter of law the court is entitled to lift the corporate veil as against the defendant company which is a member of a corporate group, merely because the corporate structure has been used so as to ensure that the legal liability (if any) in respect of particular future activities of the group . . . will fall on another member of the group rather than the defendant company. Whether or not this is desirable, the right to use a corporate structure in this manner is inherent in our corporate law.[25]

In the recent Irish case of *Allied Irish Coal Supplies Ltd v. Powell Duffryn International Fuels Ltd*[26] the Supreme Court refused to join a parent company to an action being taken against its subsidiary company just because of the relationship between them. The court held that a subsidiary could be dependent on its parent company as regards control, finance and operations and that this did not prevent it from being a separate legal entity. According to the court, the concept of limited liability was to enable some part of a person's affairs to be placed in a separate compartment.

Avoidance of Legal Obligations

In *Cape Industries* the court recognised that corporate structures are put in place to avoid potential liabilities. Indeed, it is suggested that the very use of the privilege of incorporation is motivated by a desire to reduce the potential liability for the owner should things go wrong. Similarly, the taxation concessions which are available to companies encourage their formation. However, the courts will not countenance the use of the statutory privilege as a device for avoiding existing obligations. In such circumstances the courts are willing to cast aside the veil of incorporation to examine what lies behind it. In *Jones v. Lipman*,[27] the defendant entered into an agreement to sell his house to Jones. Thereafter he changed his mind, and to avoid the contract he acquired a company and transferred the house to it. The court held that the company was a mere 'device' and 'sham' created for the sole purpose of avoiding contractual obligations. Accordingly, the company was held bound by the defendant's obligations and an order of specific performance was granted in favour of the plaintiff. In *Gilford Motor Co. Ltd v. Horne*,[28] the court also set aside the veil where a company was being used to avoid a contractual obligation. There, the defendant had, while in the employ of the

---

24 [1990] Ch 433.
25 Ibid. at 544 D, E.
26 [1997] 1 ILRM 306 (High Court); [1998] 2 ILRM 61 (Supreme Court).
27 [1962] 1 All ER 442.
28 [1933] Ch 939.

plaintiff, signed a restraint of trade agreement whereby he agreed that on leaving his employment, he would not set up a business in opposition to the plaintiff for a period of six years. Within a few weeks of his leaving his employment, his wife and son formed a company in competition with the plaintiff. Although the defendant had no shares and was not a director, the company acted on his instructions. The court held that the corporate entity was merely a 'mask', used to enable Horne to engage in business which he was contractually prevented from doing as a natural person. An injunction was granted against Horne and the company from continuing the business in competition with the plaintiff.

Fraud or Injustices

The courts will not allow the corporate personality to be used as an engine for 'fraud' or to cause on obvious injustice. The latter point was made clear in the case of *Re Bugle Press Ltd*.[29] The majority shareholders, holding 90 per cent of the issued share capital, wished to acquire the remaining 10 per cent held by a third shareholder. They formed a company which made a take-over bid, and having successfully obtained the 90 per cent shareholding it sought to enforce its right under section 209 of the UK Companies Act 1948 to acquire the minority's stake compulsorily. The minority successfully applied to the court for relief. The court viewed the transaction as one designed for the sole purpose of expropriating a minority, which is an act forbidden by company law unless permitted specifically by the articles.

Fraud was the rationale behind the court's decision to sweep aside the corporate veil in *Re Darby: ex parte Brougham*.[30] Darby and Gyde, two undischarged bankrupts, registered a company in the Channel Islands. This company then established a company in the United Kingdom and financed it by issuing debentures. The amount raised on foot of the debentures was paid to the Channel Islands company and distributed among the two bankrupts. When the UK company failed, the liquidator claimed in Darby's bankruptcy for the secret profits he had made. The court allowed the liquidator's claim, holding that Darby could not use the Channel Island company as a cloak for his fraudulent activities.

Residency

The court will often be called upon to look behind the veil of incorporation to establish the true residence of the company. This usually, but not always, occurs in relation to establishing tax liabilities. In *Daimler v. Continental Tyre Co*.,[31] the defendant owed monies to the plaintiff, a British-registered company, whose directors and shareholders were German. Under wartime laws, trading with the

---

29 [1961] Ch 270.
30 [1911] 1 KB 95.
31 [1916] 2 AC 307.

enemy was forbidden. The House of Lords looked beyond the corporate personality to those who controlled the company and concluded that the defendant was not obliged to pay the 'debt', as to do so would constitute trading with the enemy.

Quasi-Partnerships

In certain circumstances the courts look beyond the technicalities of the company's legal existence, and in doing so recognise the commercial reality of the relationship between the company, its directors and its members. Where that relationship is more akin to a partnership, whose existence is dependent upon a degree of trust and communication between the partners, and the relationship breaks down, the company may be wound up by analogy with the dissolution of a partnership.[32]

Statutory Provisions

There are several statutory provisions which have the effect of ignoring the separate existence of the company by attaching responsibility for the company's obligations to its members or, in extreme cases, to its directors. These provisions relate to the following:

1. where the company's members fall below the legal minimum;[33]
2. where there has been a failure by the company's officers to state the company's name when required by law to do so;[34]
3. the production of group accounts (see Chapter 19, Accounts and Returns);
4. where related companies are being wound up;[35] and
5. the imposition of liability on directors and other officers for the debts and obligations of the company.

Insufficient Membership

Section 36 of the Principal Act provides that where the number of members is reduced below the minimum required by law and the company continues to carry on business for more than six months with this reduced number, all members who knew of the deficit will be severally liable for any debts incurred by the company after the expiry of this period. It was held in *Brook's Wharf Ltd v. Goodman Bros*[36] that if a member incurs liability under the section, he is entitled to be indemnified by the company. It should be noted that since October 1994, with the advent of one-member companies, this provision no longer applies to private limited companies.[37]

---

32 *Re Murph's Restaurant* [1979] ILRM 141 (see Chapter 15).
33 Section 36 of the Principal Act.
34 Section 114(4) of the Principal Act.
35 Sections 140 and 141 of the Companies Act 1990: see Chapter 26, Liquidations.
36 [1937] I KB 534.
37 Regulation 7(1) of the European Communities (Single-Member Private Limited Companies) Regulations 1994 SI 275/1994.

Failure to State the Company's Name Correctly

Under section 114(4) of the Principal Act, if an officer of the company signs on the company's behalf a bill of exchange, promissory note, endorsement, cheque or order for money or goods, without the company's name being mentioned thereon, he will be liable to a fine. More importantly, if the company fails to pay the signatory shall be personally liable to the holder of the relevant instrument for the amount thereof. In *Rafsanjan Pistachio Producers Co-operative v. Reiss*,[38] the defendant director had signed cheques on the company's behalf in favour of the plaintiff. No mention of the company's name was ascribed thereon and when they were subsequently dishonoured by the company, the defendant was held personally liable for the amount unpaid. In *Durham Fancy Goods Ltd v. Michael Jackson (Fancy Goods) Ltd*,[39] it was held that the abbreviation of 'Michael' to 'M' in describing the name of the company on a bill of exchange and the form of acceptance was a misdescription and a breach of the section. However, as the plaintiff had been responsible for the misdescription and had represented that it would treat the acceptance as regular, it was estopped from enforcing the liability.

Section 114(5) of the Principal Act provides, however, that where 'Ltd' is used for 'Limited', 'Teo' for 'Teoranta', 'plc' for 'public limited company' or 'cpt' for 'cuideachta phoibli theoranta', no liability will be incurred under the section.

Accounts of Group Companies

In recognition of the phenomenon of the increasing number of groups of companies, legislative provisions have been introduced to reflect the overall group position and in certain instances, where the commercial realities of the situation so dictate, to treat some or all of the companies in a group as one entity. Accordingly, the European Communities (Companies: Group Accounts) Regulations 1992[40] require group accounts to be in the form of a consolidated balance sheet and a consolidated profit and loss. It is important to observe that ownership is not a necessary requisite to satisfying a group relationship: rather, the emphasis is on the control exercised by one company over another.

The Winding up of Related Companies

Under section 140 of the Companies Act 1990, a company may be required to contribute to the debts of related companies. The extent of a company's control over the management of the related company will be a significant factor in determining what, if any, liability should be attributed to the company. Furthermore, the court may also order that where a company is being wound up,

---

38 [1990] BCLC 352.
39 [1968] 2 QB 839.
40 SI 201/1992.

the assets of a related company which is also being wound up should be pooled between the creditors of both companies.[41]

Liability of Directors and Other Officers

Probably the most extreme example of piercing the corporate veil is when non-members are held to be responsible for the company's obligations. There are several statutory provisions which attach liability to the directors or officers of a company. These include *inter alia*:

(a) liability for failure to maintain proper books of accounts;[42]
(b) liability for acting in a fraudulent or reckless manner;[43]
(c) liability for acting in breach of the restriction and disqualification requirements of Part VII of the 1990 Act.[44]

Other Consequences of Incorporation

1. Limited Liability

All companies are liable without limit for their debts and liabilities. As long as assets are available, a company is obliged to pay its debts. However, a company, like a natural person, may not have sufficient assets to meet its debts and it is at this point that the concept of limited liability is important. Since the Limited Liability Act 1855, if a company is formed on the basis of limited liability its members are not liable to contribute to the assets of the company, except to the extent agreed. Typically, in the case of a company limited by shares, the liability of its members will be limited to the amount unpaid on those shares, if any. In the case of a company limited by guarantee, the memorandum of association will determine the amount that each member is liable to contribute. Where a company has unlimited status, its members will be liable to contribute to the assets of the company to the extent required to pay all of the company's liabilities.

2. Perpetual Succession

A company's life begins with the process of incorporation. It does not therefore have a natural birth, nor does it suffer a natural death. Its existence is perpetual and is not dependent upon the life of its members or directors. They may come and go, but the company continues until such time as it is dissolved or struck from the register.

---

41 Section 141 of the Companies Act 1990.
42 Section 202 of the Companies Act 1990: see Chapter 19.
43 Section 297 of the Principal Act: see Chapter 18.
44 Section 163(3) of the Companies Act 1990: see Chapter 16.

3. *Transferable Shares*

The member's interest in the company is a form of property which is measured in shares. These shares are freely transferable, subject to any restrictions imposed by the memorandum and articles of association. (See Chapter 8, Securities.)

4. *Floating Charge*

Companies can raise capital in the form of loans by granting by way of security a floating charge over some or all of their assets. This form of security is peculiar to companies,[45] and its advantage lies in the fact that the company can still deal with the assets charged in the ordinary course of its business. (See Chapter 11, Loan Capital.)

5. *Tax Concessions*

Companies can avail of the tax advantages afforded by various pieces of taxation legislation. A company's liability to taxation on its profits takes the form of corporation tax, which is usually at a rate below the prevailing income tax rates for individuals.

---

45 Although in theory a floating charge can be given by an individual, as in *TCB v. Gray* [1986] 1 All ER 587.

CHAPTER SEVEN

CONTRACTUAL CAPACITY OF THE COMPANY

Introduction

If a company enters into a transaction which is outside the stated objects, it is acting beyond its capacity and the transaction is said to be *ultra vires*. At common law, an *ultra vires* transaction is void and unenforceable.[1] The effect of the common law position regarding *ultra vires* was exacerbated by the fact that pre-20th century legislation only permitted the company to alter the objects clause in limited circumstances and subject to the approval of the court. Furthermore, even where the general meeting was in a position to alter the objects, its effect could not operate retrospectively to validate an *ultra vires* act.[2]

The strict application of the *ultra vires* rule often caused hardship for innocent third parties acting *bona fide*, who found themselves unable to enforce a contract against the company. This hardship was compounded by the doctrine of constructive notice which dictates that a person who deals with a company is deemed to have notice of the contents of the company's public documents. Apply both doctrines to an innocent third party and the result could not be any more severe, as the case of *Re Jon Beauforte (London) Ltd* demonstrates.[3] Here the company was established as a costumier and gown manufacturer. Without altering its objects it had engaged for several years in the business of veneer panel manufacturing. When the company failed, the liquidator disallowed a claim by a supplier of heating fuel. In fact, all but one of the creditors' claims was disallowed. The supplier argued unsuccessfully that the heating fuel could be needed for any of the company's businesses. It was held that the supplier had actual notice of the business being undertaken because it was specified on the company's headed paper. The supplier was also deemed to have constructive notice that the business was not within the company's objects, because the memorandum, which was available for public inspection, did not contain such an object. Accordingly, the contract, in furtherance of an *ultra vires* activity, was void and unenforceable. As the contract could not be enforced, the only other remedy available to the supplier was the equitable remedy of tracing, which would have been difficult to achieve, not least because the heating fuel had probably, like his chances of being paid, gone up in smoke!

---

1 *Ashbury Railway Carriage and Iron Company v. Richie* (1875) LR 7 HL 653.
2 *Attorney General v. Great Eastern Railway* (1880) 5 App Cas 473 HL. Although companies can now alter the objects by passing a special resolution, the position remains that an alteration cannot retrospectively validate an ultra vires transaction.
3 [1953] Ch 131.

Action, Judicial Reaction and Counteraction

In order to circumvent the effects of the *ultra vires* rule, the legal draftsmen departed from the model memoranda set out in the Companies Acts by registering memoranda containing a multiplicity of objects and powers. The courts responded to such initiatives by construing objects clauses strictly, and in so doing drew a distinction between the objects of the company and its powers. According to the court, the powers contained in the memorandum could only be used in furtherance of the company's main objects. Therefore, if the 'main objects' had been specified in the first few paragraphs of the objects clause, and there followed subsequent paragraphs containing wider powers, those powers could only be exercised in so far as they achieved the 'main' objects of the company.[4] Where, for example, a company's main object was to build houses, which was followed by the power to borrow money and give security, those powers could only be exercised where they were in furtherance of the company's building object.

The draftsmen responded to this 'main objects' rule by using the following devices:

1. the independent objects clause; and
2. the 'bell houses' clause.

1. The Independent Objects Clause

Memoranda were drafted whereby the 'objects clause' would end with a statement to the effect that each object and power should be treated independently and not ancillary or subordinate to the others. In other words, each object and power was a main object. The intended effect of this practice was to prevent any single object being impugned on the application of the 'main objects' test. The 'independent objects clauses' proved successful as the House of Lords, however reluctantly, upheld their validity. In *Cotman v. Broughman,*[5] the first paragraph of the objects clauses authorised the company to own and work rubber plantations. Several other paragraphs empowered the company to engage in other activities including holding and dealing in securities. The final paragraph specified that all clauses should be construed as independent substantive clauses. The company underwrote an issue of shares of an oil company, and this transaction was subsequently challenged on *ultra vires* grounds. The presence of the 'independent objects clause' was held by the court to have ensured the *intra vires* nature of the transaction. This was so despite the fact, which was acknowledged by the court in the *Cotman* case, that such clauses defeated the legislative requirement that a company's business activities should be transparent.

---

4 See *Anglo-Irish Agencies Ltd v. Green* [1960] All ER 244.
5 [1918] AC 514.

2. The 'Bell Houses' Clause

The second device used to circumvent the 'main object' rule is what is often referred to as the Bell Houses clause. This clause gives a company the capacity to enter into any contract which the directors believe would benefit the company. The effect of such a device was such that the company's objects could in practice be open ended, depending on the opinion of the directors. In *Bell Houses Ltd v. City Wall Properties Ltd*,[6] the company's objects clause specified that the business of the company was the building and development of housing estates. However, the memorandum also empowered the directors to pursue any trade or business which could, in their opinion, be advantageously carried on by the company in connection with its business. The objects also contained an 'independent objects clause'. The company, in the course of its business dealings, had made a number of useful contacts. One of these was with a group of Swiss bankers who wished to loan money for the purpose of property development. The company agreed, in return for a commission, to introduce the defendant to the Swiss bankers. The defendant later refused to pay the commission and argued that the agreement was *ultra vires* the company and void. The court held that as a result of the discretionary power given to the directors, the objects of the company were limited only by the directors' subjective opinion. As the directors genuinely believed that 'mortgage broking' could be advantageously carried on as ancillary to the general business of the company, the agreement was *intra vires*, valid and enforceable.[7]

The use of both these devices — the independent objects clause and the Bell Houses clause — had the effect of reducing the value of the objects clause which was, after all, intended to protect members as well as creditors who entered into an *intra vires* transaction with the company.

Objects v. Powers

Despite judicial acceptance of the above mentioned devices, their validity was subject to one important proviso — that regardless of what the memorandum might say, it is not possible to elevate what is by its nature a power, subordinate to a main object, into an independent object. In *Introductions Ltd v. National Provincial Bank*,[8] the company was incorporated with the object of providing foreign visitors with accommodation and entertainment but it later devoted itself totally to the business of pig breeding. It borrowed money to finance this activity and granted a debenture to secure its borrowings. The objects clause included an express power to borrow and contained an 'independent objects clause'. The bank interpreted the memorandum as meaning that the company had the power

---

6 [1966] 2 All ER 674.

7 See also *Newstead v. Frost* [1980] 1 WLR 135.

8 [1968] 2 All ER 1221.

to borrow for any purpose. When the company went into liquidation the bank sought to realise its security. The court held that borrowing as an activity was not an end in itself; rather, it was a means of achieving the company's objects. As the borrowing in question was not in furtherance of an *intra vires* activity, the entire transaction was *ultra vires* the company. Accordingly, the bank could not enforce its debenture or claim in the liquidation.[9]

According to the Court of Appeal in the *Introductions* case, ancillary powers are subject to an implied limitation in that they are exercisable only in furtherance of a stated object. In *International Sales & Agencies Ltd v. Marcus*,[10] the defendant was a licensed moneylender who made personal loans of £30,000 to F, a major shareholder in the plaintiff company. When the shareholder became ill, he told the defendants that in the event of his death his friend M would see that the loans were repaid. M was also a shareholder and director of the plaintiff company. F died insolvent and M arranged for the £30,000 to be repaid by drawing cheques on the plaintiff company's bank account. When M died, F's beneficiaries, who were now shareholders in the plaintiff company, caused the company to bring proceedings against the defendant to recover the £30,000 on the grounds that this money was paid over in respect of the obligations of F, and not the company, and therefore no benefit accrued to the company. It was held that the plaintiff company was entitled to the return of the £30,000. Although the company had the power to issue cheques, this power was not independent and could only be exercised to further the objects of the company. The payment was therefore *ultra vires* the company's objects and void.

Whether or not the exercise of a power is in furtherance of the company's objects is a matter for the court. In *Re PMPA Garage (Longmile) Ltd*,[11] certain group companies had issued guarantees in favour of another group company. The question arose as to whether the giving of guarantees for associate companies could be said to be in furtherance of the objects of the guarantor company. Although the directors had not considered the business interests of the guarantor companies, it was held that the advancement of the interests of one group company would necessarily involve a recognition that the other interests of the group should be protected. Accordingly, the exercise of the ancillary power to issue guarantees was justifiable and the guarantees were declared enforceable.

In the *Introductions* case it was held that the exercise of ancillary powers, which were themselves *intra vires* the company, for an *ultra vires* purpose rendered the exercise of the power itself *ultra vires* the company. This aspect of the decision has been criticised [12] for its failure to draw a clear distinction between

---

9 See also *Re M.J. Cummins: Barton v. Bank of Ireland* [1939] IR 60.

10 [1982] 3 All ER 551.

11 [1992] ILRM 337.

12 *Gower's Principles of Modern Company Law,* Sweet & Maxwell (6th edition) 1997 at p. 205, and Courtney, *The Law of Private Companies*, Butterworths 1994, par 6.069.

transactions which are *ultra vires* the company and those which are *intra vires* the company but if exercised for an improper purpose, such as an illegal or *ultra vires* activity, are an abuse of directors' powers. The English Court of Appeal made this distinction in *Rolled Steel Products (Holdings) Ltd v. British Steel Corporation.*[13] There, the only two directors of the plaintiff company caused the company to issue a guarantee, which was counter-covered by a charge, in respect of the obligations of a company owned by one of the directors. The plaintiff company had an express power to give guarantees for customers and others who had dealings with the company on such terms 'as may seem expedient'. The memorandum of association also contained an independent objects clause. The court held that the giving of guarantees was an ancillary power, and the relevant paragraph in the memorandum should be construed in such a manner that the company could only give a guarantee in furtherance of the company's objects. The court went on to hold that the power to give the guarantee was within the capacity of the company and this was not altered by the fact that the actual exercise of the power was in furtherance of an unauthorised purpose. It was not therefore appropriate to impugn the transaction on *ultra vires* grounds. Rather, any challenge should be based on the directors' lack of authority, if any.[14] The distinction between a transaction which is *ultra vires* a company and one which is an abuse of the directors' powers was accepted in the Irish case of *Parkes & Sons Ltd v. Hong Kong and Shanghai Banking Corporation.*[15]

Express and Implied Powers

Once a power is exercised in pursuance of the company's objects, its validity will not be questioned just because a benefit has not accrued to the company. In *Charterbridge Corporation Ltd v. Lloyds Bank Ltd,*[16] a company issued a guarantee and supporting charge in respect of obligations of an associated company. The company had an express power to guarantee the debts of persons with whom the company dealt or who had a business in which the company was interested. It was argued that as the granting of the guarantee conferred no benefit on the company; it was *ultra vires* and invalid. Although the court held on the facts that the directors had grounds for believing the company did benefit from supporting an associated company, it nevertheless concluded that an express power is not limited to transactions which benefit the company.[17] On this basis it would seem that express powers to give gifts and political donations are permitted even though they confer no benefit on the company, provided the

---

13 [1985] 3 All ER 52.
14 See Chapter 17, Directors' Power and Authority.
15 [1990] ILRM 341.
16 [1969] 2 All ER 1185.
17 See also *Re PMPA Garage (Longmile) Ltd* [1992] ILRM 337.

company was solvent at the time.[18] The solvency requirement stems from the fact that once a company is insolvent the interests of the company are displaced by the interests of the general body of creditors, and any gratuitous application of company funds would be in effect a fraud on the creditors.[19]

The courts have even gone so far as to imply powers to the company where their exercise would be incidental to or consequential upon a company's objects.[20] However, it is settled law that an implied power will not be read into the memorandum unless it benefits the company and is being exercised for a purpose which is incidental to the company's business. In *Hutton v. West Cork Railway Co.*[21] a general meeting of the company had passed a resolution to pay compensation to officials for their loss of employment. The payments were successfully challenged as being *ultra vires* the company. In a frequently cited passage Bowen LJ. stated

> The law does not say that there are no cakes and ale, but that there are to be no cakes and ale except such as are required for the benefit of the company.

Similarly, in *Parke v. Daily News Ltd*,[22] when the company's main business was sold, a decision was made to advance gratuitous payments to the employees who were being let go. The payments were successfully challenged on the basis that the express powers did not permit such a payment. Furthermore, the court refused to imply such a power to the company, as the dissipation of the company's assets in such a manner did not benefit the company.This position has also been accepted by the Irish Supreme Court. In *Re Greendale Developments Ltd*[23] the court struck down payments made to members on the grounds that in the absence of an express authorisation by the Memorandum and Articles of Association a benefit must have accrued to the company and as no such benefit did so accrue the payments were *ultra vires*. Similarly, in *Re Frederick Inns Ltd*,[24] Lardner J. in the High Court struck down excess payments to the Revenue as *ultra vires* on the ground, *inter alia*, that there was no evidence of any benefit accruing to the company.

Statutory Reform

The effect of the *ultra vires* rule on outsiders has been tempered by the introduction of two legislative provisions:

---

18 See the judgment of Bowen J. in *Hutton v. West Cork Railway Co.* (1883) 23 Ch D 654, and *Re Frederick Inns Ltd* [1991] ILRM 582 (High Court) and [1994] ILRM 387 (Supreme Court).
19 See judgment of Blayney J. in *Re Frederick Inns Ltd* [1994] ILRM 387 at 397.
20 *Attorney General v. Great Eastern Railway* (1880) 5 App Cas 473.
21 [1883] 23 Ch D 654.
22 [1962] 2 All ER 929.
23 [1998] 1 IR 8.
24 [1991] ILRM 582.

1. Section 8 of the Principal Act; and
2. Regulation 6 of the European Communities (Companies) Regulations 1973.[25]

1. Section 8 of the Principal Act

Section 8(1) of the Principal Act provides that any act or thing done by the company, shall, notwithstanding that the company had no power to do such act or thing, be effective in favour of any person relying on such act or thing provided two tests are satisfied. First, the person relying on the act is not shown to have been *'actually aware'* at the time when he so relied thereon, that such an act or thing was not within the powers of the company. Second, that the act or transaction would otherwise have been *'lawfully and effectively'* done. If the person dealing with the company can satisfy this two-pronged test then he can effectively render enforceable an *ultra vires* transaction. If the person cannot satisfy the tests then the common law position prevails, viz, the transaction being *ultra vires* is void and unenforceable.

The 'Actually Aware' Test

In order to enforce an *ultra vires* transaction against the company, the third party must not have been 'actually aware' of the *ultra vires* nature of the transaction. The term 'actually aware' has been construed quite narrowly by the courts as the case of *Northern Bank Finance Limited v Quinn & Achates Investments*[26] indicates. Quinn had borrowed £145,000 which was secured by the guarantee of an unlimited company, Achates Investments, of which he was the main shareholder. This guarantee was supported by a first legal mortgage on 56 acres of prime land in Co. Meath. The resolution was passed on 30 November 1973 and guarantee was executed on 30 November 1973. The mortgage supporting the guarantee was executed on 13 December 1973. When there was default in repayment the bank sued Quinn and the company and obtained judgment against them. It then sought an order that the mortgage was well charged on the land. Quinn's liability was not disputed. It was submitted on behalf of the company that the guarantee was *ultra vires* the objects and consequently void. The bank argued that it was protected by section 8(1) of the Principal Act. The Court heard evidence from the solicitor for the bank that although he read the Memorandum and Articles of the company he did not consciously advert to the fact that the act was *ultra vires*. The Court declared that in such circumstances a person who has read the memorandum and articles is deemed to be actually aware of its contents. Accordingly, the bank was deemed to be 'actually aware' and could not rely on section 8. The guarantee was declared void and unenforceable for being *ultra vires*.

---

25 SI 163/1973.
26 [1979] ILRM 221.

On the basis of the judgment in this case, if a party is shown to have been 'actually aware' of the contents of the memorandum but has failed to understand them he cannot avail of the protection afforded by section 8(1).

The 'Lawfully and Effectively' Test

Even where the third party is shown not to have been 'actually aware' he will not be in a position to rely on section 8(1) if the act in question, notwithstanding the fact that it is *ultra vires*, is otherwise not 'lawfully and effectively' done. This aspect of section 8(1) arose in *Re Frederick Inns Ltd.*[27] There, £2.8 million was owed to the Revenue on behalf of four companies in the Belton group. The group sold four pubs which were each of the company's main asset and applied the proceeds to the Revenue to discharge their taxation obligations. The Revenue used the funds to maximise their preferential status. The liquidator argued, *inter alia*, that the payments, in the form of gratuitous payments to the Revenue, were *ultra vires*. The court agreed with the liquidator that when a company is insolvent it is beyond its powers to alienate or transfer its property or make a gift to a third party out of its assets, even if expressly empowered to do so by the memorandum. To do so would be in disregard of the interests of the creditors which could not be lawful. Accordingly, Lardner J. held that the payments by the four companies were not 'lawfully and effectively' done within the meaning of section 8(1).

Liability of Directors

If an *ultra vires* transaction is enforced against the company, any director or officer of the company who was responsible for the *ultra vires* act shall be liable to the company for any loss or damage suffered by the company in consequence thereof.

Rights of Members and Debenture Holders

Section 8(2) of the Principal Act provides that a member or debenture holder may apply to court for an injunction restraining the company from doing any act which is *ultra vires*.

2. Regulation 6

Regulation 6 of the European Communities (Companies) Regulations 1973[28] provides that if a person deals with a company in good faith, any transaction entered into by an organ of the company, such as the board of directors or any person authorised to bind the company, shall be deemed to be within the capacity

---

27 [1994] 1 ILRM 582.
28 SI 163/1973.

of the company and any limitation of the powers of that board or person, whether imposed by the memorandum or articles, may not be relied upon as against any person so dealing with the company.

Regulation 6 supplements section 8 of the Principal Act by providing an additional defence to third parties who deal with the company. However, the requirement to show that the person acted in 'good faith' is probably more onerous than the test of 'actually aware' imposed by section 8. On the basis of the judgment in the *Northern Bank Finance* case, it would seem that if the bank had not read the memorandum at all, rather than reading it incorrectly, it could have been protected by section 8(1) of the Principal Act. It is doubtful whether such inaction would protect a person invoking Regulation 6, as the refusal to read a document for fear of what may be found therein is unlikely to constitute a *bona fide* action for the purposes of Regulation 6. Nevertheless, there is a presumption that the person was acting in good faith and, accordingly, in order to prevent a person invoking Regulation 6 the applicant must prove that he was not so acting.

Regulation 6 applies only to limited companies. Presumably it was not raised in the *Northern Bank* case because the company in that case was not a limited company. In protecting outsiders who deal with not just the company but also its authorised agents, Regulation 6 has also limited the effect of the rule in the *Turquand* case, which is considered in Chapter 17.

CHAPTER EIGHT

COMPANY SECURITIES

Introduction

Company securities fall into two main categories: shares and debentures. The most significant difference between the two is that a shareholder is a member[1] and owner of the company whereas a debenture holder is a creditor of the company. This difference in status is reflected in the legal rights conferred on the holders of each, which include *inter alia* the following:

(a) in contrast with the shareholder, who as an owner has an interest in the company, the debenture holder as a creditor has rights against the company;

(b) shareholders' rights are mostly determined by the company's articles of association and the Companies Acts whereas the debenture deed will set out the contractual rights of the debenture holder;

(c) the return on investment is measured in terms of a dividend for shareholders and interest payments for debenture holders. Dividends are only payable from distributable profits, whereas the company is contractually bound to pay interest on debentures even where profits have not been made;

(d) debenture holders can, by securing their debt, elevate themselves in the insolvency queue to a position ahead of all shareholders and some other creditors. A shareholder cannot legally contract out of his place in the insolvency queue. Even if the debenture is unsecured, the debenture holders will always be paid before the shareholders in a winding up.

In reality the distinction between the two may not be as obvious. This is because the debenture may give the holder contractual rights similar to those of shareholders, including the right to appoint a director and attend and vote at general meetings. The Companies Acts also recognise the economic reality of both shareholders and debenture holders having a vested interest in the company, by affording them similar rights in respect of the following:

(a) applying to court to have an alteration of objects clause cancelled;[2]

(b) petitioning the court to have the company wound up;[3]

(c) petitioning the court to have an examiner appointed;[4]

---

1 Technically speaking a shareholder only becomes a member on being registered in the Register of Members: Section 31 of the Principal Act.

2 Section 10(3) and (7) of the Principal Act.

3 Section 215 of the Principal Act.

4 Section 3 Companies (Amendment) Act 1990.

(d) applying to the court for an injunction restraining the company from acting *ultra vires*;[5]

(e) receiving a copy of the balance sheet and directors and auditors report which are to be laid before the annual general meeting of the company;[6] and

(f) the right to object to a proposed reduction of capital under section 72 of the Principal Act.[7]

The Legal Nature Of Shares

In *Borland's Trustee v. Steel*,[8] Farwell J. described a share as:

> the interest of a shareholder in the company measured by a sum of money, for the purpose of liability in the first place, and of interest in the second, but also consisting of a series of mutual covenants entered into by the shareholders *inter se*.[9]

As the definition suggests, a member is under a liability to the company to the extent that he must pay for his shares but he is also conferred with a bundle of rights, interests and obligations, which can be summarised as follows:

(a) those determined by the articles of association, which are capable of being enforced under section 25 of the Principal Act;[10]

(b) those determined by statute, which in many instances cannot be abridged by the company's regulations.[11]

It should be noted that while a share confers an interest in the company itself, it does not confer an interest in the property or undertaking of the company.[12]

Section 79 of the Principal Act describes a share as personal property which is transferable in the manner prescribed by the articles. A share is an intangible interest distinguishable from a share certificate, which is the document evidencing *prima facie* title to the shares. As an intangible interest, a share is a chose in action which gives the holder the right to take legal action to protect his interest therein.

---

5 Section 8(2) of the Principal Act.

6 Section 159(1) of the Principal Act.

7 Section 73 of the Principal Act.

8 [1901] Ch 279.

9 See also *IRC v. Crossman* [1937] AC 26.

10 See Chapter 5.

11 Any member can prevent re-registration of a limited company as an unlimited company: section 52(3) of the Companies (Amendment) Act 1983. Any member can apply to the Minister to have an AGM called: section 131(3) of the Principal Act. A member cannot be compelled by an alteration of the articles to subscribe for additional shares or to accept liability in respect of those shares: section 27 of the Principal Act. A member is entitled to minimum notice of general meetings: section 133 of the Principal Act.

12 *Short v. Treasury Commissioners* [1948] 1 KB 122.

Classes of Shares

Unless the articles of association expressly provide otherwise, it is presumed that all shares confer the same rights and impose the same liabilities on their holders.[13] Shareholders' rights are normally categorised in terms of the following:

(a) the right to attend and vote at meetings;
(b) the payment of dividends; and
(c) the return of capital and any surplus on a winding up of the company.

The presumption of equality may be modified by dividing shares into different classes and attaching to those classes different rights. The power to create different classes of shares and to confer on each class different rights may be provided for in the memorandum of association. However, in practice it is usually dealt with in the articles of association. Although companies do not normally complicate their capital structures by creating several different classes of shares, it is not uncommon to find at least two classes of capital to which different rights attach. Table A authorises the company, by ordinary resolution, to issue shares with 'preferred, deferred or other special rights'.[14] Accordingly, the three main classes of shares which are recognised by Table A are:

1. ordinary shares;
2. preference shares; and
3. deferred shares.

1. Ordinary Shares

Ordinary shares are those which do not confer on the holder any preferential entitlements. The holders of these shares bear the true burden of the company's fortunes, as the return on their investment is dependent upon the company's financial position. Where losses are incurred or the company is wound up because of its insolvency, the financial entitlements of the ordinary shareholders are postponed to those of the creditors and possibly those of the preference shareholders.

2. Preference Shares

Preference shares are those shares which carry preferential financial entitlements, usually in respect of dividends and return of capital. Preference shares are usually issued to attract investment in the company. Once preference shares are issued, it is usually presumed that the holder is entitled to a fixed dividend ahead of any other shareholders' entitlement in this regard. All other entitlements are conditional upon the terms of the preference share issue. Furthermore, no issue may offer preferential entitlements unless so authorised by

---

13 *Birch v. Cropper, Re Bridgewater Navigation Co.* (1889) 14 App Cas 525.
14 Model Article 2.

the articles of association. The rights of preference shareholders will now be considered in terms of:

(a) dividend entitlements;
(b) return of capital and surplus; and
(c) voting rights.

Dividend entitlements

Although preference shareholders have a priority right to receive dividends, this right cannot be invoked to compel a company to pay dividends. This is because dividends can only be paid where distributable profits are available from which they can be paid. Even where these profits are available the directors may refuse to declare a dividend, and cannot be compelled to do so because, as the court observed in *Burland v. Earle*:

> Their Lordships are not aware of any principle which compels a joint stock company while a going concern to divide the whole of its profits among its shareholders.[15]

Rather, it is a matter for the directors to decide whether or not dividends will be declared. In *Bond v. Barrow Haematite Steel Co.*[16] the company had available reserves of £240,000 but the directors did not declare a dividend. The plaintiff, a preference shareholder, argued that the dividend should have been paid given the availability of the reserves. The company claimed that it had decided to retain the reserves to make good losses arising from the disposal of current assets and a diminution of the value of the company's fixed assets. The court held that it would not interfere with the directors' discretion in relation to the declaration of dividends. However, there is nothing to prevent the articles of association from conferring an automatic right to receive a dividend, irrespective of whether or not one has been declared.[17]

Where dividends are not declared, the preference shareholder is entitled to have the arrears paid the next time dividends are declared. This is because preference shares are presumed to be cumulative unless the contrary is stated in the articles of association. Where preference shares are not issued with cumulative rights, this must be made clear. A statement to the effect that dividends will only be payable 'out of the profits made by the company in that particular year' will be sufficient to make the shares non-cumulative.[18]

Once the preference shareholder has received his dividend he is not entitled to any further share in the distributable profits unless expressly provided for in the articles of association.[19]

---

15 [1902] AC 83 at 95.
16 [1902] 1 Ch 353.
17 *Re Lafayette Ltd* [1950] IR 100.
18 *Webb v. Earle* (1875) LR 20 Eq 556.
19 *Will v. United Lankat Plantations* [1914] AC 11.

Where the company is wound up the entitlement to arrears of dividends ceases unless they were already declared, but unpaid, before the company was wound up. Alternatively, the articles may provide that the arrears are to be paid before any capital or surplus is paid to the other members.[20] However, it should be noted that if a company is insolvent dividends owing to members will not be deemed to be a debt of the company. Therefore, members will not be categorised as creditors for the purposes of the dividends owing. Accordingly, when wound up, the non-member creditors will be paid before any arrears of dividends are paid to preference shareholders.[21]

Return of capital and surplus

In the absence of an express provision to the contrary in the article, preference shareholders are not automatically entitled to the return of capital in priority to the ordinary shareholders in a winding up.[22] However, where they are entitled to a return of capital this does not necessarily exhaust their rights in this regard, and they may also be entitled to a share in the surplus assets in a winding-up situation. In *Cork Electric Supply Co. Ltd v. Concannon*,[23] the articles of association gave the preference shareholders preferred rights as to dividends and to the return of capital. When the company was being wound up because its assets had been compulsorily acquired by the newly established Electric Supply Board, the company sought directions from the court as to whether the entitlement to priority as to a return of capital exhausted the preference shareholders' rights in this regard. If such was the case it would have the effect of excluding them from participating in the surplus assets which were available. As the articles contained no limitation on the right to participate, the Supreme Court held that the preference shareholders were entitled in the same manner as the ordinary shareholders to a share in the surplus assets.[24] The decision was based on the construction of the company's articles, in particular the fact that the article providing for the dividend priority was qualified by the words 'and no such further dividend', which was regarded as an exhaustive right. No such qualification was applied to the priority right to a return of capital, which implied that this right was not exhaustive.

Voting rights

It is normal for the articles of association to restrict the voting rights of preference shareholders. However, in the absence of such provisions, the presumption of

---

20 *Re Imperial Hotel (Cork) Ltd* [1950] IR 115.
21 Section 207(1)(g) of the Principal Act.
22 *Welton v Saffery* [1897] AC 299.
23 [1932] IR 314.
24 The English courts take the position that once the articles specify an entitlement to a particular right, that entitlement is exhaustive. See *Scottish Insurance Corporation v. Wilsons and Clyde Coal Company* [1949] AC 462.

equality remains and all shareholders are entitled to equal voting rights in respect of their shares.

3. Deferred Shares

In the past it was not uncommon for the company to allot deferred or founder shares to the founders of the company. These shares carried special rights such as the right to receive a fixed dividend. However, these rights were deferred in priority to the ordinary shares. Deferred shares are rarely, if ever, issued nowadays.

Variation of Class Rights

If the articles of association attach different rights to different classes of shares, those rights can be altered by special resolution subject to the normal rules regarding the alteration of the articles.[25] However, the articles, or indeed the memorandum, may specify that a special voting procedure must be followed where such an alteration is being made. Section 78 acknowledges the company's right to alter the articles to this effect, and it provides that where such a procedure is specified and complied with, the rights of different classes of shareholders can lawfully be varied. Although the Principal Act was silent as to whether the rights of class shareholders could be varied if no such provision was made in the memorandum or articles of association, this has been rectified by section 38 of the 1983 Act which broadly provides that:

(a) where the rights attached to a class are determined otherwise than by the memorandum of association and no variation procedure is specified in the articles, the rights can only be varied with the written consent of 75 per cent of the class members or by a special resolution of that class; or
(b) where the memorandum of association determines the rights but the articles do not stipulate a variation procedure, the rights can only be varied with the consent of all the shareholders and not just the shareholders of that particular class.

Companies usually provide for their own variation rules, and Table A sets out a similar procedure to that mentioned in (a) above (Model Article 3).

Irrespective of the procedure followed, dissentient shareholders, holding at least 10 per cent of the shares of a class, may apply to the court to have the alteration cancelled.[26] If such an application is made within twenty-eight days of the authorising decision or resolution, the variation will not take effect until the court has confirmed it. The court will either confirm or reject the variation. It must confirm the variation unless it is satisfied that having regard to the circumstances, the variation would be unfairly prejudicial to the class

---

25 *Andrews v. Gas Meter Co.* [1897] 1 Ch 361.
26 Section 78(1) of the Principal Act.

represented by the applicant.[27] In *Re Holders Investment Trust Ltd*,[28] a proposal by the company to repay the 5 per cent preference shareholders by giving them unsecured loan stock was approved by the trustees who held 90 per cent of the shares of that class. The preference shareholders had a prior right to repayment of the capital ahead of the ordinary shareholders. The trustees who also held the majority of the ordinary shares would obviously benefit from the change. It was held that the resolution of the class meeting was invalid because the trustees acted in their interests as ordinary shareholders and not in the interests of the preference shareholders.

There are no statutory guidelines as to what will actually constitute a variation of class rights. A decision that adversely affects a particular class does not necessarily amount to a variation of rights. A distinction is drawn between a decision that affects the rights themselves and one that merely affects the enjoyment of those rights. In *Greenhalgh v. Arderne Cinemas*,[29] the company had two classes of ordinary shares, 50p shares and 10p shares. Each share carried one vote. A resolution was passed to subdivide the 50p shares into five 10p shares, with the result that the holders of the original 50p shares now had five votes instead of one. The subdivision had the effect of diluting the voting strength of the existing 10p shareholders. Nevertheless, the court held that the rights of the original 10p shareholders had not been varied.

Similarly, in *White v. Bristol Aeroplane Co. Ltd*,[30] the issue of bonus preference shares to ordinary shareholders was held not to be a variation of class rights, even though the allotment had the effect of reducing the existing preference shareholders' percentage holdings.[31]

It is important to remember that any alteration of the articles must be carried out *bona fide* and in the best interests of the company, and any attempt to oppress a minority shareholder under the guise of a genuine alteration will be struck down by the court as invalid. Thus in *Clemens v. Clemens Bros. Ltd*,[32] the plaintiff held 45 per cent of the issued shares and her aunt held the remaining 55 per cent. The aunt's shares were used to secure the passing of a resolution to issue new shares to directors and employees. The intended effect of the resolution was to reduce the plaintiff's shareholding to below 25 per cent, which would deprive her of the right to block special resolutions. The court set aside the resolution on the ground that it was oppressive to the plaintiff since it was designed to reduce her control over the company.

---

27 Section 78(3) of the Principal Act.
28 [1971] 1 WLR 583.
29 [1946] 1 All ER 512.
30 [1953] Ch 65.
31 See also *Re Saltdean Estate Co. Ltd* [1968] 1 WLR 1844 and *House of Fraser v. AGCE Investments Ltd* [1987] AC 387.
32 [1976] 2 All ER 268.

Other Categories of Shares

In addition to the three classes of shares mentioned above, ordinary and preference shares may be further described in terms of the following:

(a) redeemable shares are shares which must be bought back by the company after the expiry of a fixed period of time, which is usually set out in the articles of association;

(b) treasury shares are those shares that have been redeemed and having been so redeemed are retained by the company;

(c) bonus shares are shares that are issued by way of a bonus issue such as when the company capitalises profits by paying up bonus shares and issuing them to existing members in the same manner as it would pay dividends.

Legal Nature of Debentures

In its most basic form, a debenture is simply a written statement acknowledging indebtedness. The modern debenture is more likely to be a complex and formal legal document incorporating, *inter alia*, provisions for the following:

(a) an undertaking to repay the debt, subject to the terms and conditions agreed;

(b) the giving of security for the indebtedness, in such form as agreed;

(c) the events of default that will trigger the enforcement of the security; and

(d) the methods of enforcing the security.

Where the borrower defaults, the debenture holder may sue to recover the amount owing. Where the debenture is secured, which is normally the case, the debenture holder may enforce his security in the manner provided under the debenture. The enforcement of security is considered further in Chapter 24.

1. Types of Debentures

Debentures may be classified differently, but such classification only reflects the manner in which the debentures have been issued as opposed to the rights attaching to each category. This is because the rights of debenture holders are found in the underlying terms of the contract, which vary according to the bargaining position of the company and the creditor. Debentures are usually categorised as follows.

(a) Single debentures: this most common form of debenture is issued under a contractual instrument between the company and a single creditor, whereby the debenture is usually secured by a charge over some or all of the company's assets and undertaking;

(b) Series of debentures: the company may have more than one creditor, each providing a portion of an overall global loan facility. In such a case, it is usual to issue debentures as a series. As well as the standard conditions, it is normal to include in the debenture a provision for its transferability together with a *pari passu* clause whereby each debenture holder will rank equally in terms of repayment. This *pari passu* condition is essential to ensure equality between the lenders, irrespective of which loan was drawn first, or to whom the first debenture was issued.

(c) Debenture stock: it is not uncommon for public companies to raise loan capital by the issue of debenture stock to the public. The company raises a global loan which is subject to certain conditions including *inter alia* provisions for the payment of interest and the repayment of principal. Each subscriber will be issued a debenture stock certificate recording the amount and conditions of the loan. Debenture stock certificates are usually transferable.

2. The Debenture Trust Deed

Where companies are issuing a series of debentures or debenture stock, the potential subscribers may be numerous. Rather than negotiating with each subscriber individually, a trust deed is executed by the company under which a trustee is appointed to represent the debenture holders and enforce their rights. The trustee is normally vested with powers to enforce the security, if any, and to appoint a receiver. Although ordinarily appointed by the company itself, the trustee's duty is towards the debenture holder and any contractual term relieving the trustee from liability for a breach of trust is void.[33]

3. The Issue and Transfer of Debentures

Debentures are issued in the same manner as shares. Public companies can offer debentures to the public by means of a prospectus.[34] Debentures may be redeemable after a fixed period of time or they may be irredeemable.[35] They may also be convertible, which gives the holder a right to convert the debentures into shares. A debenture is transferable in the manner provided by the debenture itself. However, the company may not register a transfer of debentures unless a proper instrument of transfer has been delivered to the company. The transfer is usually in the same form as those used for share transfers.

4. Register of Debentures

Where the debenture is secured by way of a charge, the charge must be officially registered with the Registrar of Companies.[36] Furthermore, section 91 of the Principal Act requires a company to maintain a register of debenture holders and enter therein the names and addresses of the debenture holders and the amount

---

33 Section 93 of the Principal Act.
34 See Chapter 9.
35 Section 94 of the Principal Act authorises the issue of irredeemable debentures.
36 Section 99 of the Principal Act.

of debentures held by each of them. However, neither debentures which do not form part of a series ranking pari-passu nor debentures which are transferable by delivery are required to be maintained in the register. The register must ordinarily be kept at the registered office of the company and be available for inspection by the registered holder of the debentures, the shareholders and any other interested person.

CHAPTER NINE

ALLOTMENT OF SHARES

Introduction

The process by which new shares are issued and allotted by a company is subject to a number of restrictions. Some of these are prescribed by the Companies Acts and others are set out in the company's articles of association. Because public companies are permitted to issue new shares to the public they are also subject to additional requirements and restrictions in this regard. These rules will now be considered under the following headings:

(a) allotment of shares generally; and
(b) allotment of shares to the public.

Allotment of Shares Generally

Prior to 1983 the authority to allot shares was usually considered to be within the remit of the directors, as a power delegated to them by the articles of association. This authority is now restricted by section 20 of the Companies (Amendment) Act 1983. It provides that the directors shall not exercise any powers of allotting shares unless so authorised by the company in general meeting or by the company's articles. Where the authorisation is granted by the general meeting, a copy of the authorising resolution must be delivered to the Registrar of Companies within fifteen days of it being passed.[1] Furthermore, notice of the delivery of the resolution to the Registrar must be published in *Iris Oifigiúil*.[2] The authorisation to the directors, whatever its form, must state the maximum number of shares to be allotted and the date upon which the authority will expire.[3] The authority cannot be granted for an indefinite period because section 20(3) of the Companies (Amendment) Act stipulates that the authority must not exceed five years from the date of incorporation or the date of the resolution. Even where the authority is vested in the directors, it may be revoked, varied or renewed for a further five years by an ordinary resolution of the company.[4] Although an allotment in contravention of section 20 will usually be valid, any director who knowingly and wilfully contravened the section will be guilty of an offence and liable to a fine not exceeding £2,500 (€3,174).

---

1 Section 20(6) of the Companies (Amendment) Act 1983.
2 Section 55 of the Companies (Amendment) Act 1983.
3 Section 20(3) of the Companies (Amendment) Act 1983.
4 Section 20(4) of the Companies (Amendment) Act 1983.

Section 89 of the Principal Act empowers the court to validate an otherwise invalid issue of shares if the court is satisfied that it would be just and equitable to do so. Conversely, it will not validate the issue if it is not so satisfied. This provision was considered in the case of *Re Sugar Distributors Ltd.*[5] Here, the company's secretary prepared minutes which recorded that the requisite general meeting and board meeting had been held and resolutions had been passed thereat to enable the company to issue and allot additional shares to a majority corporate shareholder. In fact, the meeting of the shareholders to pass the resolution had never taken place, nor had the board meeting at which the decision to allot the shares was purportedly taken. The secretary had taken the decision on foot of instructions from the majority shareholder to issue new preference shares in order that both companies might avail of tax concessions. When an inspector was subsequently appointed to the company he found that the correct procedures had not been followed in issuing the preference shares. The company brought an application for an order under section 89 that the allotment was valid. Keane J. held that the object of the application was to enable the company to gain a tax advantage rather than to validate a defective title to shares already issued. Such an objective, he observed, was never contemplated by the section 89 procedure which gave the court a discretionary power that would only be exercised where it considered it just and equitable to do so. Accordingly, the court would not permit it to be used for such a purpose.

1. The Allotment Process

The allotment of shares is primarily governed by principles of contract law. Allotment occurs when an application for newly issued shares has been accepted by the directors and the acceptance has been notified to the applicant. Private companies typically expedite the allotment process by the straightforward issuance of a share certificate. Public companies usually adopt a more formal approach which commences with the issuance of a letter of allotment. This letter of allotment may contain a form of renunciation which allows the allottee to renounce the allotment in favour of another person. The allottee, provided he does not renounce, will then return the allotment letter together with an application for the registration of the shares in his name. On receipt of this the company will enter the name in the register of members and issue a share certificate.

By virtue of section 31(2) of the Principal Act, once the name of a person is entered in the register, that person becomes a member of the company. If, having issued a letter of allotment, a company fails to register the name, the person concerned may sue to enforce his contractual entitlement to have his name so registered.

---

5 [1995] 2 IR 195, [1996] 1 ILRM 342.

Where new shares have been allotted, the company is required, within one month, to make a return to the Registrar of Companies detailing the following:

(a) the number and nominal value of the shares comprised in the allotment;
(b) the names and addresses of the allottees; and
(c) the amount, if any, paid or due and payable on each share or in the case of shares allotted for non-cash consideration, details of the appropriate contract and consideration.[6]

2. Pre-emption Rights of Existing Shareholders

Where a company proposes to allot shares wholly for cash, the shares must first be offered to existing members in proportion to their respective holdings.[7] Not all members are entitled to a pre-emption right. Section 23 limits the right to those members who hold shares which do not confer any priority preference as to a dividend payment or a return of capital in a winding-up. This effectively removes all preference shareholders from the enjoyment of the statutory pre-emption right.

The right of first refusal only applies where an allotment of 'equity securities' is proposed. Equity securities are essentially all shares other than the following:

(a) shares, including preference shares, which confer restricted rights in respect to dividends or capital distributions;[8]
(b) shares allotted under an employee share scheme — this is an important exception as otherwise these schemes would become impossible to work if all existing shareholders were entitled to a right of first refusal;
(c) shares allotted for consideration otherwise than in cash — therefore where it is proposed to allot shares as consideration for the acquisition of a business undertaking, there is no requirement to make an offer to existing shareholders on the same terms.

Where such an allotment of equity securities is proposed, the offer must be served in the same manner as a notice of a general meeting.[9] It must specify a period of not less than twenty-one days during which the offer may be accepted, and the offer may not be withdrawn before the expiry of this period.[10] Where an offer has been made, the directors shall not allot those securities to any other person until the offer has expired or has been rejected.[11]

---

6 Section 58(1) of the Principal Act.
7 Section 23 of the Companies (Amendment) Act 1983.
8 A restriction on voting rights is, therefore, irrelevant for the purpose of defining equity securities.
9 Section 23(7) of the Companies (Amendment) Act 1983.
10 Section 23(8) of the Companies (Amendment) Act 1983.
11 Section 23(1)(b) of the Companies (Amendment) Act 1983.

A member cannot exercise a pre-emption right on only part of the offer. He either accepts the offer in full or rejects the offer. In *Ocean Coal Co. v. Powell Duffryn Steam Coal Co.*,[12] the plaintiff and defendant each held equal shares in the company. The articles provided that where a member wished to transfer his shares to outsiders, he must first offer them to existing shareholders at the same price. The defendant wished to sell his shares but the plaintiff only wished to purchase enough of them to ensure that he would retain control of the company. It was held that his pre-emption right did not entitle him to any portion of the shares offered. Accordingly the plaintiff was obliged to purchase all the shares or reject the offer.

The statutory pre-emption right of members may in the case of private companies be permanently excluded by the memorandum or articles of association.[13] Indeed, all companies may, where the directors of the company are authorised to allot shares, exclude the right in any of the following ways:

(a) directors may be given power under the articles or by a special resolution to disapply the pre-emption right or modify it to the extent permitted by that resolution; and

(b) directors may, by special resolution, be given the power to exclude or modify the right in relation to a particular allotment.[14] Where such a resolution is proposed, it must be recommended by the directors and the notice of the meeting must contain an explanation from the directors as to the reasons for their recommendation, the amount to be paid as consideration for the shares and the directors' justification for that amount.

However, the directors' power to disapply the pre-emptive right will cease when their authority to allot has been revoked or has expired. In any case, a company may provide in its memorandum or articles for its own pre-emption scheme which may even give entitlements to preference shareholders.

Failure to comply with the statutory requirements will not invalidate the allotment. However, it will render the company, and any officer who knowingly authorised or permitted the contravention, liable to compensate the members to whom the offer ought to have been made, subject to a two year statutory limit on the right to claim such compensation.[15]

3. Consideration for the Allotment of Shares

Generally, all shares must be allotted with a nominal or par value. This value will be determined by the capital clause in the memorandum of association, which specifies the authorised share capital, the number of shares into which it is divided and the amount of each share. The nominal value will rarely reflect the

---

12 [1932] 1 Ch 654.
13 Section 23(10) of the Companies (Amendment) Act 1983.
14 Section 24 of the Companies (Amendment) Act 1983.
15 Section 23(11) of the Companies (Amendment) Act 1983.

market value of the company's shares, which will vary depending on the company's fortunes. Section 27 of the Companies (Amendment) Act 1983 requires that when a company is allotting shares it must obtain, in money or money's worth, consideration of a value at least equal to the nominal value of the shares. This statutory prohibition on allotting shares at a discount reflects the common law position illustrated by the case of *Ooregum Gold Mining Co. of India v. Roper*.[16] In this case the market value of the company's shares had fallen below the nominal value. In an attempt to raise much needed capital the company resolved at a general meeting to allot preference shares, a portion of which was deemed as having been paid. A shareholder successfully challenged the allotment on the ground that the company could not allot shares at a discount.

Consideration need not be paid in full at the time of allotment. However, a public company may not allot shares unless they are paid up to the extent of one quarter of the nominal value in addition to the whole, if any, of the share premium. Where the full amount of a share is not payable and has in fact not been paid, the holder of the share, even if not the original allottee, remains liable for the unpaid amounts until such time as they are called in by the company or a liquidator. In *Re Munster Bank (Re Dillon's claim)*[17] a bank manager, as part of a security arrangement with a customer, became the registered holder of partly paid-up shares previously held by the customer. It was held that he was personally obliged to pay for the outstanding amounts due on the shares when a call was subsequently made.

Non-cash consideration

When shares are allotted for non-cash consideration, different rules apply depending on the company's status. In the case of a private company the statutory dictates are few and relate to notification and delivery requirements.[18] Although the Companies (Amendment) Act 1983 acknowledges the right of private companies to allot shares for non-cash consideration, including goodwill and services, it does not prescribe any preconditions for such an allotment.[19] In the absence of such provisions the general principles of contract law apply. Accordingly, the courts will not inquire into the adequacy of consideration provided it is real and not tainted by fraud or dishonesty. Thus in *Re Wragg Ltd*,[20] two former business associates sold their business undertaking to a newly incorporated company in which they were the shareholders. The consideration price of £46,300 was paid by the allotment of £20,000 in shares and the balance in cash and debentures. When the company was subsequently wound up, the

16 [1892] AC 125.
17 (1886) 17 LR Ir 341.
18 Section 58(1)(b) of the Principal Act.
19 Section 26.
20 [1897] 1 Ch 796.

liquidator contended that the business had been over-valued to the extent of £18,000 and that the company should be entitled to recover the excess amount from the shareholders. Although the court accepted that shares could not be issued at a discount, it held that a company was entitled to put its own value on the worth of property and pay for it in fully paid shares. As there was no element of dishonesty and the shareholders had agreed to the purchase price, the court would not interfere in the arrangement. Accordingly, the liquidator's claim failed.[21] Similarly, in *Re Leinster Contract Corporation*,[22] the court refused to set aside an allotment just because the consideration, which was in the form of patents, ultimately proved worthless. However, where there is evidence of bad faith or dishonesty, the allotment may be invalidated.[23] Furthermore, where consideration is past or illusory the allotment will fail on the basis of principles of contract law.[24]

In the case of public companies the statutory rules demand a more stringent approach. First, a public company is barred from accepting, in consideration for its shares, an undertaking for future services.[25] Second, it may not allot shares in consideration for any undertaking which will not be performed until after five years from the date of the allotment.[26] Contravention of these requirements will render the holder of the shares liable to pay an amount equal to the nominal value together with any premium and interest which applies. If an undertaking ought to have been performed within five years from the date of the allotment but is not, the allottee or the holder of the shares, if he had notice of the contravention, becomes immediately liable to pay for his shares in cash. Third, to avoid the difficulties inherent in establishing the adequacy of consideration, the Companies (Amendment) Act 1983 requires that where non-cash consideration is being obtained, it must be independently valued except in the case of a take-over bid where the consideration involves a share exchange.[27] The valuation report must be made to the company, within the six months prior to the allotment, by an independent person qualified to be an auditor of the company. The expert is entitled to require from the company's officers such information and explanations as he thinks necessary to enable him to carry out the valuation and make the report.[28] He is also entitled, where he believes it necessary, to obtain a further report from another expert, such as a valuer. Any person who knowingly

---

21 See also *Salomon v. Salomon* [1897] AC 22.
22 [1902] IR 349.
23 *Tintin Exploration Syndicate v. Sandys* (1947) 177 LT 412.
24 Re White Star Line [1938] Ch 458 and *Re Eddystone Marine Insurance Co.* [1893] 3 Ch 9.
25 Section 26(2) of the Companies (Amendment) Act 1983.
26 Section 29(1) of the Companies (Amendment) Act 1983.
27 Section 30 of the Companies (Amendment) Act 1983.
28 Section 31 of the Companies (Amendment) Act 1983.

or recklessly makes a statement, as to a material particular, which is misleading, false or deceptive will be guilty of an offence.[29] The expert's report must contain the following information:

(a) the nominal value of the shares to be wholly or partly paid for by the consideration in question;
(b) the amount of any premium payable on those shares;
(c) the description of any premium payable on those shares;
(d) the extent to which the nominal value of the shares and any premium are to be treated as paid up by the consideration or by cash.

The company must, on receipt of the expert's report, send a copy to the allottee and the Registrar of Companies. Finally, a public company may not, within two years of receiving its trading certificate, receive a transfer of a non-cash asset from a subscriber to the memorandum, where the consideration to be given is equal to or greater than one-tenth of the nominal value of the company's share capital issued at that time, other than those assets normally acquired in the ordinary course of business, unless it has been independently valued and it has been agreed by the company by way of ordinary resolution.[30]

4. Share Premium

Where companies allot shares for a consideration greater than their nominal value, the excess amount must be credited to a share premium account.[31] Where non-cash consideration is obtained the same obligation is imposed although a relief is provided where merger accounting principles apply. There is no obligation on directors to obtain the best possible price or a premium when allotting shares to members. However, where the allotment is to non-members, it was suggested in *Hilder v. Dexter*[32] that in exercising their powers in the best interests of the company, directors may be obliged to obtain a premium for the company. Although the share premium account is a reserve separate from the share capital account, for the purpose of capital maintenance rules they are treated similarly. Accordingly, the share premium account can only be applied in the following ways:

(a) where a return to members is authorised by the reduction of capital rules in the Companies Act; or
(b) for the payment of bonus shares; or
(c) for writing off a company's preliminary expenses or the expenses of, or the commissions paid or discount allowed on, any issue of the company's shares; or

---

29 Section 31(3) of the Companies (Amendment) Act 1983.
30 Section 32 of the Companies (Amendment) Act 1983.
31 Section 62 of the Principal Act.
32 [1902] AC 474.

(d) in providing for any premium payable on the redemption of redeemable preference shares or debentures of the company. (See Chapter 10, Maintenance of Capital.)

Allotment of Shares to the Public

Private companies can only raise capital from their members, or alternatively from company borrowings.[33] By contrast, public companies may, and usually do, raise capital by offering their shares or debentures to the public. Although a public company may sell its shares directly to the public, it is usual for such a company to be *floated* on the Stock Exchange through which medium it can trade its shares. An issue of shares to the public may be achieved by any of the following methods.

1. Issuing a Prospectus

An offer is made directly through the issue of a prospectus which invites the public to subscribe for shares. The prospectus is usually published in a newspaper and the prospective investor applies for shares on foot of same.

2. By Offer for Sale

In this instance the company sells all the securities on issue to an intermediary, which is usually an issuing house, whose business is that of corporate finance. The issuing house publishes a document called an offer for sale, with an application form attached, offering the shares to the public at a higher price than it paid for them. This method of issue is advantageous for a company for two reasons. First, the company is relieved of the responsibility of selling the shares. Second, the endorsement of the new issue by a reputable issuing house is bound to create public interest and confidence in the issue. Securities are deemed to be allotted under an offer for sale in either of the following circumstances:

(a) they are offered to the public within six months after the allotment to the issuing house; or
(b) at the date when the offer to sell the securities to the public is made, the company has not received the full consideration due from the issuing house.

An offer for sale is an offer to which the prospectus rules apply because the ultimate purpose of the issue is not to sell the shares privately to an issuing house but to sell them to the public. In addition to the normal prescribed contents, a prospectus which is also an 'offer for sale' must state the net amount of consideration for the securities and a place and time at which the contract between the company and the issuing house may be inspected.

---

33 Section 21 of the Companies (Amendment) Act 1983.

3. By Placement

The securities are issued in large quantities to a number of financial institutions or clients of the issuing house. The placement is generally effected by an issuing house by way of private negotiations.

4. A Rights Issue

The company may wish to raise fresh capital without either offering the shares to the public at large or availing of a placing. In these circumstances, it may decide to raise the necessary funds by allotting shares to the existing shareholders, who are given the right to apply for a given number of new shares in proportion to their existing holdings. A rights issue is usually made renounceable. Unless the issue is made non-renounceable, the prospectus rules will apply.

5. By Tender

Shares may be offered by tender, i.e. a minimum price is fixed below which the shares will not be allotted and bids are invited. The shares will then normally be allotted to the highest bidder. A tender may not be submitted by way of a referential bid. In *Harvela Investments v. Royal Trust Company of Canada*[34] the company invited purchasers to submit sealed bids for shares. One of the bids stated that the bidder would pay a certain amount over any other offer received by the company. The House of Lords held that such bids were unacceptable as one bidder could not lose and the others could not win.

The Prospectus

A prospectus is defined by section 2(1) of the Principal Act as 'any prospectus, notice, circular, advertisement or other invitation, offering to the public for subscription or purchase any shares or debentures of a company'. The prospectus may, and often does, take the form of a large newspaper advertisement which describes the company, its prospects and the terms of the offer. The use of the word 'offer' is strictly inaccurate from a contract law viewpoint, as a prospectus merely invites the public to make offers for the company's shares. Once the offer is made and the company accepts the application for shares, it is at that point that agreement is reached.

A document, which on the face of it appears to be a prospectus by giving the public an opportunity to subscribe for shares, will still be deemed to be a prospectus even if it is circulated among a restricted number of people. Section 61(1) of the Principal Act gives effect to this rule by providing that an offer of shares to the public shall also include an offer of shares to any section of the public.

---

34 [1986] AC 139.

1. Contents of the Prospectus

In general the prospectus must include all the necessary information that investors would reasonably require to make an informed decision as to whether to purchase the company securities. The Third Schedule to the Principal Act sets out the specific information and reports which must be contained in the prospectus. These requirements have been supplemented by the European Communities (Transferable Securities and Stock Exchange) Regulations 1992.[35] Prospectuses must include, *inter alia,* the following:

(a) details of the share and loan capital of the company;
(b) details of the directors, including such provisions in the articles which relate to their qualification shares, remuneration and their interests, if any, in the company and its assets;
(c) details of the promoters and auditors of the company;
(d) details of the property acquired or to be acquired from the proceeds of the issue;
(e) a report by the auditors on the profits and losses of the company and its subsidiaries in the preceding five years, and a statement of their respective assets and liabilities at the latest date to which accounts have been made up;
(f) if any business is to be acquired from the proceeds of the issue, similar reports are required in respect of the profits and losses and the assets and liabilities of the business;
(g) if a company is to be acquired from the proceeds of the issue, further reports relating to the financial position of that company are required;
(h) if the prospectus is an offer of shares to the public, it must state the minimum subscription amount which must be raised to cover the purchase price of any property to be acquired, any preliminary expenses or commissions payable, the repayments of any borrowings and any working capital;
(i) details of all material contracts entered into by the company within the preceding five years other than those entered into in the ordinary course of business.

Where a report included in the prospectus contains a statement purporting to be made by an expert, the expert's consent to the issue of the report must be attached to the prospectus.

2. Registration of the Prospectus

Before a prospectus can be issued, a copy signed by every person named therein as a director or proposed director of the company or by his agent authorised in writing, must be delivered to the Registrar of Companies on or before the date of its publication.[36] Furthermore, the following documents must be attached to the copy of the prospectus which is filed in the Companies Office:

---

35 SI 202 of 1992.
36 Section 47(1) of the Principal Act.

(a) the consent to the issue of the prospectus required from any person as an expert;[37] and

(b) a copy of every material contract or an explanatory memorandum required to be stated therein.[38]

3. Date of the Prospectus

Section 43 of the Principal Act requires a prospectus to be dated and that date shall, unless the contrary is proved, be taken as the date of publication of the prospectus.

4. Statement in Lieu of Prospectus

Where a private company applies to be re-registered as an unlimited public company, the company must deliver to the Registrar of Companies, with its application to re-register, a document called a statement in lieu of prospectus which in turn must comply with the requirements set out in the Second Schedule to the Principal Act.

5. Exemptions to the Requirement to have a Prospectus

Public companies may be exempted from the requirement to issue a prospectus in any of the following circumstances.

1. Where there is a *bona fide* invitation to enter into an underwriting agreement.[39] Under such an agreement the underwriter agrees to subscribe for all the securities for which the public does not apply. The agreement usually provides that if the offer is over-subscribed, the underwriters take no shares or debentures unless they have applied for them. Payment of underwriting commission in respect of an issue of shares must be authorised by the company's articles of association and must not exceed 10 per cent of the offer price.[40]

2. Where the form of application in relation to the securities was not offered to the public.[41] Whether the offer is a public or a private one will depend on the circumstances of each case. In *Nash v. Lynde*,[42] the directors of a private company had some copies made of a document intended to interest possible investors. Although marked 'strictly private and confidential', a copy was handed to a solicitor who gave it to his client who further passed it to his brother-in-law. On the basis of the document the brother-in-law subscribed for shares and also became a director of the company. The court held that in

---

37 Section 47(1)(a) of the Principal Act.
38 Section 47(1)(b) of the Principal Act.
39 Section 44(4)(a) of the Principal Act.
40 Section 59 of the Principal Act.
41 Section 44(4)(b) of the Principal Act.
42 [1929] AC 158.

the circumstances, the document was merely a private communication between persons who knew each other, and it was therefore deemed not to have been issued to the public. However, in *Re South of England Natural Gas and Petroleum Co.*[43] the circulation of 3,000 copies of a document among shareholders was held to be a prospectus even though it was printed with the heading 'for private circulation only'.

3. Where the issue of securities is limited to the company's existing members or debenture holders, whether such issue is renounceable or not.[44] It is usual in practice to issue renounceable letters of allotment which provide that the securities can be transferred, for a limited period, without formal transfer documents. Transfers which occur during the 'renounceable' period are not subject to stamp duty.

4. Where the issued securities are in all respects 'uniform' with securities that have been issued in the preceding two years and are dealt in or quoted on a recognised Stock Exchange.[45]

5. The Stock Exchange may grant a certificate of exemption to a company, where the requirements of the Third Schedule would be unduly burdensome.[46] Where such an exemption is granted an advertisement complying with the regulations of the Stock Exchange relating to quotations will be deemed to be a prospectus.

6. Where the Stock Exchange has approved Listing Particulars.[47]

7. Where debentures are issued and must be repaid within five years of the date of issue, an offer for subscription or sale to a person whose ordinary business is to buy and sell shares.[48]

6. *Restrictions on Allotment*

Once the prospectus has been issued, the company must wait four clear business days before it may allot shares or debentures in response to applications received. Any allotments made in breach of this rule are valid, but the company and its officers may be fined.[49] The interval permits prospective investors to consider their options before deciding whether to apply for the securities. An application for shares in pursuance of a prospectus issued generally cannot be revoked until nine days after the issue of the prospectus.

---

43 [1911] 1 Ch 573.
44 Section 44(7)(a) of the Principal Act.
45 Section 44(7)(b) of the Principal Act.
46 Section 45 of the Principal Act.
47 European Communities (Stock Exchange) Regulations 1984 (SI 282/1984) as amended by European Communities (Stock Exchange) (Amendment) Regulations 1991 (SI 18/1991).
48 Section 61(3) of the Principal Act.
49 Section 56 of the Principal Act.

Section 22 of the Companies (Amendment) Act 1983 provides that any offer for shares in a public limited company must be fully subscribed unless the offer states that a part subscription may be acceptable. If these conditions are not satisfied within forty days from the issue of the prospectus or the listing particulars, the money received must be repaid. If it is not repaid by the forty-eighth day, the directors of the company shall be jointly and severally liable to repay that money, with interest on it from that day at the rate of 5 per cent per annum.

An allotment made in contravention of section 22 shall be voidable at the instance of the applicant within one month after the date of the allotment, and not later, and shall be so voidable even if the company is being wound up.

Liability for Mis-statements in a Prospectus

1. Civil Liability

Where a prospectus contains a mis-statement, any person who, having subscribed for securities on the face of the prospectus and by reason of any untrue statement included therein, suffered a loss, may claim that loss against any of the following:

(a) every person who is a director of the company at the time of the issue of the prospectus;
(b) every person who has authorised himself to be named and is named in the prospectus as a director or as having agreed to become a director either immediately or after an interval of time;
(c) every person being a promoter of the company;
(d) every person who has authorised the issue of the prospectus.[50]

Section 49(3) of the Principal Act provides that a defence will be available for persons other than experts in the following circumstances:

(a) the person concerned withdrew his consent to acting as director before the prospectus was issued and it was issued without his consent;
(b) the prospectus was issued without his knowledge or consent and on becoming aware of it he gave reasonable public notice that it was issued without his knowledge or consent;
(c) after the issue of the prospectus and before allotment thereunder he, on becoming aware of any untrue statements therein, withdrew his consent thereto and gave reasonable public notice of their withdrawal and the reason therefore;
(d) in making the statement he had reasonable grounds for believing it to be true, or relied on a statement in a report by an expert whom he reasonably believed to be competent, or relied on a statement made in an official public document.

An expert who has given his consent to the inclusion of the statement which proves to be untrue may escape liability if he can demonstrate that:

---

50 Section 49(1) of the Principal Act.

(a) he withdrew his consent before a copy of the prospectus was delivered to the Registrar of Companies; or

(b) he withdrew his consent before any allotment was made under the prospectus and gave reasonable public notice stating the reason for his withdrawal; or

(c) he was competent to make the statement and up to the time of allotment believed on reasonable grounds that the statement was true.[51]

2. *Criminal Liability*

Where a prospectus includes an untrue statement, any person who authorised the issue of the prospectus shall on summary conviction be liable to imprisonment for a term not exceeding six months or a fine not exceeding £500 (€635), or to both, and on indictment, to imprisonment for a term not exceeding two years, or a fine not exceeding £2,500 (€3,174), or to both. The person may escape liability if he can demonstrate that the statement was immaterial or that he believed on reasonable grounds up to the time of the issue of the prospectus that the statement was true.[52]

Other Remedies for Mis-Statements in Prospectuses

If a prospectus is misleading, the common law remedies available to a subscriber for securities are as follows:

1. rescission of the contract on the ground of misrepresentation;
2. an action for damages for deceit against those who issued the prospectus; and
3. an action for damages based on negligent misrepresentation.

1. *Rescission*

An allottee may be entitled to rescind the contract if he can demonstrate the following:

(a) that the prospectus included a material false statement of fact;
(b) that the prospectus was issued by or on behalf of the company and that he was one of the persons to whom it was addressed; and
(c) that the false statement induced him to subscribe for shares.

However, the right to rescind will not be available if the allottee discovers the true facts and then by his conduct affirms the contract. This is so even if this was not his intention. Therefore, his right to rescind may be lost if he, having discovered the true facts, exercises any of his rights as a member including selling shares and receiving dividends. As the right to rescind is an equitable remedy, it will also be lost in the following circumstances:

---

51 Section 49(5) of the Principal Act.
52 Section 50 of the Principal Act.

(a) if, on discovering the truth, he fails to rescind promptly;
(b) if it is no longer possible to restore both parties to their pre-contractual position;
(c) if, in seeking the equitable remedy, he does not come to the courts 'with clean hands'.

2. Negligent Misrepresentation

Damages may also be recovered for negligent misrepresentation.[53] To succeed in such an action the plaintiff must demonstrate the following:

1. there was a sufficient degree of proximity between the defendant and the plaintiff;
2. the person who made the statement did so in a professional capacity which made it reasonably foreseeable that the plaintiff would rely on what he said; and
3. the plaintiff did rely on what was said and in doing so suffered a loss which was reasonably foreseeable.[54]

3. Damages for the Tort of Deceit or Fraud

This remedy is not often successful, as the allottee has to prove that the false statement was made knowingly, without belief in its truth or with reckless carelessness as to whether the statement was true or false.[55] The action for deceit will be brought against those responsible for the issue of a prospectus with intent to defraud, including the directors, the issuing house and the company.

Stock Exchange Requirements

Where, as is usual, the shares are the subject of a flotation, the issue must also comply with the requirements of the Stock Exchange. While it is possible to invite the public to subscribe for shares and debentures without seeking Stock Exchange approval, this is uncommon, for two reasons. First, unless shares are dealt with on the Stock Exchange, they will have little attraction for the investor. Second, where an offer is made or a placement effected with the assistance of an issuing house, there will usually be an insistence that the Stock Exchange requirements are met in so far as they are applicable. The minimum requirements laid down by the Stock Exchange in this regard have now been given the force of law by the European Communities (Stock Exchange) Regulations 1984.[56] These regulations implemented the following EEC Directives:

1. The Admissions Directive, which concerns the conditions for the admission of securities to official listing on a Stock Exchange operating within a Member

---

53 *Hedley Byrne v. Heller & Partners* [1964] AC 465.
54 Ibid.
55 *Derry v. Peek* (1889) 14 App Cas 337.
56 SI 282/1984.

State. In Ireland, a company must have a minimum market value of £700,000 (€888,818) and at least 25 per cent of the equity capital should already be in the hands of the public before it can be listed. However, an exemption from these requirements can be granted. Responsibility for deciding on the admission of securities to listing rests with the Stock Exchange.

2. The Listing Particulars Directive, which sets out the requirements for the drawing up, scrutiny and distribution of listing particulars in respect of securities admitted to official Stock Exchange listing. The Directive imposes an obligation on Member States to ensure that the admission of company securities to the official listing is conditional upon the publication of information referred to as the 'listing particulars'. These particulars must contain *inter alia* such information as is necessary to enable investors and their investment advisers to make an informed assessment of the assets and liabilities, financial position, profits and losses, and prospects of the issuer and of the rights attaching to such securities. Again, the Stock Exchange is the authority which decides whether the requirements imposed by the Directive are met. A copy of the listing particulars must be delivered to the Registrar of Companies before the date of publication.[57]

3. The Interim Reports Directive, which sets out the information to be published on a regular basis by companies whose shares have been admitted to an official Stock Exchange listing.

The Listing Rules

Where a company seeks an official listing on the Listed Market in Ireland, it must produce Listing particulars as set out in the Yellow Book. These Listing requirements are a substitute for the statutory requirements relating to prospectuses. The Listing particulars include *inter alia*:

(a) the names of the issuer, person responsible for listing particulars, the auditors and other advisors;
(b) the relevant securities and any underwriting arrangements;
(c) details relating to the issuer and its capital;
(d) details of the group's activities, financial information and management information;
(e) recent development and future prospects; and
(f) information on debt securities.

In addition to the above, an applicant must disclose all such information as investors and advisers may reasonably require and make an informed assessment of the issuer's financial position and prospects, and the rights attaching to the securities.

---

57 The Regulations were amended by the European Communities (Stock Exchange) Regulations 1991 (SI 18/1991) which in turn had revised the EC Listing Particulars Directive.

CHAPTER TEN

MAINTENANCE OF SHARE CAPITAL

Introduction

As mentioned in Chapter 8, a company will raise its capital from its own members in the form of equity and from creditors in the form of loan capital. It relies on this capital to expand its business. Without it, the coffers of the company will run dry and the business will stagnate. The extent of the company's share capital is a primary indicator of the company's credit worthiness. If the company's owners are not prepared to invest more than the legal minimum, which can be as little as €1 in the case of a single-member private limited company, what message does that send to prospective creditors of the company? The law jealously guards the capital base of the company and will not permit indiscriminate accretions from that base except in the most limited of circumstances. Before considering the legal provisions relating to the maintenance of share capital, it is appropriate at this stage to distinguish between a company's authorised share capital and its issued share capital.

1. Authorised Share Capital

In the case of a company with a share capital, the capital clause must state the amount of the share capital with which the company proposes to be registered and the division of that share capital into shares of fixed amounts. This 'authorised' share capital is itself of little significance because it represents merely a notional amount, which the company may issue without having to go through the formalities of increasing the capital. It is not unusual to find grossly undercapitalised companies with an authorised share capital of millions.

2. Issued Share Capital

Issued share capital is the nominal value of the shares which have been allotted and issued to members and for which they have paid or have agreed to pay. In practice it is usual to pay the full price on shares shortly after they have been issued, although on occasion prospective investors may be encouraged to take up a new issue on the basis that payment will be by way of instalments. In any case, it is the issued share capital of the company that reflects the true level of capitalisation, and it is this capital base that the law regards as next to sacrosanct, so much so that as far back as 1892 it was a judicial decision, as opposed to a legislative one, which prohibited the issuance of a company's shares at a discount.[1] Fortunately this rule is now enshrined in legislation.[2]

---

1 *Ooregum Gold Mining Co. v. Roper* [1892] AC 125. See Chapter 9.
2 Section 27(1) of the Companies (Amendment) Act 1983.

Alteration of Share Capital

Section 68 of the Principal Act provides that a company, if authorised to do so by its articles, may in general meeting alter its existing share capital in any of the following ways:

(a) increase its share capital by new shares of such amount agreed by the company;

(b) consolidate and divide all or any of its share capital into shares of a larger amount than its existing shares;

(c) convert its paid-up shares, if any, into stock, and reconvert that stock into paid-up shares of any denominations;

(d) subdivide any or all of its shares into shares of a smaller amount, provided that in the subdivision the proportion between the amount paid and the amount, if any, unpaid on each reduced share shall be the same as it was in the case of the share from which the reduced share is derived;

(e) cancel shares which have not been taken or agreed to be taken by any person and diminish the amount of its share capital by the amount of the shares so cancelled.

1. Increase in Share Capital

A company may resolve, if so authorised by its articles of association, to increase the amount of its authorised share capital. Table A only requires the passing of an ordinary resolution to effect such a change. Within one month of making any increase above the registered capital, the company must deliver to the Registrar of Companies notice of the increase and the Registrar must record the increase.[3] Obviously, where a change is being made to the memorandum of association to reflect the increased capital a copy of the altered memorandum must also be sent to the Registrar.

2. Reduction of Share Capital

Section 72(1) of the Principal Act contains an express prohibition on the reduction of share capital by a limited company. However, the general prohibition is subject to a number of exceptions and section 72(2) provides that, subject to confirmation by the court, a company may by special resolution, where the articles of association so permit (Table A does so permit), reduce its share capital by any of the following means:

(a) extinguish or reduce the liability on partly paid shares;

(b) cancel any paid-up share capital which is lost or is no longer represented by available assets;

---

3 Section 70(1) of the Principal Act.

(c) pay off any paid-up share capital which is in excess of the needs of the company.

When the company passes the resolution to reduce its share capital it must then apply to the court for a confirmation of the reduction.[4] When the company petitions the court to confirm the reduction, the procedure to be followed will vary depending on the potential effect of the reduction on the company's ability to pay its debts. In certain circumstances the reduction will not be confirmed unless the creditors have agreed to it, or they have had their debts discharged or secured.[5] Those circumstances are where the reduction involves:

(a) a diminution of liability in respect of unpaid share capital; or
(b) the payment to shareholders of any paid-up share capital; or
(c) any other reduction where the court so directs.

The court may decide that these provisions will not apply as regards any class or class of creditors.[6]

Once the court is satisfied that every creditor has either consented to the reduction or has had their debt discharged or secured it may make the order confirming the reduction on such terms and conditions as it thinks fit.[7] The court in making such an order may authorise the company to be re-registered as another form of company without it having passed a special resolution. The court may also specify the change to be made to the company's memorandum and articles of association. The court may also order the company to add the words 'and reduced', or the Irish equivalent, to its name or to publish the reasons for the reduction.[8]

Even if the statutory formalities have been satisfied, the court will not sanction the reduction unless the majority shareholders in authorising the reduction were exercising their powers in good faith.[9] Similarly, the reduction must be equitable between the various classes of shareholders involved.[10]

Where the reduction involves a variation of class rights the consent of the class must be obtained.[11] In *Re Old Silkstone Collieries*[12] the company purported to repay part of its capital and in doing so agreed that the preference shareholders would obtain a priority claim in the final distribution of any surplus assets. When the second reduction of share capital was proposed which would have the effect

---

4 Section 73(1) of the Principal Act.
5 Section 73(2) of the Principal Act.
6 Section 73(3) of the Principal Act.
7 Section 74(1) of the Principal Act.
8 Section 74(2) of the Principal Act
9 Re John Power & Sons Ltd [1934] IR 412.
10 *Re Holders Investment Trust* [1971] 2 All ER 289.
11 Section 38 of the Companies (Amendment) Act 1983. See variation of class rights in Chapter 8.
12 [1954] 1 All ER 68.

of repaying the preference shareholders, they objected on the basis that the total repayment would prevent them from obtaining their interest in the remaining assets. It was held that this was a variation of class rights and since the necessary consent of the class had not been obtained the reduction would not be approved.

Where a reduction is approved a copy of the court order confirming the reduction and of a court-approved minute showing the altered share capital must be delivered to the Registrar of Companies who must then register the order and minute.[13] The Registrar will then issue a certificate of registration which is conclusive evidence that all the requirements of the Act relating to the reduction have been complied with and that the share capital of the company is such as is stated in the minute. On registration the resolution for reducing the share capital takes effect. Where the reduction brings the allotted share capital of the company below the authorised minimum, it must be re-registered as another form of company.[14]

As well as the formal methods described above, the capital of a company may be reduced without the need for court confirmation. Shares may be forfeited or surrendered for non-payment of a call, provided the articles of association so authorise. The court is also empowered under certain provisions of the Companies Acts to order a company to purchase the shares of its members.

3. Loss of Capital

When a company incurs trading losses the capital base of the company will be diminished. Such an occurrence is involuntary and cannot therefore be the subject of any legislative prohibition. However, section 40 of the Companies (Amendment) Act 1983 requires that where the net assets of the company fall below half or less of the company's called-up share capital, the directors must convene an extraordinary general meeting of the company, for the purpose of considering what measures, if any, should be taken to deal with the situation. The meeting must be held not later than twenty-eight days from the date on which such a situation became known to any director.

4. Purchase by a Company of its Own Shares

As far back as 1887 the House of Lords held in *Trevor v. Whitworth*[15] that a company could not purchase its own shares because this would cause a reduction of capital. This common law prohibition did not apply where the shares were given to a company by way of a gift and held by a nominee.[16] Thus in *Re*

---

13 Section 75(1) of the Principal Act.

14 Section 17(3) of the Companies (Amendment) Act 1983.

15 (1887) 12 App Cas 409 HL.

16 Section 42 of the Companies (Amendment) Act 1983 extends the prohibition to the purchase of shares by a nominee of a company. Section 42(5) and (6) does provide for exceptions to this rule in limited circumstances.

Castigliones Will Trusts [17] a will provided that 1,000 fully paid-up shares were to be held in trust for the testator's son, but in the event that his son died without issue, the shares were to be transferred to the company. Following the death of the son the gift to the company was upheld provided the shares were transferred to a nominee for the company.

The modern statutory prohibition on a limited company purchasing its own shares is found in section 41 of the Companies (Amendment) Act 1983.[18] If a company purports to do so, the transaction is void and the company and every officer in default is guilty of an offence.[19] Despite the general prohibition, there are statutory exceptions:

(a) the acquisition of fully paid shares otherwise than for valuable consideration;
(b) the redemption of shares in pursuance of section 65 of the Principal Act or the redemption or purchase of shares in pursuance of Part XI of the 1990 Companies Act;
(c) the purchase of shares in pursuance of a court order under section 15 of the 1983 Act or under section 205(10) of the Principal Act;
(d) the forfeiture or the acceptance of shares surrendered in lieu of forfeiture.

Despite the general prohibition contained in section 41, section 211 of the Companies Act 1990 permits a company, if so authorised by its articles of association, to purchase its own shares subject to certain conditions which also attach to the redemption of shares, which are discussed below. However, the purchase must not cause the nominal value of the non-redeemable share capital to be reduced below one-tenth of the total issued share capital.[20] Public limited companies which purchase their own shares must also comply with the additional requirements of the European Communities (Public Limited Companies Subsidiaries) Regulations 1997.[21] The rules in relation to a purchase differ depending on whether the company is buying the shares in a market or off-market purchase.

Off-Market Purchases

An off-market purchase is one where the shares are purchased otherwise than on a recognised Stock Exchange or on a Stock Exchange but are not subject to a marketing arrangement on that Stock Exchange.[22] Shares are subject to a

---

17 [1958] Ch 549.
18 As amended by section 232(a) of the Companies Act 1990. A similar statutory prohibition had appeared in section 72 of the Principal Act along with the prohibition on reducing capital, but that part of the section was repealed by section 231(2) of the Companies Act 1990.
19 Section 41(3) of the Companies (Amendment) Act 1983.
20 Section 211(3) of the Companies Act 1990.
21 SI 67/1997 which gives effect to Council Directive 92/101/EEC which amends the Second Company Directive.
22 Section 212(1)(a) of the Companies Act 1990.

marketing arrangement if they are listed on the Stock Exchange or the company has been afforded ongoing dealing facilities on the Stock Exchange.[23] A company can only buy its own shares off-market in pursuance of an authorised contract, the terms of which have been approved in advance by a special resolution of the company.[24] Such a resolution will not be effective if:

(a) the seller, where he is a member of the company, carries the vote by exercising his voting right over those shares which are the subject of the resolution;[25] or

(b) a copy of the proposed contract, or a memorandum of its details where the contract is not in writing, is not available for inspection at the company's registered office for twenty-one days before the meeting at which the authorising resolution is to be passed and at the meeting itself.[26]

Contingent Purchase Contracts

A contingent purchase contract is one whereby the company may at some future time become entitled to, or obliged to, purchase its own shares. Such a purchase can only occur on a contingent basis, if the contract has been approved in advance and the off-market purchase rules have been observed.

Market Purchases

A market purchase is one where the shares are purchased on a recognised Stock Exchange and are subject to a marketing arrangement.[27] The conditions attached to market purchases are less onerous than those attached to off-market purchases. A company can only buy its shares in a market purchase if it has been authorised in advance by an ordinary resolution of the company in general meeting.[28] There is no requirement that the contract itself must be authorised. The authority must, however, specify the maximum number of shares which may be acquired and the minimum prices which must be paid for the shares. A printed copy of the resolution must be forwarded to the Registrar of Companies.[29]

Additional Rules for PLCs

Where a public company proposes to make either a market or a non-market purchase, the authorisation by the general meeting must specify the date on which the authority is to expire, which must not exceed eighteen months after the

---

23 Section 212(2) of the Companies Act 1990.
24 Section 213 of the Companies Act 1990.
25 Section 213(3) of the Companies Act 1990.
26 Section 213(5) of the Companies Act 1990.
27 Section 212(b) of the Companies Act 1990.
28 Section 215(1) of the Companies Act 1990.
29 Section 215(2) of the Companies Act 1990.

date on which the resolution granting the authority is passed.[30] In the event that the contract to purchase the shares was concluded before the authority expired, and the authority had provided for such an exigency, the contract may be executed wholly or partly after the expiry date.[31]

Purchase by subsidiary of shares in its holding company.

A company may acquire and hold shares in a company which is its holding company subject to the following provisions:

(a) the consideration for this purchase is provided out of the profits of the subsidiary available for distribution;

(b) from the time of the acquisition, and while the subsidiary holds the shares, the profits of the subsidiary available for distribution shall be restricted by a sum equal to the total cost of the shares acquired, the shares are treated for consolidating accounting purposes as treasury shares and the subsidiary shall not exercise any voting rights in respect of those shares;

(c) the contract for the acquisition of the shares is authorised in advance by the subsidiary and the holding company.

5. Redemption of Shares

Section 207 of the Companies Act 1990 empowers any company, where the articles so authorise, to issue redeemable shares and redeem them accordingly. Redeemable shares can only be issued provided that at least 10 per cent of the nominal value of the issued shares is non-redeemable and the terms of any redemption offer provide for payment on redemption. Once issued, the shares can only be redeemed in the manner provided for by the articles and where each of the following conditions is satisfied:

(a) the shares must be fully paid;

(b) the redemption can only be made out of the profits available for distribution or, in the case of a proposed cancellation of the shares, on redemption out of the proceeds of a fresh issue of redeemable shares;

(c) at the time of redemption the nominal value of the issued share capital which is not redeemable must be not less that 10 per cent of the total issued share capital.

Cancellation on Redemption

Redeemed shares may be cancelled on redemption. Where they are cancelled on redemption then the company's issued share capital can be reduced by the nominal value of the shares redeemed.[32] However, an amount equal to the nominal value

---

30 Section 216(1) of the Companies Act 1990.
31 Section 216(2) of the Companies Act 1990.
32 Section 208 of the Companies Act 1990.

of the shares redeemed or, if there has been an issue made to fund the redemption and the value of the new shares is less than the value of the redeemed shares, the difference in value between the shares redeemed and the new shares issued for the purpose of the redemption, must be transferred to the fund called the Capital Redemption Reserve Fund. Accordingly, the company's former capital is not reduced, as one type of capital is substituted for another. This fund, like the share premium account, is treated in the same manner as paid-up capital but it may be applied in paying up bonus issues, thus converting it to share capital. When shares are redeemed from a fresh issue of shares they must be cancelled on redemption.

Treasury Shares

If shares are not cancelled on redemption or if a company purchases its own shares under section 211 of the Companies Act 1990, they may be retained by the company as treasury shares. Treasury shares are of little use as they do not confer any of the typical rights of a shareholder on the company that now holds them. The company cannot vote using those shares, it cannot receive dividends on the basis of those shares and they confer no rights in a winding up. The value of treasury shares cannot exceed 10 per cent of the nominal value of the issued share capital. Shares which have been retained as treasury shares can be re-issued provided certain conditions are complied with.[33]

Redemption at a Premium

If the shares are being repaid at a premium, then the premium can only be paid out of distributable profits[34] unless the redemption is being paid for out of the proceeds of a fresh issue of shares for that purpose, and in that case the premium can only be paid up to an amount equal to the lesser of:

(a) the aggregate of the premiums received by the company on the issue of the shares being redeemed; or

(b) the current amount in the company's share premium account including the amount transferred to that account in respect of premiums on the newly issued shares.

Notification to the Registrar

Where a company has purchased shares or redeemed shares in the manner described above, it must, within twenty-eight days after delivery to the company of those shares, deliver to the Registrar for registration a return in the prescribed form that states, with respect to shares of each class purchased, the number and nominal value of those shares and the date on which they were delivered to the

---

33 Section 209(6) of the Companies Act 1990.
34 See Chapter 13.

company.[35] A copy of the purchase contract must also be kept at the company's registered office for ten years.[36]

Section 89 Validation

Where a company has acquired shares by redemption or purchase and those shares were invalidly acquired, the court may, under section 89 of the Principal Act, declare the acquisition valid if it considers it just and equitable to do so.[37] The court will not make such a declaration in relation to redeemable shares in the following circumstances:

(a) where they are redeemed otherwise than out of profits available for distribution; or

(b) where the premium payable on redemption, if any, is paid for otherwise than out of profits available for distribution; or

(c) where the premium payable on the redemption of shares issued at a premium is made out of a fresh issue of shares and exceeds the lessor of either the aggregate premiums received by the company on the issue of the shares redeemed, or the current amount of the company's share premium account; or

(d) if a special resolution authorising the issue has not been passed.

Furthermore, the court in granting relief, under section 89, may direct that the company and its officers are not relieved of liability in relation to the purchase by a company of its own shares.

Duty to Notify the Stock Exchange

Where a company has dealing facilities or a recognised stock exchange and its shares have been purchased in the manner described above, it must notify the Stock Exchange which may publish information received by it. In certain instances, the Stock Exchange must notify the Director of Corporate Enforcement of unlawful purchases which come to its attention.

6. Financial Assistance for Purchasing Shares

The general prohibition on a company giving financial assistance to enable a third party to purchase its shares is found in section 60(1) of the Principal Act. For the purpose of the section, the prohibition applies to financial assistance given directly or indirectly, whether by way of a loan, a guarantee or the provision of security. What will constitute financial assistance for the purposes of section 60

---

35 Section 226 Companies Act 90 public limited companies must comply with further notification requirements in this regard.

36 Section 222 Companies Act 90.

37 See Chapter 9 and *Re Sugar Distributors Ltd.* [1995] 2 IR 195.

is not exhaustively defined, although some examples are given. In *Charterhouse Investment Trust Limited v. Tempest Diesels Ltd,*[38] Hoffman J. stated:

> the words have no technical meaning and their frame of reference is in my judgment the language of ordinary commerce. One must examine the commercial realities of the transaction and decide whether it can possibly be described as the giving of financial assistance by the company.[39]

The commercial reality test was applied by the High Court in *Re CH (Ireland) (in liquidation).*[40] It found that a circuitous set of transactions entered into by a number of parties, which began with the deposit by CHI of certain monies and ended with the purchase by another company of shares in CHI, was the giving of financial assistance within the meaning of section 60. Section 60(14) declares that any transaction in breach of the section is voidable at the instance of the company against any person who had notice of the facts constituting a breach. In *Bank of Ireland v. Rockfield,*[41] the Supreme Court held that 'notice' for the purpose of the subsection meant 'actual' rather than constructive notice.[42] A sanction is also imposed by section 60(15) of the Principal Act, which provides that every officer in default is liable to a fine or imprisonment, or to both.

Because the giving of financial assistance may in certain circumstances be unobjectionable, section 60 provides for a number of exceptions to the general rule. The principal exception is contained in section 60(2), which only applies to private companies.[43] Under this subsection the prohibition on a company providing financial assistance for the purchase of its own shares will not apply if the following conditions are satisfied. First, an authorising special resolution must be passed by the members in general meeting and second, a statutory declaration of solvency must be sworn by the directors of the company. In *Re Northside Motors Co. Ltd,*[44] Eddison owned half the shares in the plaintiff company in advance of the purchase. Wishing to acquire the remainder, the defendant advanced finance to another company which was owned by Eddison. The security for the loan was a guarantee from the plaintiff company. When the bank became aware that the procedures under section 60(2) had not been observed, it demanded that the company pass the appropriate resolution and that the directors make the necessary statutory declaration of solvency. The company acquiesced with the

---

38 [1987] BCLC 7.

39 Ibid. at 10.

40 Unreported, High Court, 12 December 1997.

41 [1979] 2 IR 21.

42 See also *Eccles Hall Ltd v. Bank of Nova Scotia High Court,* 3 February 1995 (Murphy J.).

43 Section 60(15A) of the Principal Act as inserted by para. 10 of the First Schedule of the Companies (Amendment) Act 1983 excluded this right from public limited companies.

44 Unreported, High Court, 24 July 1985 (Costello J.).

bank's request. Some time later the company honoured its commitments under the guarantee. When it was subsequently wound up, the liquidator sought the recovery of the money paid out under the guarantee. Costello J. held that the company had given financial assistance within the meaning of section 60 and the resolution and statutory declaration could not retrospectively validate the breach.

The special resolution must be passed within twelve months prior to the financial assistance being provided.[45] Every member of the company, notwithstanding any provisions in the articles to the contrary, must be given notice of the meeting at which the special resolution will be proposed.[46] The notice must be accompanied by a copy of the statutory declaration by the directors.[47] In the event that the members do not unanimously vote in favour of the resolution, the assistance must not be provided for at least thirty days to enable dissenting shareholders, holding at least 10 per cent of the nominal value of the company's issued share capital, to apply to the court for the cancellation of the special resolution.[48] In the event that such an application is made within twenty-eight days from the date of passing of the resolution, the special resolution will have no effect until confirmed by the court.[49] In *Lombard & Ulster Banking Ltd v Bank of Ireland*[50], it was held that an informal agreement by all the shareholders would not be an appropriate substitute for a special resolution authorising the giving of financial assistance. Therefore a subsequent verification of those acts could not substitute for the formal procedure required under section 60. However, section 60 has since been amended and provides that a resolution in writing signed by all the members shall be as valid as a special resolution passed at a duly convened meeting.[51]

The statutory declaration of solvency must be sworn by the directors of the company not more than twenty-four days before the meeting at which the special resolution is proposed.[52] The declaration must state the following:

(a) the form which the assistance is to take;
(b) the persons to whom such assistance is to be given;
(c) the purpose for which the company intends those persons to use such assistance;
(d) that the declarants, having made a full enquiry into the affairs of the company, have formed the opinion that the company, having given the financial assistance, will be able to pay its debts as they become due.[53]

---

45 Section 60(2)(a) of the Principal Act.
46 Section 60(6) of the Principal Act.
47 Section 60(2)(b) of the Principal Act.
48 Section 60(7) of the Principal Act.
49 Section 60(8) of the Principal Act.
50 Unreported, High Court, 2 June 1987 (Costello J.)
51 Applying section 141(8) relating to informal resolutions to section 60.
52 Section 60(3) of the Principal Act.
53 Section 60(4) of the Principal Act.

A copy of the statutory declaration must be sent to the Registrar of Companies within 21 days after the date on which the financial assistance was given. Where any director makes the statutory declaration without having reasonable grounds for their opinion as to the solvency of the company, the penalties are severe. Such directors will be liable to a fine not exceeding £500 (€635) or imprisonment for a period not exceeding six months, or to both.[54] In the event that a company is wound up within twelve months after the making of the statutory declaration and its debts are not paid within the twelve months from the commencement of the winding up, it shall be presumed, until the contrary is shown, that the director did not have reasonable grounds for his opinion. Of course, this presumption may be rebutted.

Transactions which are not prohibited

The prohibition contained in section 60 does not apply to any of the following transactions:

(a) the payment of a dividend declared by the company or the discharge of a liability lawfully incurred by it;[55]
(b) the lending of money in the ordinary course of business;[56]
(c) the provision of money for the purchase of fully paid shares where such is for the benefit of employees, former employees and salaried directors or former salaried directors; [57] and
(d) the making by a company of loans to persons, other than directors, who are employed by the company to enable them to purchase shares.[58]

These exemptions apply to private and public companies.

Re-nominalisation of Share Capital in Euro

Section 26 of the Economic and Monetary Union Act 1998 provides mechanisms for companies to re-nominalise their share capital in convenient Euro amounts, if re-denomination into Euro has resulted in inconvenient uneven amounts. Companies may elect to re-nominalise their share capital during the period up to and including the 30 June 2003. However, any adjustments shall not reduce the nominal value of any share to zero. Re-nominalisation is effected by amending the company's share capital provisions in its memorandum and articles of association.

Where re-nominalisation would result in an increase in share capital, an ordinary resolution must be passed by the general meeting, or a class meeting,

54 Section 60(5) of the Principal Act.
55 Section 60(12) of the Principal Act.
56 Section 60(13)(a) of the Principal Act
57 Section 60(13)(b) of the Principal Act.
58 Section 13(c) of the Principal Act.

where appropriate. The following must then be forwarded to the registrar of companies within fifteen days of the passing of the resolution:

(a) notification of the increase;
(b) the authorising resolution;
(c) the amended memorandum and articles of association; and
(d) the appropriate registration fee.

A Company may also, by ordinary resolution, effect re-nominalisation of its share capital by altering the memorandum and articles of association in order to round up the value of each share. Such an alteration will only be permitted if there is an appropriate adjustment in distributable reserves or an introduction of additional capital which is reflected in an increase in the amount of issued share capital.

Where re-nominalisation would result in a decrease in share capital, a special resolution is required. This resolution must provide that an amount equal to the decrease will be paid into a fund to be known as the Capital Conversion Reserve Fund. The amount transferred must not represent more than 10 per cent of the reduced share capital. The authorising resolution, together with the amended memorandum and articles, must be sent to the Registrar.

CHAPTER ELEVEN

Loan Capital

Introduction

The company's capacity to borrow will be determined by the objects clause of the memorandum. In the absence of an express power, a trading company is assumed to have an implied power to borrow for a purpose incidental to that trade.[1] If a company has an express or implied power to borrow, it will also have an implied power to give security for those borrowings. While the company is usually conferred with unlimited borrowing powers, it is normal, and obligatory in the case of listed companies, to impose restrictions on the amount that directors can borrow on the company's behalf. Article 79, Table A, confers an express authority on directors to borrow and to secure those borrowings by way of mortgage or charge. However, limits are imposed on the amount that can be borrowed, and these can only be exceeded with the prior sanction of the general meeting.

When a company borrows money it will in normal circumstances be required to provide security for the repayment of the amounts borrowed. Usually the company will issue debentures which are secured by a charge over some or all of the company's assets. From the lender's point of view a charge is an attractive form of security for the following reasons:

(a) the secured creditor may obtain a measure of control over the business of the debtor by the imposition of certain restrictive conditions and events of default in the loan and security documentation;

(b) in the event that the company defaults, the secured creditor will generally have a right of enforcement;

(c) in the event that the company becomes insolvent, a secured creditor will enjoy a priority over an unsecured creditor as to repayment;

(d) if the charge is fixed the charge holder will generally have a priority over the preferential creditors.[2]

Charges may be categorised in terms of either fixed charges or floating charges. However, it is not uncommon for security arrangements to incorporate both types of charges.

---

1 See Chapter 7.

2 However, fixed charges over book debts may be subordinated to certain preferential creditors: see section 115 of the Finance Act 1986 as amended by section 174 of the Finance Act 1995, now section 1001 of the Taxes Consolidated Act 1997.

Fixed Charges

A fixed charge is so called because it is essentially a charge on identifiable property. It attaches, from the moment of its creation, to the property in question. Accordingly, provided the charge is properly registered, the holder has an immediate security over the property.

If the company disposes of the asset which is the subject matter of the charge, it must either repay the loan amount out of the proceeds of the sale before legal ownership is transferred, or pass the asset over to the purchaser still subject to the charge. The latter would be a most unusual occurrence. Therefore a fixed charge is best suited to long-term assets which are not changing on a frequent basis. Otherwise, every time a charged asset is disposed of the company would need to obtain the consent of the charge holder and draw up and register the appropriate deeds of release and memoranda of satisfaction. Furthermore, any new asset acquired would then have to be charged to replace the old security. The expenses involved in such a process would be prohibitive.

Floating Charges

A floating charge is a charge on the property of a company which is constantly changing, for example the stock-in-trade of a business or the assets or undertaking for the time being of a company. The advantage of this form of security is that it allows companies which do not have a solid asset base, in the form of identifiable long-term assets, to raise debt capital on the back of stock-in-trade, raw materials and work-in-progress. The nature of the floating charge was described by Romer LJ. in the case of *Re Yorkshire Woolcombers Association*[3] as:

(a) a charge on a class of assets of a company present and future;
(b) which class is, in the ordinary course of the company's business, changing from time to time; and
(c) until the holder enforces the charge, the company may carry on business and deal with the assets charged.

Although all three characteristics are usually essential, it would appear from one Irish decision that this is not necessarily the case. In *Welch v. Bowmaker (Ireland) Ltd and Bank of Ireland*,[4] a debenture was issued in favour of Bowmaker which created a specific charge over three of four parcels of land owned by the company, together with a floating charge over its other assets. The terms of the debenture included a 'negative pledge' clause whereby the company pledged not to create any other security over the property which would take priority over the existing charge. One month later the company deposited the title deeds of the fourth parcel of land as security with the Bank of Ireland, which was

---

3 1903] 2 Ch 284 at 295.
4 [1980] IR 251.

unaware of the terms of the debenture. The company subsequently failed. The court held that a floating charge had been created over the fourth parcel of land and that the fixed charge created by deposit of deeds in favour of the Bank of Ireland took priority. Therefore, although it is unusual to create a floating charge over land, it was held possible to do so.

Crystallisation of The Floating Charge

Up until the point when the holder enforces the security, the floating charge 'hovers' over the assets in question, thus allowing the company to retain autonomy over, and continue to deal with those assets. Once the security is enforced, the floating charge is said to crystallise. This does not involve any physical change in the nature of the assets — rather it is a process by which the floating charge is converted into a fixed charge on the happening of certain events. It has traditionally been accepted that one of the following events will trigger the crystallisation of a floating charge:

(a) the company ceases to trade usually by the intervention of the debenture-holder;[5]

(b) the appointment of a receiver;[6]

(c) the liquidation of the company.[7]

When crystallisation occurs the charge is no longer said to be hovering, as it now attaches to the assets. From that point the company is no longer free to deal with those assets without the permission of the charge holder. Generally, the holder of the floating charge will appoint a receiver to collect and realise the assets. However, the receiver must first account to the preferential creditors for the amounts owed by the company.[8] This provision is necessary to safeguard the company from pre-emptive actions by floating charge holders who attempt to realise their security at a time which maximises their position but not that of the company or the other creditors. By virtue of section 98, a receiver will therefore be required to pay off the preferential creditors before he can apply any of the proceeds in discharge of the floating charge holders' debts.[9]

1. The Floating Charge as a Primary Security

While the floating charge was at its inception an adequate solution to the need for secured debt-capital, it has one major flaw, which is its susceptibility to having its priority postponed to subsequent fixed charges over the company's property[10] or to

---

5 *Re Woodroffes (Musical Instruments) Ltd* [1985] BCLC 227.

6 *Halpin v. Cremin* [1954] IR 19.

7 *Re Crompton & Co. Ltd* [1914] 1 Ch 954.

8 Section 98 of the Principal Act.

9 See Chapter 24, Receivers.

10 *Wheatley v. Silkstone and Haigh Moor Coal Co.* [1985] 29 Ch D 715.

an increasing number of statutorily preferred creditors.[11] Furthermore, if a company is wound up before a floating charge is realised, the costs of the liquidation must be paid from the assets of the company in priority to all claims, including floating charges.[12] Taken together, these priority positions could represent a substantial erosion in the assets that would otherwise be available to the floating charge holder.

2. Negative Pledge Clauses

One technique employed to protect the holder of the floating charge against any subsequent security interest was the insertion of a clause — referred to as a 'negative pledge' clause — into the charge. The effect of such a clause is that the company is restricted from creating any further security interests which would have priority over the floating charge. The clause, which now appears in most standard charges, merely attempts to limit the authority of the company to issue any further security over the assets in question. If the company subsequently breaches the pledge and grants a fixed charge over the assets in question, that holder of the fixed charge will enjoy a priority position over the floating charge holder. This is because even though the holder of the fixed charge is deemed to have constructive knowledge of the existence of the floating charge, he is not deemed to have knowledge of the contents of that charge and therefore will not have knowledge of the 'negative pledge' made by the company.

In *Wilson v. Kelland*[13] the company had issued a floating charge to a creditor which incorporated a negative pledge clause. The company later, in breach of the negative pledge, granted a fixed charge over the same assets. The fixed charge holder had not made a search in the Companies Office and was unaware of the existence of the previous charge. It was argued that the fixed charge holder had constructive notice of the floating charge and its contents. The court accepted that the holder of the fixed charge had constructive notice of the floating charge, but he was not deemed to have notice of the negative pledge clause as this information was not required by law to be registered. The only way the floating charge holder will retain a priority position is to prove that the fixed charge holder had actual knowledge of the 'negative pledge' clause.[14] If the floating charge holder cannot prove this actual knowledge, then the only other recourse available is to sue the company for breach of contract. As the company is likely to be insolvent at that stage, any damages payable for the breach will form only part of the unsecured claims. On this basis the use of the negative pledge clauses in charges can be viewed as a source of comfort only.

---

11 Section 285 of the Principal Act: see Chapter 27.
12 See Chapter 26 with respect to the distribution of assets in a winding up.
13 [1910] 2 Ch 306.
14 *English & Scottish Mercantile Investment Co. Ltd v. Brunton* [1892] 2 QB 700.

3. Other Devices

The continued deterioration of the floating charge holder's position has forced creditors to take account of the risks involved in employing a floating charge as the primary security. The alternative solution of relying on non-security devices such as 'retention of title' clauses is not an option available to a lending bank which is supplying loans rather than goods. The solutions which have been developed to circumvent the diminishing effect of the floating charge have been twofold. First, attempts were made to revert to the pre-1880 method of employing the fixed charge. The difficulty here was that while the fixed charge was readily acceptable when it related to land and buildings, when it came to extending it to include revolving assets, particularly book debts, controversy arose. The other solution was to stipulate in the debenture that a floating charge would automatically crystallise on the occurrence of a specified event or events of default, thus converting it to a fixed charge without any action needed on the part of the charge holder.

Fixed Charges over Book Debts

The ability of a creditor to create a floating charge over future book debts received judicial support as far back as 1883.[15] However, it is only in the past thirty years that the position with respect to taking fixed security over such assets has been addressed, although some confusion stills surrounds the issue. Traditionally, it was considered impossible to take a fixed charge over assets, such as book debts, which are by their very nature changing from day to day. It is for this reason that it was always considered more appropriate to take a floating charge over such assets. However, in the English decision of *Siebe Gorman v. Barclay's Bank Ltd*[16] the validity of a fixed charge over book debts was upheld. The charge in question provided that the proceeds of the book debts should be placed into a specially designated bank account, withdrawals from which were permitted only with the consent of the charge holder. It was this element of 'control', a necessary feature of the fixed charge, that persuaded the court that the charge was fixed.

The first Irish case which addressed the issue was *Re Keenan Bros Ltd.*[17] There, the charge was taken over the company's book debts, the proceeds of which were lodged to a bank account under the terms of the debenture. The charge also provided that withdrawals could not be made from that account without the consent of the charge holder. When the company was subsequently wound up, the Revenue Commissioners argued that despite the description of the charge, it was in substance a floating charge because the bank, while retaining control over the

---

15 *Tailby v. Official Receiver* (1883) 13 App Cas 523.
16 [1979] 2 Lloyd's Reports 142.
17 [1985] IR 401.

asset, continually gave the company permission to withdraw monies from that account. According to the Revenue, this continued use by the company of the assets charged was a feature of a floating charge and not a fixed charge. Although the Supreme Court accepted the validity of the substance over form argument, it concluded that the charge in question was a fixed charge. The court was persuaded that an essential feature of a fixed charge — its immediate attachment to the assets — was a feature of the charge in question because the company was only permitted to deal with the assets charged to the extent permitted by the charge holder. Furthermore, the charged assets were so withdrawn from their ordinary trade use by putting them in the 'control' of the debenture holder that the charge constituted a fixed charge. On the basis of the decision in *Re Keenan Bros*[18] it seemed that a necessary requisite of a fixed charge over book debts was that the book debts, having been collected, should be paid into a designated bank account. This would seem to be the only method of maintaining control over the assets by the charge holder. However, in *Re Wogan's (Drogheda) Ltd*[19] this requirement appeared to be disregarded by Finlay C.J. who held that any delay or suspension in the operation of the proceeds account should not deprive a lender of his rights under a fixed charge. Rather, it was sufficient that the charge gave the holder the right to designate a proceeds account which he would control.[20]

The advantage of obtaining a fixed charge over book debts has been eroded to some degree by the enactment of section 115 of the Finance Act 1986, as amended.[21] The effect of this section is that the holder of a fixed charge over book debts will be primarily liable for certain VAT and PAYE amounts owed by the company which issued the charge unless certain qualifications arise.[22] However, the charge over book debts is still used by lenders for practical as well as legal reasons. First, it gives lenders control over the assets charged. Second, as the proceeds are lodged to the bank account, the charge holder can see the weekly income stream building up. This gives a very accurate insight into the business of the company which the normal creditor is not privy to. Finally, a fixed charge over book debts cannot be avoided by a liquidator under section 288 of the Principal Act. (See Chapter 26, Liquidations.)

Automatic Crystallisation Clauses

There has been considerable controversy in recent years about the validity of what are termed 'automatic crystallisation' clauses in a debenture. These clauses effectively crystallise the floating charge in an event other than the cessation of

---

18 See also *Re Armagh Shoes Ltd* [1984] BCLC 405.

19 [1993] 1 IR 157.

20 But see judgment of Blayney J. in *Re Holidair Ltd* [1994] 1 IR 416.

21 Section 174 of the 1995 Finance Act. See section 1001 Taxes Consolidated Act 1997.

22 For an interesting critique of section 115, as amended, see Courtney, *Company Law Review* (Round Hall Sweet & Maxwell) 1995.

trade, the appointment of a receiver and the winding up of a company. In *Re Griffin Hotel Co.*[23] it was held that if a floating charge crystallised before a winding up had commenced, it would not lose its priority to preferential creditors in the event that the liquidator was subsequently appointed. In other words, if the debenture contains provisions which trigger the automatic crystallisation of a floating charge upon the happening of an event, other than those events which cause a floating charge to crystallise at law, does that floating charge become a fixed charge for the purposes of the insolvency queue? The idea behind the automatic crystallisation clauses is that the floating charge is crystallised without the appointment of a receiver. Therefore, the obligation to pay preferential creditors before the floating charge holder which is imposed on a receiver by section 98 of the Principal Act has no application if a receiver has not been appointed. In *Re Brightlife Ltd*,[24] Hoffman J. held that the appointment of a receiver, liquidator or the cessation of business was not an exhaustive list of the events which cause a floating charge to crystallise, and he could not see any reason why parties could not contract their own terms into the debenture or charge.

The public policy arguments against validating such crystallisation clauses are twofold. First no other party would have notice of the crystallising events and, second and more importantly, the party would not be aware that the floating charge has in fact crystallised. In the UK the legislature has intervened with the introduction of the 1986 Insolvency Act. It provides that once a charge is created as a floating charge it will always be considered a floating charge for the purpose of establishing its place in the insolvency queue. The issue has yet to be determined in Ireland, but Keane J. has stated extra-judicially[25] that such clauses are unlikely to be accepted in Ireland for the policy reasons mentioned above.

4. Other Disadvantages of Floating Charges

The other disadvantages of the floating charge can be summarised as follows.

(a) A floating charge is in effect a charge over future assets as it does not create immediate rights over identifiable assets. By contrast, a fixed charge is usually a more satisfactory form of security since it confers immediate rights over specific assets. If a creditor has obtained a fixed charge over a building, a quick visit will ensure that the building exists. Of course, the sensible fixed charge holder will ensure that the building is insured and insist on seeing a copy of the insurance certificate. On the other hand, even if the holder of a floating charge inspects the charged assets he will know that those assets will not necessarily be available to him if at some future date he is required to realise his security. As the company is free to deal with them, the holder of a

---

23 [1940] Ch 87.
24 [1986] 3 All ER 673.
25 Keane, *Company Law in the Republic of Ireland* (Butterworths) 1991.

floating charge cannot be certain, until the company fails, which assets will actually form part of his security.

(b) Even when the floating charge crystallises, there is no guarantee that the assets, which fit the generic description of those charged, are in fact subject to the security. A supplier, who in normal circumstances would be an unsecured creditor of the company, may have sold goods only on condition that he is to retain legal ownership until he has been paid. The validity of these 'reservation or retention of title' clauses was recognised as far back as 1893.[26] The proliferation of 'retention of title' clauses clearly causes a problem for the floating charge holder because he is faced with a competing and superior claim, in the form of a supplier, to some of the assets in the company's possession. This problem is exacerbated by the fact that accounting practices dictate that assets, subject to retention of title clauses, should still appear on the buyer's balance sheet. This gives rise to an increased difficulty on the part of the floating charge holder to ascertain, at any particular time, the true worth of his security.

(c) A floating charge, unlike a fixed charge, created in the twelve months (or two years where it is in favour of a connected person) prior to the commencement of a winding up will be avoided by a liquidator under section 288 of the Principal Act as amended, unless certain conditions prevailed at the time. Essentially, if money was paid or goods or services supplied at the time of or subsequently to the creation of the charge and in consideration of the charge, it will not be impunged. Nor will the charge be avoided if it can be shown that the company was solvent immediately after the giving of the charge. The purpose of this statutory provision is to prevent creditors who realise that the insolvent company is on the brink of liquidation from obtaining a priority position by taking security over the company's remaining unencumbered assets which would otherwise have been available for the unsecured creditors.[27]

Registration of Charges

Section 99(1) of the Principal Act requires almost every type of charge to be registered with the Registrar of Companies within twenty-one days of its creation. Section 100(1) of the Principal Act places the onus of registration on the company which creates the charge. Section 99(2) sets out the types of charges which must be registered.[28] It is open to the Minister to alter this list by statutory instrument.[29]

---

26 Sections 17 and 19 of the Sale of Goods Act 1893. See *Aluminium Industrie Vaassen BV v. Romalpa Aluminium Ltd* [1976] 2 All ER 552.

27 See Chapter 26 for a detailed account of section 288.

28 Not all charges are registrable: those that arise by operation of law, for example a banker's lien, do not fall into the category of charges required to be registered under section 99 of the Principal Act.

29 Section 99(2A) and (2B) of the Principal Act.

The requirement that all charges are registered ensures that creditors can discover the extent to which the assets of a company are used to fund its borrowings. Indeed, this information is equally informative for the members of a company. Having imposed a duty on companies to register their charges, section 103 of the Principal Act imposes an obligation on the Registrar of Companies to keep, in respect of all companies, a register of charges.

A charge is registered by delivery to the Registrar of Companies, in the prescribed form, particulars of the charge including, *inter alia,* the following:

(a) the date the charge was created;
(b) the amount of the debt to which the charge applies;
(c) the property to which the charge applies;
(d) the person entitled to it.

If the Registrar is satisfied with the particulars, he will issue a certificate of registration to the effect that the charge has been registered in accordance with section 99. The Registrar's certificate is conclusive that the charge has been duly registered.[30]

This is so even if the charge had been incorrectly dated. In *Lombard & Ulster Banking Ltd v. Amurec Ltd,*[31] the defendant company issued an undated mortgage over a ballroom premises to the plaintiff bank in November 1972 together with a commitment to provide the appropriate stamping fee. In March 1974, when the stamping fee had not been provided, the bank, using its own funds, had the mortgage stamped and lodged in the Companies Registry Office. The Registrar issued the certificate of registration which certified that the charge was created in March 1974. When the defendant company was subsequently wound up, the liquidator argued that the charge was void because it had not been registered within twenty-one days of its creation. The court held that the certificate of registration was conclusive proof that the registration requirements had been complied with and the charge was valid. Even where other registered particulars are incorrect, such as the amount of the debt to which the charge applies, this will not invalidate the certificate of registration. This is because the court is only giving effect to the document creating the charge and not to the particulars contained in the certificate of registration In *Re Mechanisations (Eaglecliffe) Ltd,*[32] the certificate of registration mis-stated an amount of £18,000 as the debt to which the charge applied. In fact, the charge also applied to further unspecified amounts owing to the creditor in respect of any goods supplied. When the company was subsequently liquidated the charge holder claimed an amount of £23,000. The liquidator argued that the maximum entitlement was the amount specified in the certificate of registration. The court held that the charge covered

---

30 Section 104 of the Principal Act.
31 [1976–1977] ILRM 222.
32 [1964] 3 All ER 840.

the extra sums owing to the creditor, and the fact that incorrect particulars were registered did not affect the creditor's entitlement. This decision has been followed in Ireland in *Re Shannonside Holdings Ltd.*[33]

If the charge is not registered within the specific time frame it becomes void against the liquidator and any creditor of the company. In such a circumstance the loan which has been secured by the charge becomes immediately repayable. If the charge holder demands repayment and the company is not in a position to oblige, the charge holder has the same rights against the company as any unsecured creditor. He may petition the court to have the company wound up.

It is possible to apply to the court for an order to extend the time for registration. Under section 106(1) of the Principal Act the court may order that the time for registration be extended provided it is satisfied that:

(a) the omission was accidental; or
(b) the omission is not of a nature to prejudice the position of the company's creditors or shareholders; or
(c) it is just and equitable to grant such relief.

The court will usually grant such an order unless there is evidence of *male fides* on the part of the applicant.[34] However, it is unlikely to grant the extension where no useful purpose will be served by such an order.[35]

The Register of Charges

Every company is obliged to keep at its registered office a copy of every instrument which creates a registrable charge.[36] Copies of such instruments must be available for inspection by any of the company's creditors or members for at least two hours per working day.[37]

Satisfaction of the Charge

When a charge is satisfied, a memorandum of satisfaction of charge, in the prescribed form, should be delivered to the Registrar of Companies. Once the Registrar is satisfied that the debt has been paid in whole or in part and that all or part of the assets or undertaking charged have been released from the charge, he may then enter on the register a memorandum of satisfaction in whole or in part.[38]

---

33 Unreported, High Court, 20 May 1993 (Costello J.).
34 *Re Teleomatic Ltd* [1994] 1 BCLC 90.
35 *Re Farm Fresh Frozen Foods Ltd* [1980] ILRM 131.
36 Section 109 of the Principal Act.
37 Section 110(1) of the Principal Act.
38 Section 105 of the Principal Act.

CHAPTER TWELVE

MEMBERSHIP

Introduction

Because ownership and control of the company are often separated — a phenomenon more applicable to public companies and large private companies than small private companies — a number of problems arise. These problems range from the loss by the company's primary organ — the general meeting — of its decision-making powers to the potential abuse by the company's officers of their day-to-day control and management of the company's business and undertaking. Both common law and statute have long recognised these problems of corporate governance and have attempted to eliminate them by a series of provisions which make the controllers more accountable to the shareholders while at the same time protects the position of the shareholder, even where his interest in the company is a minority one. In this and the following three chapters the position of shareholders and their rights, duties and obligations are discussed. Chapters 16–18 deal with the general law relating to the company's management. Chapters 19–22 deal with specific aspects of the law which attempt to improve management's accountability to shareholders.

The Register of Members

Before persons are entitled to any rights in relation to their shares, their name must be entered on the register of members.[1] Section 116 of the Principal Act requires every company to keep a register of members which must contain the following particulars:

(a) the names, addresses and occupations of the members and, in the case of a company having a share capital, a statement of the shares held by each member, the number of each share (where the shares are numbered) and the amount paid or considered as paid on the shares of each member;
(b) the date at which each person was entered in the register as a member;
(c) the date at which any person ceased to be a member.

The register must be kept within the state at the company's registered office or such other place if work is being done on it. If it is kept at any place other than the registered office, the Registrar of Companies must be notified of its location. Where a company has more than fifty members, an index of members must also be maintained unless the register itself is in the form of an index. The register of

---

1 Section 31 of the Principal Act. See *Arulchelvan v. Wright*, High Court, 7 February 1996 (Carroll J.), where the beneficiary of a deceased member's shares was held not to have the right to attend and form part of the quorum at an extraordinary general meeting.

members must be available for inspection free of charge by members and, subject to a nominal fee, by non-members for at least two hours every business day. Requested copies of the register or a part thereof must be provided within ten days subject to a scrivenery charge. The register may be closed for up to thirty days in each year provided that the closure is advertised.

The register may be rectified by the company where any error or omission has occurred.[2] However, any rectification may not adversely affect any person unless he agrees to the rectification. Notice of any rectification must be sent to the Registrar within twenty-one days where any such error or omission appears on any document already sent to him.

The court is also given the power to order the rectification of the register on an application by any aggrieved person, member of the company or the company itself.[3] The court may make such an order where:

(a) the name of any person is, without sufficient cause, entered into or omitted from the register, in contravention of section 116; or

(b) default is made in entering on the register the fact of any person having ceased to be a member within the period fixed by section 116.

In considering whether to make an order under the section the court may decide on any question relating to the title to the shares. If any order for rectification is made, the court may direct that compensation be paid by the company for any loss suffered by the aggrieved party.

Section 123 provides that the register of members shall not be concerned with any trust arrangements relating to shares. Therefore the company will usually only have to deal with those rights pertaining to the registered owner of the shares irrespective of any underlying arrangements between the registered owner and another party.[4]

Section 124 provides that the register of members shall be *prima facie* evidence of any matters directed or authorised by the Companies Acts to be inserted therein. It is not conclusive evidence and therefore persons who become aware of inaccuracies may apply for rectifications. However, an application for rectification must be made promptly on discovering the error or omission or a person may be estopped from denying the accuracy of its contents.

Transfer of Shares

Shares are by their nature the transferable personal property of the company member.[5] However, the right to transfer shares is not absolute and may be restricted

---

2 Section 122 of The Principal Act.
3 Section 122 of the Principal Act.
4 There are exceptional circumstances whereby a company must take account of such underlying arrangements, for example where it receives a 'stop notice' from a third party holding shares as security: see 'Shares as Security for a Loan' later in this chapter.
5 Section 79 of the Principal Act.

by the articles of association or the Companies Acts. Indeed, private companies are obliged to include restrictions on the transfer of shares in their articles of association.[6] This is usually achieved by the inclusion of a pre-emption clause which gives existing shareholders a right of first refusal to shares being sold by other members or to new shares being issued by the company and a clause empowering directors to refuse to register a transfer.

1. Restrictions on Transfers

A transfer of shares will not occur by operation of the law. A formal transfer must be completed. Section 81 of the Principal Act prohibits a company from registering a transfer of shares unless a proper instrument of transfer has been delivered to the company. Furthermore, the transfer must also be executed by the transferor.[7] Although Table A also requires that the instrument of transfer be executed by the transferee, companies usually dispense with this requirement in their own articles of association. Until a share transfer is registered, the transferor remains the holder of the shares. However, he holds them as nominee for the transferee who holds an equitable interest in those shares (Act 22 Table A).

2. Directors' Powers to Refuse Registration

Because a transferee has no legal right to the shares until his name has been entered in the register of members, it is imperative that his name be so registered as soon as possible. However, he is not automatically entitled to have his name registered because the directors may only register shares in the manner permitted by the articles of association.

Table A empowers directors to refuse to register a transfer of shares. In the case of a public company this power is limited to a right to refuse a transfer of unpaid shares, but in the case of private companies the power is not so restricted. Instead, under Article 3 of Part II of Table A directors may, in their absolute discretion, and without assigning any reason therefor, decline to register any transfer of any share, whether or not it is a fully paid share. Where the articles provide such a wide power to directors, it will be difficult to challenge any decision arising thereon.

However, the power must, as with all directors' powers, be exercised in good faith and for a proper purpose. In *Re Hafner*,[8] the directors exercised their powers under a Table A type article and refused to register the plaintiff as a member of the company. The plaintiff produced evidence that the directors' powers were exercised for the improper purpose of preventing him from asking questions about exorbitant payments being made to the directors. The directors, during the

---

6 Section 33(1)(a) of the Principal Act.
7 *Re Green* [1949] 1 All ER 167.
8 [1943] IR 426.

course of the proceedings, argued that they were not required to give reasons for their decision but the court held that once improper motivations were established the directors were estopped from relying on this right.[9] Accordingly, the court drew an inference from the directors' silence that the allegations were well founded and the directors' decision was invalidated. In *Popely v Planarrive Ltd*[10] the directors exercised their discretion under Table A and refused to register the shares in the plaintiff's name. Evidence was provided that the plaintiff was not an ideal character to control the company, as many of his former actions were detrimental to the company. The court held that the board had, in refusing to register the plaintiff, acted in good faith and in the best interests of the company.

However, the court will presume that the directors have acted in good faith and the onus is on the plaintiff to prove otherwise. In *Re Smith & Fawcett Ltd*,[11] the directors refused to register a transfer of the shares of a deceased director but agreed that they would register a transfer of part of the shareholding if the transferor agreed to sell the balance to the surviving director at a fixed price. This decision was later justified as being in the company's best interests in that it ensured that the existing management remained in control. The court held that there was insufficient evidence of bad faith on the director's behalf and refused to invalidate the decision.[12]

Where the articles contain restrictions other than those provided for in Table A, the extent of the restriction is solely a matter of construction by the courts who tend, where the language is uncertain or ambiguous, to lean in favour of the shareholders' freedom to transfer. However, the courts will not defeat the obvious purpose of the restriction, as the case of *Lyle & Scott Ltd v. Scott's Trustees*[13] demonstrates. The company's articles conferred a pre-emption right on the other shareholders when any shareholder was 'desirous of transferring his ordinary shares'. Some of the existing shareholders attempted to avoid the articles by selling the beneficial interest in their shares to a prospective take-over bidder who would use his proxy cards to vote on their behalf. The court held that the articles must be construed to include a restriction on the transfer of the beneficial interest and not just a restriction on the process of having the transfer registered.

Where the directors are only entitled to reject a transfer on specified grounds, reliance on other grounds will invalidate the decision. In *Re Bede Steam Shipping Co. Ltd*,[14] the directors were authorised to refuse transfers if they were of the opinion that it was in the company's best interests that the transferee would not become a member. The directors refused to register transfers of shares on the

---

9 See Chapter 17, Directors' Powers.
10 [1997] 1 BCLC 8.
11 [1942] 1 All ER 452.
12 Nowadays such a decision might constitute oppression under section 205 of the Principal Act: see Chapter 15.
13 [1959] AC 763.
14 [1917] 1 Ch 123.

stated ground that it was prejudicial to the company to have its issued share capital fragmented. The court held that the decision was invalid as it was not within the reasons prescribed by the articles of association. In *Tangney v. The Clarence Hotel Co. Ltd*[15] a similar provision was contained in the articles. Accordingly, the directors refused to register a transfer to a person on the grounds that it was not in the company's interest to have him admitted to its membership. In fact, the transferee was already a member of the company and the court held that the directors could therefore not invoke this ground in refusing the transfer.

Directors must exercise their power to refuse to register a transfer within a reasonable period. In *Re Swaledale Cleaners Ltd,*[16] due to technical difficulties in holding a board meeting, the directors took over four months to exercise their power of refusal. The court held that the delay was unreasonable and the transfer should, accordingly, be registered. In any case section 84 of the Principal Act requires a company to notify the transferee of a refusal to transfer the shares within two months from the date the transfer is lodged. As a result of this provision, the maximum reasonable period is two months. If a director fails to notify the transferor within that period he can be compelled to register the transfer.

3. The Transfer Procedure

In practice, the transfer of fully paid shares is effected by the use of the standard stock transfer form.[17] The transfer form is signed by the transferor and given to the transferee together with the share certificate. The transferee sends the transfer form, which must be stamped for the purposes of stamp duty,[18] to the company directors who must only register the transfer in accordance with the provisions of the articles of association. Once registered, the old share certificate is cancelled and a new one is issued to the transferee.

The above mentioned procedure may not be possible where only part of the shares comprised in the share certificate are being transferred. This is because it would be unwise to hand over the share certificate when the transferor wishes to retain some of the shares. Similarly, it would be unfair to the transferee to pay for his shares if the transferor retained the certificate. In such a situation a certification of transfer must take place which involves the following procedure:

(a) the transferor executes the transfer and sends it, together with the share certificate, to the company;

(b) the company retains the share certificate and endorses the transfer form with the words 'certificate lodged' which is returned to the transferor;

---

15 [1933] IR 51.

16 [1968] 1 WLR 1710.

17 As permitted by section 22 of the Stock Transfer Act 1963.

18 Normally 1 per cent *ad valorem* on the consideration paid on the shares.

(c) the transferor delivers the transfer to the transferee who stamps it and presents it to the company; and

(d) the company then issues two new share certificates, one representing the amount of shares transferred to the transferree and the other representing those shares retained by the transferor.

A certification of transfer by the company estops it from denying the truth of the essential facts stated therein. Furthermore, the certification is a representation by the company to any person acting on the faith of the certification, that documents have been produced to the company which on the face of them show a *prima facie* title to the shares comprised in the instrument of transfer.[19] However, it is not a representation that he has in fact title to them. A person who accepts a certified transfer may claim damages from the company if it did not retain the share certificate or indeed if it certified the transfer without ever having received the certificate. However, in order to succeed in such a claim the person must show that he relied on the certification of transfer. In *Longman v. Bath Electric Tramways*,[20] the company mistakenly sent the share certificate together with the certification of transfer to the transferor. The transferor proceeded to deposit the share certificate with the plaintiff as security for a loan. The plaintiff later claimed that he was entitled to the shares. The plaintiff's claim failed as he never knew of the existence of the certification of the transfer and had not relied upon it in his dealings with the transferor.

4. Forged Transfers

Where a company registers a transfer made on foot of a forged transfer form and a stolen share certificate, the consequences are as follows:

1. the original transferor can have his name restored to the register of members because a forged document is a nullity which cannot deprive him of his title to the shares — this is so even if he failed to reply to a notice from the company advising him of the transfer;

2. the person who lodged the forged transfer cannot rely on the share certificate and he is further liable to indemnify the company for any loss it may have suffered from having to pay compensation — this is so even if he did not know of the forgery;

3. where a third party takes the transfer of the 'forged' shares in good faith and for value, the company is estopped from denying the title to the new transferee. If this person suffers a loss as a result of the restoration of the true owner to the register, the company must compensate him for this loss.

In *Re Bahia and San Francisco Railway*,[21] the holder of shares deposited his share certificate with a broker. The broker forged the holder's signature and

---

19 Section 85(1) of the Principal Act.
20 [1905] 1 Ch 646.
21 (1868) LR 3 QB 584.

transferred the shares to X. X then presented the share certificate and transfer to the company. Before registering the transfer to X the company notified the original holder. As he did not respond, X was duly registered as the holder. X subsequently sold his shares to Y who was then registered as the new holder. When the forgery was discovered the court held that the original holder should be restored to the register and that Y was entitled to damages from the company. Furthermore, X, although unaware of the forgery, had presented the forged transfer and was held liable to indemnify the company for its liability to Y.

5. *Automated Transfers*

The Companies Act 1990 (Uncertificated Securities) Regulations 1996[22] introduced provisions for the automated transfer of company securities. As the process is intended to be paperless, the regulations provide that instead of a share certificate the buyer will receive an 'uncertified unit'. The regulations further provide for the transfer and registration of these units.

Transmission of Shares

Transmission of shares occurs by operation of law. This will occur in any of the following circumstances:

(a) where a member dies his shares will automatically vest in his personal representative who may be registered as the member or may transfer the shares without becoming a member;
(b) where shares are held jointly, the surviving owner becomes the registered owner on the death of the other;
(c) on the bankruptcy of a member, the beneficial ownership (not the legal ownership) passes to the official assignee.

Share Certificates

Although the share certificate is not a document of title, it is *prima facie* evidence of title.[23] A share certificate is a formal statement by the company, under seal, stating that the person named holds the shares specified and the extent to which the specified shares are paid up. The company may be estopped from denying any aspect of this statement if a third party relies in it to his detriment. In *Balkis Consolidated Co. v. Tomkinson*[24] P, who had no title to the shares, sold them to T and induced the company by fraud to issue a new share certificate to T. T later resold the shares but on discovering the original fraud, the company refused to register the transfer to the new purchaser on the ground that T had no title to the shares. In order to satisfy the claims of those to whom he had sold the shares,

---

22 SI 68/1996.
23 Section 87 of the Principal Act.
24 [1893] AC 396.

T purchased additional shares and brought an action against the company to recover the price paid for those shares. His action succeeded because he had changed his position in reliance on the share certificate. Similarly, in *Bloomenthal v. Forde*,[25] the company, in consideration of obtaining a loan from B, issued him a share certificate in which the shares were described as fully paid. When the company went into liquidation, the liquidator claimed from B the unpaid amount on his shares. It was held that the company was estopped from denying that the shares were fully paid. Accordingly, the liquidator's claim failed.

It has been held that the company may be able to deny the effect of the certificate where it was issued by a person who was not authorised by the company to do so. In *Ruben v. Great Fingall Consolidated*,[26] the company secretary had forged a director's signature on a share certificate which was issued to the plaintiff. The court held that the company could deny the correctness of the certificate as it had not been issued by an authorised person and, accordingly, was not issued by the company. However, the basis of this decision was rejected in *Lloyd v. Grace Smith & Co.*[27]

Share Warrants

By virtue of section 88 of the Principal Act, a public company may issue share warrants where so authorised by the articles of association. A share warrant is a negotiable instrument which entitles the bearer of the warrant to the shares in question. An instrument of transfer is therefore not required as the title can be passed by simple delivery. Share warrants are rarely used in this jurisdiction.

Shares as Security for a Loan

Shares may be used as security for borrowings. Where a legal mortgage is taken over the shares, the shares are transferred to the mortgagee who is registered as a member. The mortgagee will usually undertake to re-transfer the shares when the loan has been repaid. A lender may prefer not to take a legal mortgage for the following reasons:

(a) stamp duty is payable on each transfer; and
(b) if the shares are not fully paid, the mortgagee is liable to pay the calls while his name is on the register.

Alternatively, a lender may take an equitable mortgage, which is evidenced by a simple deposit of the share certificate and a blank transfer form with the lender. If the borrower defaults, the lender has an implied power to fill in his name on the blank transfer form and then dispose of the shares. The disadvantage

---

25 [1897] AC 156.
26 [1906] AC 439.
27 [1911] 2 KB 489.

of the equitable mortgage is that the borrower's name remains on the register. The borrower may falsely claim that his certificate has been lost and may obtain a new certificate. The mortgagee may protect himself by serving a 'stop notice' on the company, which has the effect of compelling the company to notify him if any attempt is made to transfer the shares.

Calls

A call is a demand by the company for money due on shares. Unless shares are fully paid, the holder, who need not be the original allottee, is liable to pay the balance when called upon by the company. The procedure for making calls is usually contained in the articles of association. Table A makes the following provisions in this regard:

(a) the power to make calls is vested in the directors;
(b) no call shall exceed one-quarter of the nominal value of the share;
(c) members must be given at least fourteen days' notice of the time and place of payment;
(d) a call is deemed to be made when the directors' resolution is passed;
(e) the joint holders of shares shall be jointly and severally liable to pay all calls in respect thereof;
(f) the directors may, on the issue of shares, differentiate between the holders as to the amount of calls to be paid and the time of payment;
(g) directors may, if they think fit, receive advance payments for calls.

Non-payment of calls

Table A provides for interest to be paid, from the date the call was due, at a rate of 5 per cent. However, the directors may waive payment of interest wholly or in part. Table A also provides that a member's shares may be forfeited for non-payment of a call. Where the directors propose to forfeit the member's shares, they must first serve a notice calling for the payment of the sum due within fourteen days of the date of the notice. Where the member does not comply with the terms of the notice, the directors may then resolve to forfeit the shares. The shareholder ceases to be a member on the forfeiture of his shares but he remains liable for all amounts owing to the company at the date of forfeiture. Forfeited shares may be re-issued or cancelled. To avoid a forfeiture, shareholders may decide to surrender their shares and this is permitted by the Companies Acts as an authorised reduction of capital.

Liens

It is usual for the articles to give the company a lien on a member's shares for non-payment of calls. A public company's articles can only create a lien on partly paid shares or in the ordinary course of the company's business.[28] The lien gives the company a first claim on the shares unless it has notice of some pre-existing claim such as an equitable mortgage.[29]

---

28 Section 44 of the Companies (Amendment) Act 1983.
29 *Bradford Banking Co. v. Briggs & Co.* (1886) 12 App Cas 29.

CHAPTER THIRTEEN

DIVIDENDS

Introduction

A dividend represents the cash return to a shareholder whereas a debenture holder is paid interest. A dividend is a proportion of the distributable profits of the company. It may be a fixed annual percentage, as in the case of preference shares, or it may be variable depending on the fortunes of the company during a particular period. But because a dividend is only payable from the distributable profits of the company, it follows that if no profits are made, or if no profits are available for distribution, no dividend will be declared. At the outset it should be noted that the rules regarding the payment of dividends are incorporated into the general rules regarding the making of distributions, which cover a much wider range of transactions.[1]

Distributable Profits

Dividends may only be paid out of the company's profits that are available for distribution.[2] The reasoning behind this requirement is to ensure that the capital of the company is not eroded by distributions to members.[3] Central to an understanding of a company's ability to pay dividends are the definitions of 'profits' and 'distribution'.

1. Profits

Section 45(2) of the Companies (Amendment) Act 1983 defines profits available for distribution as the company's accumulated realised profits, so far as they have not previously been distributed or capitalised, less its accumulated, realised losses, so far as they have not been previously written off in a reduction or reorganisation of capital. Under this definition dividends can only be made where there has been a surplus of profits for the current and past years, in so far as they have not already been distributed, over losses for those years, in so far as they have not already been written off. For the accountant the concept of 'realised profits' poses no great difficulty. For those who are not familiar with accounting, the matter is more complex. In general terms a 'realised profit' is a tangible profit as opposed to an artificial profit. Where for example a company makes a profit from a sale of goods, having deducted the cost of the goods sold

---

1 See *Aveling Barford Ltd v. Perion Ltd* [1989] BCLC 626 and *Re Greendale Developments Ltd* [1998] 1 IR 8.
2 Section 45(1) of the Companies (Amendment) Act 1983.
3 See Chapter 10.

and any other deductions required by accounting practices, this will constitute a tangible or realised profit. On the other hand, an unrealised profit would arise where, for example, a company revalues one of its buildings at a greater value than it had previously been shown in the company's audited balance sheet.

Accumulated realised losses include *inter alia* such things as a debit balance on a profit and loss account and amounts written off in respect of the depreciation of assets. Furthermore, except in limited circumstances, where development costs are shown as an asset in the company's accounts, those amounts shall be treated as a realised loss.[4]

2. Distributions

Section 51(2) of the Companies (Amendment) Act 1983 defines a distribution as every description of a distribution of a company's assets to its members, whether in cash or otherwise, except those distributions made for the following:

(a) the issue of fully or partly paid-up bonus shares;
(b) the redemption or purchase of shares where authorised under the Companies Acts;
(c) the reduction of share capital by extinguishing or reducing the liability of any of the members on any of their shares as authorised under section 72 of the Principal Act; and
(d) a distribution of assets to members of the company on its winding up.

Additional Restrictions for Public Limited Companies

A public limited company is subject to further limitations in that section 46(1) of the Companies (Amendment) Act 1983 provides that it can only make a distribution where:

(a) its net assets are not less than the aggregate of its called-up share capital and its undistributable reserves;
(b) the distribution does not result in its net assets falling below that aggregate.

For the purposes of section 46(1) the undistributable reserves of a public limited company are the following:

(a) the share premium account;
(b) the capital redemption reserve;
(c) the amount by which the company's accumulated unrealised profits, so far as they have not previously been utilised by any capitalisation, exceed its accumulated unrealised losses, so far as they have not already been written off in a reduction or reorganisation of the company's capital;

---

4 Section 45(A) of the Companies (Amendment) Act 1983 as inserted by section 20 of the Companies (Amendment) Act 1986.

(d) any other reserve which the company is prohibited from distributing by the law or the company's memorandum or articles of association.

Where a public company is an investment company, section 47 of the Companies (Amendment) Act 1983 provides that it may make a distribution from its accumulated realised revenue profits, so far as they have not already been distributed or capitalised, less its accumulated revenue losses, whether they are realised or unrealised, and in so far as they have not already been written off in relation to a reduction or reorganisation of capital if:

(a) the amount of its assets is at least equal to one and a half times the aggregate of its liabilities; and
(b) the distribution does not reduce its assets to less than one and a half times its liabilities.

It is clear that section 47 makes special provision for investment companies because it draws a distinction between revenue profits and capital profits. Furthermore, the distribution can only be made after realised and unrealised losses have been deducted from the company's profits.

General Provisions for all Companies

Section 49 of the Companies (Amendment) Act 1983 sets out the requirements in relation to the relevant accounts which must be used before a decision, in relation to whether a distribution should be made and the amount of such a distribution, should be made.

Consequences of Making an Unlawful Distribution

A member who receives a dividend payment, knowing at the time that it amounted to an unlawful distribution, is obliged to repay the amount which he received.[5] Furthermore, directors may also be held liable for breach of their duties. In *Re Exchange Banking Co.*[6] the directors for several years laid before the meeting accounts which, as the directors knew, inaccurately stated the position with respect to certain assets. In reliance on those accounts the shareholders passed resolutions to declare dividends out of the profits shown in the accounts. The truth of the matter was that the company had made losses. The company ultimately failed and the liquidator successfully claimed from the directors the amount which they had knowingly paid by way of dividend.

It is not only directors that may be held liable. In *Re Thomas Gerrard & Sons Ltd*[7] the managing director falsified accounts by including non-existent stock. As

---

5 Section 50 of the Companies (Amendment) Act 1983.
6 (1882) 21 Ch D 519.
7 [1967] 2 All ER 525.

a result of the overstated profits, additional taxes were paid by the company and dividends were declared which otherwise would not have been. The auditors became suspicious when they discovered that invoices relating to the stock had been altered. Rather than investigate the matter, they accepted the managing director's explanation. The auditors were held liable to the company for the amounts paid by way of dividends and excess taxes.

Declaration of Dividends

Even when distributable profits are available for distribution there is no mandatory requirement on companies to pay dividends. In *Bond v. Barrow Haematite Steel Co.*[8] the company had available reserves of £240,000 but the directors did not declare a dividend. The plaintiff, a preference shareholder, argued that the dividend should have been paid given the availability of the reserves. The company claimed that it had decided to retain the reserves to make good losses arising from the disposal of current assets and a diminution of the value of the company's fixed assets. The court held that it would not interfere with the directors' discretion in relation to the declaration of dividends. However, there is nothing to prevent the articles of association conferring an automatic right to receive a dividend, irrespective of whether or not one has been declared.[9]

The power to declare a dividend is given in the articles of association. Table A makes the following provisions in this regard:

(a) the company in general meeting may declare dividends but no dividend may exceed the amount recommended by the directors;
(b) the directors may declare such interim dividends as they consider justifiable;
(c) dividends are normally payable on the paid-up amount of the share capital;
(d) a dividend must be paid in cash unless the contrary is specified in the company's regulations;
(e) if shares are held jointly, the dividend is payable to the first named joint holder on the register.

Since the recommendation of the general meeting must not exceed the amount recommended by the directors, it is the directors who in effect have the last say as to when a dividend is to be declared and how much will be paid. The shareholders cannot force the directors to recommend a dividend. However, the directors will be conscious of the general meeting's power to remove them under section 182 of the Principal Act. Furthermore, the company may alter the articles to provide for alternative rules relating to the declaration of dividends.

---

8 [1902] 1 Ch 353.
9 *Re Lafayette Ltd* [1950] IR 100.

Dividend Payments

Although dividends are generally payable in cash, the articles may permit a company to pay them by way of non-cash assets such as shares or debentures. Indeed, many public companies now give their shareholders the option of taking shares in the company in lieu of cash dividends. In any case, Table A provides that dividends may be payable by way of cheque. Where the articles are silent on the manner in which dividends must be paid, then payment must be in the form of cash. In *Wood v. Odessa Waterworks Company*,[10] the articles authorised the company to declare a dividend to be paid to shareholders. It did not specify the form of payment. The general meeting resolved that the dividends should be declared in the form of debentures on which the company would pay interest pending the redemption of the debentures. A shareholder sued the company, claiming that the articles required payment to be in cash. The court upheld the claim and an injunction was issued preventing the company from paying the dividend otherwise than in cash.

Limitation Period for Claims

Where a dividend has been declared, it then becomes a debt owing to the shareholder who may sue to enforce his right to the dividend. The time limit for bringing an action against the company for unpaid dividends is twelve years from the date of declaration or the declared date of the payment, whichever is the later. A balance sheet duly signed by the directors has been held to have constituted a written acknowledgment of the debt due by the company.[11] The articles may provide for the forfeiture of dividends which are not claimed within a lesser period of time. Where the company is wound up, any unclaimed dividends are subject to a six year limitation period unless the articles of the company provide otherwise.[12]

---

10 (1889) 42 Ch D 636.

11 *Jones v. Bellgrove Properties Ltd* [1949] 2 All ER 198 and *Re Gee & Co. (Woolwich) Ltd* [1974] 1 All ER 1149, but cf. *Re Companiea de Electricidad de la Provincia de Buenos Aires Ltd* [1978] 3 All ER 668.

12 Section 283(2) of the Principal Act.

CHAPTER FOURTEEN

SHAREHOLDERS' MEETINGS

Types of Meetings

1. Annual General Meeting

The first Annual General Meeting ('AGM') of a company must be held within eighteen months of incorporation. Thereafter the AGM must be held every year with not more than fifteen months elapsing between each meeting.[1] A newly formed company need not hold an AGM in the year of incorporation or the following year, provided an AGM is held within eighteen months of incorporation.[2]

Unless otherwise provided by the articles, the AGM must be held within the State.[3] If default is made in holding the AGM within the prescribed time, the Director of Corporate Enforcement may, on the application of any member of the company, call a meeting or direct that one be held.[4] He may also issue such directions as he thinks expedient for the holding of the meeting, including fixing the meeting's quorum at one member. A meeting called by the Director will be deemed to be the AGM if held in the year in which the default in holding the meeting occurred. Otherwise it will only be deemed to be the AGM if the company so resolves. A copy of such an authorising resolution must be forwarded to the Registrar within fifteen days of its being passed. Default in complying with the requirement to hold an AGM will render every director who is knowingly and wilfully guilty of the default — or, in the case of default by the company, every officer in default — liable to a fine.

Where it is impractical to call a meeting in the manner normally followed, or to conduct a meeting in the manner prescribed by the articles, the court may, on the application of a member or director of the company, order that a meeting be called, held and conducted in such manner as it thinks fit.[5] In *Re El Sombrero*,[6] the applicant held 90 per cent of the shares in a private company but was not a director. The rest of the shares were held equally between two other persons who were the company's directors. The applicant convened a meeting with the stated object of removing the directors. The articles fixed the quorum at two persons and, as the directors did not attend, the meeting was denied a quorum. An application was made to the court,

---

1 Section 131 of the Principal Act.
2 Section 131(2) of the Principal Act.
3 Even where articles do provide that meetings should be held in the State, if all the members agree to hold it outside the State the meeting will be valid: *Re Shannonside Holdings Ltd*, High Court, 20 May 1993 (Costello J.).
4 Section 131(3) of the Principal Act.
5 Section 135(1) of the Principal Act.
6 [1958] 3 All ER 1.

which directed that a meeting be held with a quorum of one member, thus allowing the applicant member his statutory right to remove a director.

The Business of the AGM

The articles of association determine for the most part the business of the AGM. However, section 148 of the Principal Act makes it incumbent on the directors to lay before the AGM a profit and loss account (or income and expenditure account in the case of a company not trading for profit) and a balance sheet. Furthermore, section 158 of the Principal Act requires that a report of the directors, concerning the state of the company's affairs, should be attached to the balance sheet. Section 163 of the Principal Act requires the auditors of the company to make a report to the members on the accounts examined by them, and this report must be read at the AGM. Group accounts must also be laid before the meeting in the case of parent companies.

Article 53 of Table A provides that the following matters be considered as the ordinary business of the AGM:

(a) the declaration of a dividend;
(b) the consideration of the accounts and balance sheet;
(c) the consideration of the directors' and auditors' report;
(d) the election of directors in the place of these retiring;
(e) the reappointment and remuneration of the auditor.

All other business is deemed by Table A to be the special business of the meeting.

Single-Member Companies

Since the coming into force of the European Communities (Single Member Private Limited Companies) Regulations 1994 ('the 1994 Regulations'), the above provisions relating to the AGM are no longer mandatory for all companies. Instead, single-member companies may dispense with the holding of an AGM if the sole member so decides.[7] Alternatively, the sole member or the auditors of a single-member company may, by notice to the company not later than three months before the end of the year, require the holding of an AGM in that year. Rather than laying the accounts and reports before the AGM, it is sufficient to have sent the accounts and reports to the sole member at least twenty-one days before the date of the AGM.

2. Extraordinary General Meetings

Any meeting which is not an AGM is an Extraordinary General Meeting ('EGM'). Table A provides that the directors may convene an EGM whenever

---

7 Section 8(1) of the European Communities (Single Member Private Limited Companies) Regulations 1994 SI 275/1994.

they think fit. Section 40(1) of the 1983 Act requires directors to convene an EGM when it becomes known to them that the net assets of the company have fallen to half or less of the company's called-up share capital. A company auditor, who gives reasons for his resignation in his written notice, may also requisition a meeting under section 186 of the Companies Act 1990. Members are also given a statutory right to requisition an EGM.[8] The members' requisition must satisfy each of the following criteria:

(a) it must be supported by members holding at least one-tenth of the paid-up share capital in the case of a company having a share capital, or, in the case of a company having no share capital, by members holding at least one-tenth of the total voting rights;
(b) it must state the objects of the meeting;
(c) it must be signed by all the requisitionists; and
(d) it must be deposited at the registered office of the company.

Presuming compliance with the statutory formalities, the directors must within twenty-one days from the date of deposit of the requisition convene a meeting to be held within two months. Failing this, either all the requisitionists or those representing more than half of their total voting rights may do so, provided that the meeting shall be held within three months. The company must repay any reasonable expenses incurred by the requisitionists in convening such a meeting. The company can recover any such payments by retaining any sums due by the company to the defaulting directors, by way of fees or remuneration.

3. Class Meetings

Meetings of the holders of different classes of shares are usually convened when it is necessary to obtain approval from that class. Class approval is prescribed by the Companies Acts in a number of situations including, *inter alia*, a proposed variation or abrogation of class rights or a proposal for a scheme of arrangement under the Companies (Amendment) Act 1990. Although class meetings may be held at the same time as general meetings, it has been suggested that where there is likely to be intimidation by non-class members, the class members may seek to have a separate meeting.[9]

Notice of Meetings

The Companies Acts and the articles of association provide for different notice requirements depending on the type of meeting and the nature of the business to be transacted thereat. Under section 133 of the Principal Act, every member is entitled to twenty-one days' written notice of the AGM. All other meetings

---

8 Section 132 of the Principal Act.
9 *Carruth v. ICI* [1937] AC 707.

require seven days' notice in the case of a private company and fourteen days notice in the case of a public company.[10] These notice periods may be waived, provided that the auditors and all the members entitled to attend and vote are in agreement.[11] If a special resolution is proposed at any meeting, the twenty-one day notice period is required unless 90 per cent of the members, entitled to attend and vote, agree otherwise.[12] On account of this rule where a resolution requiring a minimum of twenty-one days' notice is proposed, the shorter notice periods may become irrelevant. The company's articles may provide for longer periods of notice, although Table A adopts the statutory notice periods.

1. Table A Requirements

Section 134(a) of the Principal Act requires notice to be served on every member, subject to any contrary provisions in the articles. The provisions of Table A that apply to notices of meetings are as follows:

(a) notice must be given to every member, those persons to whom shares have devolved by reasons of his being a personal representative or the official assignee in bankruptcy of a member or deceased member and the auditor of the company;

(b) notice may be given to the joint holders of a share by giving the notice to the first named holder in the register of shares;

(c) notice may be given either personally or by post — if the notice is properly addressed and stamped the addressee is deemed to have received it twenty-four hours after posting;

(d) notice must be clear notice, in that the day of serving the notice and the day for which the notice is given are not counted in calculating the notice period;

(e) accidental failure to give notice of a meeting, or non-receipt of a notice by any person entitled to receive notice, will not invalidate the proceedings at the meeting.

A member may give notice to the company of his intention to propose a resolution to remove a director, or remove or appoint an auditor, or to fill a casual vacancy in the office of auditor. Where such a resolution is proposed the company must be given extended notice of twenty-eight days.[13] However, if the company, on receipt of such a notice, calls the meeting for a date less than twenty-eight days after receiving the notice, the notice is deemed to have been properly given.

---

10 Section 133(2) of the Principal Act.
11 Section 133(3) of the Principal Act.
12 Section 141(2) of the Principal Act.
13 Section 142 of the Principal Act. Members may not waive the extended notice requirements.

2. Form and Content of Notice

The notice convening an AGM must be in writing and in accordance with the provisions of the articles. The form of the notice will depend on the business being proposed at the meeting. Table A requires that the notice specify the place, the day and the hour of the meeting. It would appear that where the ordinary business is being conducted, it is not necessary to give specified details in the notice of the meeting. This would seem to be the case even where an ordinary resolution is required. In *Choppington Collieries v. Johnson*,[14] a notice for an AGM specified the election of directors as ordinary business of the meeting. At the meeting a member proposed a resolution to elect new directors in place of those that were retiring. The chairman refused to accept the resolution on the basis that no notice had been given of the member's resolution. The court held that the member's resolution constituted the ordinary business of the meeting and therefore no notice of it was required.

Table A requires that where special business is to be transacted, the notice of the meeting should include the general nature of that business. Where that special business requires a special resolution to be moved, section 141(1) of the Principal Act provides that the notice should also specify the intention to propose a special resolution. The wording of the resolution contained in the notice must be precise and if an amendment to the terms of a resolution is later proposed at the meeting, it cannot be carried unless a majority agree and provided the terms of the resolution as amended are still such that adequate notice of the intention to pass the same can be deemed to have been given.[15] Typographical changes are usually acceptable, but even the most insignificant amendments to the substantive content may invalidate the resolution. In *Re Mooregate Mercantile Holdings Ltd*,[16] notices were issued of a resolution to cancel the entire share premium account of £1,356,900 which had been lost. On discovering that the share premium account stood at £321 more than the notice specified, the chairman proposed to amend the resolution to one reducing the share premium account to £321, and the resolution was carried. The resolution was held to be invalid as it was not the same as that which the notice had described.

It is also necessary to disclose all material information which is relevant to the proposed resolution in the relevant notice, even when it does not form part of the text of the resolution. In *Kaye v. Croydon Tramways Co.*,[17] the notice set out a resolution which if approved would involve the sale of the company's business. It did not, however, make any disclosure of an agreement to pay the directors compensation if the sale proceeded. It was held that the notice did not properly disclose the nature of the business being transacted at the meeting, and the

---

14 [1944] 1 All ER 762.
15 Section 141(5).
16 [1980] 1 All ER 40.
17 [1898] 1 Ch 358.

authorising resolution was therefore invalid. Similarly in *Baillie v. Oriental Telephone & Electric Co.*,[18] a special resolution was proposed and subsequently accepted, whose effect was to give retrospective approval to the payment of increased directors' remuneration. Although the notice and the accompanying circular had set out the text of the resolution and the reasons for it, it was silent on the matter of the sizeable amounts already paid to the directors. The resolution was held to be invalid as the notice did not give sufficient information concerning the transaction.

Where a company has been given extended notice of a resolution under section 142 of the Principal Act, it must give notice to the members of the resolution at the same time and in the same manner as it gives notice of the meeting to which the resolution is proposed. If this is impracticable, it must give notice in the manner provided by the articles not less than twenty-one days before the meeting. It is usual to do so by way of an advertisement in a newspaper circulating in the district in which the registered office is situated. The company must also send a copy of the proposed resolution to the director or auditor who is the subject of the resolution.

Proceedings at General Meetings

In order to be valid, a meeting must be properly convened by notice, a quorum must be present and the meeting must be presided over by a chairman. Furthermore, all resolutions must be passed in accordance with the requirements of the Companies Acts and the articles of association.

1. The Quorum

A quorum is the minimum number of persons whose presence is necessary before a meeting can be held. At common law, one person cannot constitute a meeting, even if he holds proxies for other members. However, there are now exceptions to that rule and a single person may constitute a quorum for any of the following meetings:

(a) class meetings where all the shares in that class are held by one member; or
(b) meetings called by the Minister or the court where the quorum has been fixed at one person; or
(c) meetings of single-member companies;[19] or
(d) creditors' meetings if there is only one creditor; or
(e) an adjourned meeting.

In the case of all other meetings, unless the articles otherwise provide, the quorum is fixed at three members for a public company and two for a private

---

18 [1915] 1 Ch 503.
19 Regulation 10 of the European Communities (Single-Member Private Limited Companies) Regulations 1994: SI 275 of 1994.

company.[20] Table A provides that no business shall be transacted at any general meeting unless a quorum is present when the meeting proceeds to business. A similar type of article was the subject of judicial construction in *Re Hartley Baird Ltd.*[21] The company's articles fixed the quorum at ten members who were present when the meeting began. During the course of the meeting, and before all decisions were taken, some members left, causing the numbers remaining to fall below ten. It was held that once the meeting was quorate when it proceeded, it was not necessary that the quorum remained until all the business had been conducted. However, if the number of members at the meeting fall below two, except in those cases provided for by law, the common law principle is that a meeting no longer exists and any purported resolutions will be invalid.

Only members can constitute a meeting. As membership is dependent on entry to the register of members, a person who is the beneficiary of a deceased member's shares but has not procured registration of those shares in their own name cannot form part of the quorum for the purposes of the statutory requirement.[22]

Table A provides that if within half an hour from the time fixed for the meeting a quorum is not present, the meeting, if convened by the members, shall be dissolved. In any other case the meeting shall stand adjourned to the same day of the following week, at the same time and place or to such other day, time and place as may be determined by the directors. Table A further provides that if at the adjourned meeting a quorum is not present within half an hour, the members present shall constitute the quorum.

2. Chairman

The meeting must be presided over by a chairman. The company's articles will determine who the chairman will be. Table A provides that the chairman of the board of directors or, failing him, another director nominated by the directors shall be the presiding chairman. Where no director is present and willing to act as chairman, the members may elect a chairman. The chairman's duties include the following:

(a) conducting the meeting in accordance with the Companies Acts and the articles;
(b) preserving the order of a meeting and adjourning it where necessary;[23]
(c) deciding on matters relating to motions and amendments;[24]
(d) demanding a poll, if appropriate;[25] and
(e) declaring the result of a poll.

---

20 Section 134(c) of the Principal Act.
21 [1954] Ch 143.
22 *Arulchelvan v. Wright,* unreported, High Court, 7 February 1996 (Carroll J.).
23 *Byng v. London Life Association Ltd* [1989] 1 All ER 560.
24 See *Re Moorgate Mercantile Holdings Ltd* [1980] 1 All ER 40.
25 See *MacDougall v. Gardiner* (1875) 1 Ch D 13.

3. *Voting and Polls*

Unless the articles provide otherwise, voting in the first instance is decided on a show of hands. This is the position adopted by Table A, which also provides that a poll may be demanded before or on the declaration of the result of the show of hands. Section 137 of the Principal Act makes void any provision contained in a company's articles which would have the effect of:

(a) excluding the right to demand a poll on any question other than –
     (i) the election of the chairman; or
     (ii) the adjournment of the meeting; and
(b) requiring more persons to demand a poll than any of the following –
     (i) five or more members having a right to vote;
     (ii) members representing 10 per cent of the voting rights;
     (iii) members holding 10 per cent of the paid-up capital who are entitled to vote.

Table A provides that in addition to those categories mentioned in (b) above, the chairman of the meeting may also demand a poll.

Although voting by a show of hands has the advantage of saving time, a poll is more effective because it allows shareholders to exercise their voting rights in proportion to their shares in the company and it gives members who are unable to attend the opportunity to influence the decision-making by authorising a proxy to attend and vote on their behalf.

Unless the articles provide otherwise, the voting rights in a poll are determined as follows:

(a) in the case of a company having a share capital, one vote per share or one vote per £10 (€12.70) of stock; and
(b) in any other case, one vote per member.[26]

The procedure for taking a poll is governed by the articles, but it is usual to ask members and proxies to sign voting cards or lists. The votes are then checked against the register of members and the result is declared.

If a poll is not demanded the chairman will decide the outcome by counting the show of hands. Section 141(3) of the Principal Act provides that a declaration by the chairman that the resolution is carried is conclusive evidence of the fact of the number or proportion of the votes recorded in favour of or against the resolution. Table A goes further than the statutory provision by requiring that a record of the result be entered in a book containing the minutes of the proceedings of the meeting. It is possible to challenge the chairman's declaration on the grounds that it was blatantly wrong. In *Re Caratal (New) Mines Ltd*,[27] a

---

26 Section 134(e) of the Principal Act.
27 [1902] 2 Ch 498.

special resolution was proposed and put to the vote on a show of hands. The chairman counted the raised hands and declared that six were for the proposal and twenty-three were against it. He further declared that as a result of the 200 proxy votes the resolution was carried. The declaration was successfully challenged in court on the basis that the proxies could not be used for a vote by a show of hands.

The articles usually provide the chairman with a casting vote, although he is not obliged to exercise it. If he is not already a shareholder in the company, this will be his only vote.

4. Proxies

Members entitled to attend and vote at meetings have a right to appoint one 'proxy' to attend, speak and vote on their behalf.[28] However, unless the articles otherwise provide, the right to appoint a proxy shall not apply in the case of a company not having a share capital. Every notice calling a meeting must state that the member has the right to appoint a proxy and the proxy does not need to be a member of the company.

The articles may require that the instrument appointing the proxy shall only be valid if received in advance of the meeting, but the articles cannot fix a longer interval than 48 hours before the meeting for the receipt of same. Where the directors are authorised to issue 'proxy cards' at the company's expense, they must issue them either to all members or to none. However, this does not apply if a member requests in writing a proxy form and such forms are available on request in writing for all members. The form that the instrument appointing a proxy must take is detailed in Table A. It must be in writing, under the hand of the appointer or, if the appointer is a corporation, under the company seal or the hand of an authorised signatory.

5. Minutes

Section 145 of the Principal Act requires every company to keep minutes of all proceedings at general meetings. Any such minutes, if purported to be signed by the chairman of the meeting at which the proceedings were held or by the chairman of the next meeting, shall be evidence of the proceedings. Furthermore, unless the contrary is proved, the meeting is presumed to have been duly held and all appointments of directors or liquidators are deemed to be valid. The books containing the minutes must be kept at the registered office and be open to inspection by any member without charge for at least two hours per day.[29] A company shall, if required by the Director of Corporate Enforcement, produce to the Director the books containing such minutes.

---

28 Section 136 of the Principal Act.
29 Section 146 of the Principal Act.

6. Decision Making by Shareholders

Decisions taken by the company in general meeting are in the form of ordinary resolutions and special resolutions.

Ordinary Resolutions

Ordinary resolutions are those that are approved by a simple majority of members, present in person or by proxy, who are entitled to attend and vote. An ordinary resolution is the type used whenever the provisions of the Companies Acts or the articles of the company do not require a special resolution. The rules regarding notice of resolutions must be complied with in order to ensure their validity.

Special Resolutions

Special resolutions are those that are passed by at least a 75 per cent majority of members, present in person or by proxy, who are entitled to attend and vote. A special resolution is required by statute when certain decisions are being made, including *inter alia* decisions to:

(a) alter the name and objects clause of the memorandum of association;
(b) alter the articles of association;
(c) reduce the share capital of the company;
(d) wind up the company voluntarily unless the company is insolvent;
(e) present a petition for a compulsory winding-up order, where the company is the petitioner under section 213 of the Principal Act;
(f) to approve the giving of financial assistance for the acquisition of shares in a private company;
(g) to approve the purchase by a company of its own shares in an off-market purchase.

Notification to the Registrar

Section143 of the Principal Act requires the following resolutions to be notified to the Registrar of Companies:

(a) special resolutions;
(b) unanimous resolutions which, had they not been unanimous, could not have been passed other than by special resolution;
(c) resolutions agreed unanimously by a class of members which, had they not been so agreed, could not have been passed other than by a particular majority or in a particular manner;
(d) all resolutions which bind the members of a particular class though not agreed to by all those members;
(e) resolutions increasing the share capital of a company;
(f) resolutions that a company be wound up voluntarily.

The Registrar must be notified within fifteen days from the date of passing of the resolution. Furthermore, a copy of these resolutions must be made available for a nominal fee to a member on request. Where articles have been registered, a copy of every such resolution must be embodied in or annexed to all articles thereafter issued.

Default in complying with these provisions does not render them invalid. Rather, the company and every officer in default shall be liable to a fine.

Decisions of Single-Member Companies

In the case of single-member companies, there is no requirement to pass resolutions. Instead of a resolution, a written decision notified to the company will suffice.[30] However, the sole member cannot use this power to remove an auditor of the company.

7. Shareholders' Discretion in Decision-making

Assuming the procedure for voting and taking decisions complies with the law, the question arises as to whether shareholders may vote as they please. In Chapter 18, we see where directors who are in a fiduciary position towards the company cannot put themselves into a conflict between personal interests and duty to the company. A member, on the other hand, owes no such fiduciary duty and need not avoid a conflict between their own interests and those of the company. In *Pender v Lushington*,[31] Jessel M.R. observed: 'a man may be actuated in giving his vote by interests entirely adverse to the interests of the company as a whole ... but he cannot be restrained from giving his vote in what way he pleases.' These comments restate what the courts and indeed company legislation have always recognised, namely, the principle of majority rule. However, this rule is not absolute and is subject to limitations discussed in the next chapter, in the context of minority shareholder protection. Furthermore, while an individual shareholder may vote as he pleases, certain decisions taken by the company in the general meeting of the shareholders collectively must be taken *bona fide* and in the best interests of the company including *inter alia* the following:

(a) where the members are exercising their statutory power to alter the articles of association;[32]
(b) where directors are being appointed, such appointments must be for the benefit of the company as a whole, and not for an ulterior motive;[33]

---

30 Regulation 9(1) of the European Communities (Single-Member Private Limited Companies) Regulations 1994.
31 [1877] 6 Ch 70.
32 *Re Allen v Gold Reefs of West Africa Ltd.* [1900] 1 Ch 656 discussed in Chapter 5.
33 *Re H.R. Harmer Ltd.* [1959] 1 WLR 62.

(c) at a class meeting where the power of a majority must be exercised for the purpose of benefiting the class as a whole, and not the individual majority shareholder.[34]

8. *Company Decisions Taken Informally*

The common law recognised that a unanimous decision taken by shareholders in an informal manner was a valid and effective method of adopting a resolution.[35] In *Parker & Cooper v. Reading*,[36] the directors had issued a debenture on behalf of the company, which for technical reasons was invalid. All the shareholders had over a period of time discussed the transaction and had acquiesced in it, though not through the medium of a formal resolution. The liquidator of the company later sought to repudiate the transaction. The court held that as all the shareholders had agreed to the transaction, it was valid, irrespective of the fact that no meeting had been held. The legal principles applicable to such a decision were summarised by Kingsmill Moore J. in the Irish case of *Buchanan Ltd v. McVey*[37] as follows:

> If all the corporators agree to a certain course then, however informal the manner of their agreement, it is an act of the company and binds the company subject to only two prerequisites . . . The two necessary prerequisites are (1) that the transaction to which the corporators agree should be *intra vires* the company; and (2) that the transaction should be honest.[38]

The 'assent principle' may also apply to decisions where every member had the opportunity to state their objections but did not do so. In *Re Bailey Hay & Co. Ltd*,[39] a notice of a meeting to consider a resolution to wind up the company had been given which was one day short of the notice required by law. All five shareholders attended, two voted for the resolution, three abstained and the resolution was carried. Some time later, in an attempt to undermine the liquidation process, it was claimed that the authorising resolution was invalid because of the defective notice. This argument was rejected by the court on the grounds, *inter alia*, that by not attempting to stop the winding up by voting against it, all members had agreed to it.[40]

The assent principle has been given a statutory footing by virtue of section 141(8) of the Principal Act. This provides that where a company is so authorised by its articles, a resolution in writing signed by all the company's members shall

---

34 *Re Holders Investment Trust Ltd.* [1971] 1 WLR 583.
35 See *Cane v. Jones* [1981] 1 All ER 426.
36 [1926] Ch 975.
37 [1954] IR 89.
38 Restated with approval in *Re Greendale Developments Ltd (in Liquidation)* [1998] 1 IR 8.
39 [1971] 1 WLR 1357.
40 See also *Re Home Treat Ltd* [1991] BCLC 705.

be as valid and effective as if the resolution had been passed at a general meeting of the company, and if described as such shall be deemed to be such. This statutory provision is more rigorous than the common law 'assent principle' because it requires the agreement to be in writing. Whether or not section 141(8) overrides the common law position remains to be seen. However, one High Court judge has suggested that in the absence of an express agreement, the circumstances may imply that an agreement was in fact reached.[41] This would seem to give credence to the belief that the statutory provision supplements rather than replaces the common law rule.

---

41 Per Costello J. in *Re Shannonside Holdings Ltd*, unreported, High Court, 20 May 1993. Noted in Courtney, *The Law of Private Companies*, Butterworths (1994). See also Supreme Court in *Re Greendale Developments Ltd (in Liquidation)* [1998] 1 IR 8.

CHAPTER FIFTEEN

MINORITY PROTECTION

Introduction

If a wrong is done to a company, it follows from its separate legal personality that the proper plaintiff in any subsequent action is the company itself. The agency to decide on such a course will be the board of directors or, failing this, the company in general meeting. This rule of company law was established in *Foss v. Harbottle*.[1]

The Rule in *Foss v. Harbottle*

In that case the defendant directors had sold land to the company at an exorbitant price. Two shareholders took an action against them to make good the loss caused to the company. The action failed on the grounds that the wrongs committed were against the company, so any action against the wrongdoers ought to be taken by the company and not by the individual shareholders. As Wigham VC observed, it was not

> for any individual members of a corporation thus to assume to themselves the right of suing in the name of the corporation. In law, the corporation and the aggregate members of the corporation are not the same thing. . . .[2]

The rule in *Foss v. Harbottle* is a logical one for the following reasons:

(a) it preserves the principle of majority decision-making;
(b) it prevents a multiplicity of actions by aggrieved shareholders; and
(c) it deters futile actions by shareholders against irregularities and wrongdoings which are capable of being ratified by the general meeting.

The rule does not, however, prevent individual members from bringing actions to defend their own personal interests. What constitutes a personal wrong to a member, as opposed to a wrong to a company, will not always be obvious, as the case of *MacDougall v. Gardiner*[3] demonstrates. The chairman of the company, in breach of the articles of association, refused a request by some shareholders that a poll be held on the question of whether or not a general meeting should be adjourned. The plaintiff sought a declaration that the chairman's action was improper. The declaration was refused on the grounds that the 'irregularity' in the internal procedures of the company was one which could have been ratified by the majority.

---

1 (1843) 2 Hare 261.
2 Ibid. 490.
3 (1875) 1 Ch D 13.

Since this case there has been a growing acceptance by the courts that the failure to comply with the terms of the articles may be an infringement of the 'personal' rights of a shareholder. In *Pender v. Lushington*[4] the court was persuaded by such an argument. The plaintiffs had proposed a resolution but the chairman, in breach of the articles, refused to count the votes attaching to the plaintiffs' nominee shares and the resolution was not carried. The plaintiffs successfully applied for an injunction against the directors who proposed acting on the basis that the resolution had not been passed. The court held that, as a shareholder, the plaintiffs were entitled to have their votes recorded, and failing this they had a right to sue.

Similarly in *Edwards v. Halliwell*[5] the court held that a breach of the internal procedures as set out by the articles of association was a breach of a member's personal rights. The case concerned a trade union, whose rules provided that no increase could be placed on membership subscriptions unless approved by two-thirds of a ballot of members. A decision was taken to increase the subscriptions without holding a ballot. The court held that the rule in *Foss v. Harbottle* had no application to the case, as the decision to increase the subscriptions constituted a wrong done to the members and not to the union.

Exceptions to the Rule in *Foss v. Harbottle*

It has always been recognised that exceptions to the rule in *Foss v. Harbottle* may be permitted. In *Foss v. Harbottle* itself Wigham VC alluded to this possibility, but the facts did not justify an exception being made. It is now accepted that the following circumstances justify a departure from the rule.

1. Where the transaction is one not capable of being ratified by the majority, including criminal acts or acts which are *ultra vires* the company. In *Cockburn v. Newbridge Sanitary Steam Laundry Company*,[6] the company's managing director had paid bribes to officials in the War Office in order to obtain contracts for the company. Two of the company's shareholders instituted proceedings to compel the managing director to repay the bribe amounts to the company. The managing director's defence, that any cause of action ought to be by the company and not the shareholders, failed. The court, in holding for the plaintiffs, stated that acts which are beyond the powers of the company may be challenged by a shareholder. Similarly, in *Parke v. Daily News*,[7] a minority shareholder successfully claimed that gratuitous payments made to employees of the company were *ultra vires*. In any case, section 8(2)

---

4 (1877) 6 Ch D 13.
5 [1950] 2 All ER 1064.
6 [1915] 1 IR 237.
7 [1962] 2 All ER 929.

of the Principal Act specifically provides that a member may apply to court for an order restraining the company from carrying out *ultra vires* acts.

2. Where an act could only be validly approved by a special resolution, and this has not been the case. In *Byng v. London Life Association*,[8] a member succeeded in obtaining a declaration that a purported meeting and special resolutions were void because the correct procedure for adjourning the meeting had not been followed. In *Merill v. Hooper's Telegraph Works*,[9] the company directors settled an action by the company on terms that were favourable to the majority shareholders but not to the company itself. The general meeting then purported to ratify by way of resolution the directors' action. The minority shareholders succeeded in an action claiming that the resolution was invalid and that any benefits made by the majority shareholders should be returned to the company.

3. Where there is a fraud on the minority. In *Cook v. Deeks*,[10] directors of the company had diverted profitable contracts away from the company to themselves. The minority shareholders sought an order directing that the directors' account to the company for the profits they made. Although a general meeting had purported to ratify the wrong done by the directors, this was held to be ineffective as it constituted a 'fraud on the minority'. Similarly, in *Daniels v. Daniels*,[11] two directors who were also the majority shareholders had caused the company to sell land to themselves at an undervalue. Although no fraud was alleged, the court held that the transactions should be set aside on the grounds that the directors' negligence had benefited themselves at the expense of the company. However, if the negligent act of the directors did not benefit themselves, then their actions may be capable of ratification, as occurred in *Pavlides v. Jensen*.[12] The plaintiff, a minority shareholder, claimed that the directors had negligently sold the company's principal asset, a mine, to a third party at a gross undervalue. The action was dismissed on the grounds that the controlling shareholders who were represented by the directors had not benefited and their actions were accordingly ratifiable by the general meeting.

4. Where the justice of the case requires it.[13]

It should be noted that a shareholder will not be entitled to bring a derivative action on behalf of a company unless that shareholder is acting *bona fide* for the benefit of the company in respect of wrongs done to that company.[14] Furthermore,

---

8 [1990] 1 Ch 170.

9 (1974) LR 9 Ch App 350.

10 [1916] 1 AC 554.

11 [1978] Ch 406.

12 [1956] 2 All ER 518.

13 *Moylan v. Irish Whiting Manufacturers Ltd*, High Court, 14 April 1980 (Hamilton J.).

14 *Barrett v. Duckett & Others* [1995] 1 BCLC 243.

the courts will not countenance a derivative action if the applicant shareholder has an ulterior motive. As Lawton LJ. stated:

> It is pertinent to remember, however, that a minority shareholder's action in form is nothing more than a procedural device for enabling the court to do justice to a company controlled by miscreant directors or shareholders. Since the procedural device has evolved so that justice can be done for the benefit of the company, whoever comes forward to start the proceedings must be doing so for the benefit of the company and not for some other purpose. It follows that the court has to satisfy itself that the person coming forward is a proper person to do so.[15]

Finally, if another adequate remedy is available the court will not allow the derivative action to succeed. In *Fargo v. Godfrey*[16] a minority shareholder brought a derivative action on behalf of the company alleging that the other shareholder and directors had diverted assets and business opportunities belonging to the company for their own personal use. By the time the plaintiff had issued the writ a liquidator had been appointed over the company. In striking out the writ the Court of Appeal held that once a liquidator is appointed the situation changes because neither the board nor the general meeting can control any longer the activities of the company.

Rather than pursuing a derivative action based on an exception to the rule in *Foss v. Harbottle*, the aggrieved shareholder may opt instead for the statutory remedy afforded by section 205 of the Principal Act.

Section 205 of the Principal Act

Section 205(1) of the Principal Act provides that:

> Any member of a company who complains that the affairs of the company are being conducted or that the powers of the directors of the company are being exercised in a manner oppressive to him or any of the members (including himself) or in disregard of his or their interests as members, may apply to the court for an order under this section.

1. Presenting the Petition

Section 205(1) specifically gives members the *locus standi* in regard to petitioning the court for a remedy. However the definition of 'member' for the purposes of section 205 is much broader than the normal definition attributable to a member.[17] Section 205(6) gives the personal representative of a person who, at the date of his death was a member of a company, or any trustee of, or person beneficially

---

15 *Nurcombe v. Nurcombe* [1984] BCLC 557 at 562.

16 [1986] BCLC 370.

17 By virtue of section 31 of the Principal Act a person will not become a member until his name has been registered in the register of members.

interested in, the shares of a company by virtue of the will or intestacy of the deceased, the right to apply for an order under section 205(1). Furthermore, a member's right to petition the court is not dependent on his showing that the oppressive conduct affected him only in his capacity as a member.[18] The Companies (Amendment) Act 1990 has introduced some limitation on the discretion of a member to bring an action under section 205. It provides that complaints concerning the conduct of the affairs of the company while it is under the protection of the court, shall not constitute the basis for the making of an order for relief under section 205.

All petitions must be presented for the genuine purpose of obtaining the relief claimed and not for any collateral purpose; otherwise, the petitioner will be abusing the process of the court.[19]

2. *Oppression*

What will constitute oppressive behaviour within the meaning of section 205(1) will be determined by an objective judgment based on the facts. It is irrelevant that no evidence of *male fides* on the part of the 'oppressor' can be found.[20] In *Scottish Wholesale Co-operative Society Ltd v. Meyer*[21] a subsidiary company was formed by a co-operative society in which the plaintiff became a minority shareholder. When the majority no longer required the plaintiff as a shareholder it sought to purchase the minority shareholding. The plaintiff refused to sell its shares and the co-operative transferred the subsidiary's business to itself. Without a business, the subsidiary was worthless. The plaintiff petitioned the court under the UK equivalent of section 205(1). The Court of Appeal held that the actions of the majority shareholder were oppressive as it had exercised its majority power in a manner which was 'burdensome, harsh and wrongful'.

This definition was accepted by Keane J. in *Re Greenore Trading Co. Ltd*[22] Here the plaintiff and two other shareholders, B and V, each held one third of the issued share capital of the company. Later B agreed to sell his shares to V for a consideration which represented, *inter alia*, £14,500 payable by the company as compensation for B's loss of office. The plaintiff sought relief under section 205, claiming that V's control over the company was being used in an oppressive manner. Keane J. held that the payment of £14,500 either represented an unauthorised payment of company monies which had not been approved by the company in general meeting or it represented the giving of financial assistance

---

18 In *Re Murph's Restaurant Ltd* [1979] ILRM 141. But see *Re Unisoft Group Ltd No. 30* [1994] 1 BCLC 609 where Harman J. took the contrary view that the shareholder must be affected *qua* shareholder.
19 *Re Bellador Silk Ltd* [1965] 1 All ER 667.
20 *Re Irish Visiting Motorist's Bureau Ltd*, High Court, 7 February 1972.
21 [1959] AC 324.
22 [1980] ILRM 94.

by the company to purchase its shares which is contrary to section 60 of the Principal Act. In either scenario the payment was unlawful and a misapplication of the company's monies for the purpose of giving V an increased shareholding. Accordingly, he granted the relief sought and made an order that the plaintiff's shares be purchased by V.

Although the behaviour in the above mentioned case was deemed to be 'unlawful', this is not a requisite to an order under section 205. In *Re a Company* (No. 00789 of 1987),[23] the court held that continuous failure to hold AGMs and lay accounts before the members was conduct unfairly prejudicial to the interests of the members. However, failure to comply with the statutory requirements with regard to the holding of AGMs and the production of accounts will be treated as conduct which is negligent and careless; this does not mean it will also constitute oppressive conduct within the meaing of section 205.[24] Repudiation of an agreement may also constitute 'oppression' within the meaning of section 205(1). Accordingly, in *Irish Press plc v. Ingersoll Irish Publications Ltd*[25] Barron J. held that the failure to operate a management agreement between the petitioner and respondents amounted to a repudiation of the agreement which was oppressive behaviour within the meaning of the act. Accordingly, the respondent was ordered to sell its shares in the company to the petitioner. Similarly in *Crindle Investments v. Wymes*[26] the Supreme Court considered a failure by the majority shareholders to accept offers of a compromise in relation to legal proceedings as being oppressive conduct within the meaning of the section 205(1).

It would seem that the oppressive conduct does not necessarily have to be continuous. In *Re Westwinds Holding Co. Ltd*[27] the manner in which the company's assets were sold was held by the High Court to be a suffcient act of oppression to invoke section 205.

However, it would seem that section 205(1) cannot be invoked on the basis of a mere possibility of oppression. In *Re a Company* (No. 004475 of 1982)[28] a majority of shareholders had indicated their wish to acquire a wine bar using company funds. A petition by a minority shareholder failed on the ground that it was premature to bring such an action before any final decision to proceed with the purchase was actually taken.

3. *Disregarding Members' Interests*

Even where no oppressive conduct is said to exist, section 205 may still be invoked where the petitioner can demonstrate that the affairs of the company or

---

23 [1990] BCLC 384.
24 *Re Clubman Shirts* [1983] ILRM 323.
25 Unreported, High Court, 16 December 1993 (Barron J.).
26 [1998] 2 ILRM 275.
27 Unreported, High Court. 21 May 1974 (Kenny J.).
28 [1983] 2 All ER 36.

the powers of the directors are being conducted in disregard of the member's interests. In *Re Williams Group Tullamore Ltd*[29] the company's articles of association provided that as long as there were preference shareholders the ordinary shareholders could not attend and vote at general meetings. The articles further provided that the preference shareholders received a fixed dividend which they duly did on an annual basis. The ordinary shareholders on the other hand fared much better, as they received substantial dividends. The preference shareholders, obviously tired of this imbalance, proposed a special resolution whereby a new class of share would be issued which would qualify for a dividend payment over and above the existing preference shareholder's dividend. Despite the fact that the new issue would be distributed to all shareholders, the effect of the proposal would be to distribute profits of the company to the preference shareholders which otherwise would have been available to ordinary shareholders under the original distribution scheme. Even though the correct procedures were followed and the proposal was put forward in good faith, Barrington J. held that the resolutions were in disregard of the ordinary shareholders' interests. This case gives some indication of the Irish courts' recognition that a member may have a 'legitimate expectation' that the status quo is maintained, a certain course of action followed or indeed that he will share in the management and profits of the company which is outside the scope of the memorandum and articles of association.[30]

4. Courts' Discretionary Powers under S.205

If the court is satisfied that the claim is well founded it may, with a view to bringing to an end the matters complained of, make any order it deems fit, including the following:

(a) direct or prohibit any act; or
(b) cancel or vary any transaction; or
(c) provide for the future regulation of the conduct of the company; or
(d) order the purchase of the shares of any member by the other members or by the company itself.

In the *Scottish Wholesale* case the Court of Appeal ordered that the co-operative purchase the plaintiff's shares at the value they would have had if the business of the company had not been transferred. Similarly, in the recent Irish case *of Re NEW-AD Advertising Company Limited*[31] the court ordered the oppressor, a majority shareholder, to purchase the shares of the minority at a value that they would have been at but for the oppressive conduct. Even where

---

29 [1985] IR 613.
30 *Re Westbourne Galleries Ltd* [1973] AC 360, *Re Blue Arrow plc* [1987] BCLC 585 and *Re Saul D Harrison & Sons plc* [1994] BCC 475.
31 High Court, 1 July 1997 (Costello P.).

the oppressor is in discussion with the petitioner with a view to acquiring the petitioner's shares at a fair value, this will not prevent a petition being presented.[32] Furthermore, the court may even order the respondent to sell his shares to the petitioner.[33] In the *Crindle* case the court ordered that the minority shareholder should be in control of negotiations which were to be conducted in relation to certain legal proceedings to which the company was a party. However, it stopped short of ordering the majority shareholders to join in an acceptance of an offer to compromise the proceedings in their own personal capacity.

While the remedy is discretionary it would appear that the court will not consider damages as an appropriate remedy under section 205. In *Irish Press v. Ingersoll*[34] Barron J. in the High Court awarded damages for the oppressive conduct. However the Supreme Court[35] reversed the decision on the following grounds:

(a) the award of damages could not achieve the objective of section 205 which was to bring the oppression complained of to an end;

(b) awarding damages was a common law remedy and was not appropriate for actions under section 205; and

(c) if damages could have been awarded the legislature would have made such a provision in section 205.

Winding Up — Section 213(f) and (g)

Another remedy available to a shareholder is the radical step of applying to the court to have the company wound up. Ever since 1848 the courts have been empowered to order that a company be wound up on 'just and equitable grounds'. Examples are where the *raison d'être* of the company has gone, where a majority has defrauded the company and where there was a complete deadlock in its affairs. The case-law has set out the following basic principles:

(a) a complaint does not have to be brought within any fixed set of categories or situations in order for it to afford grounds for ordering a winding up;

(b) the section is not confined to circumstances which affect the petitioner *qua* member — while he must be a member, the circumstances may relate to his relationship with the company or the other shareholders as an employee, a director or a creditor;

(c) the action complained of, even though consistent with the company's own regulations, may be outside what can fairly be regarded as having been in the contemplation of the parties when they become members of the company,

---

32 *Horgan v, Murray*, Supreme Court, 9 July 1997.
33 *Irish Press plc v. Ingersoll Irish Publications Ltd*, High Court, 16 December 1993.
34 Unreported, High Court, 13 May 1994 (Barron J.).
35 *Irish Press plc v. Ingersoll Irish Publications Ltd* [1995] 2 IR 175; [1995] 2 ILRM 270.

and the fact that such an action is within the powers of the company will not necessarily be an answer to a claim for winding up.

Where the company has been formed and is being operated in a manner similar to a partnership, and the relationship of trust and mutual confidence has broken down, the court may also make an order on the just and equitable ground. In *Re Westbourne Galleries Ltd*,[36] E and N had carried on business together for over twenty years. They had done so originally as business partners and subsequently as equal shareholders and joint directors of a company. Eventually they agreed to bring N's son into the business, and he was given 100 shares from each of them and appointed to the board. Following a disagreement between the original shareholders, the father and son used their majority at a general meeting to oust E from the board. E petitioned the court to have the company wound up on the just and equitable ground. Despite the fact that the shareholders had exercised a statutory power, the court, in allowing the petition, held that it was not equitable to insist on legal rights as the company had been set up on the understanding that the business relationship would remain the same.

The breakdown of the 'quasi-partnership' relationship was accepted as a 'just and equitable reason' to wind up the company in the Irish case of *Re Murph's Restaurant Ltd*.[37] The company was formed by two brothers and a friend. One brother and the friend each invested £800 and also advanced £400 each on behalf of the other brother so that they would all be equal 'partners' in the business. They were each directors of the company. The business prospered and the friend ultimately gave up his job to work full-time in the business. The business expanded from Dublin to Cork, and it was the Cork branch that was run by the friend. While the business was well run and organised, the same could not be said of the company's administrative affairs. No general meetings were held, no accounts were maintained, but the directors took great care to draw equal amounts in drawings from the company. The two brothers expanded their business horizons and purchased a hotel in Cork which, unknown to the friend, was partly financed by money from the company. Eventually, the two brothers decided to 'break' from the friend, and they notified him of a meeting at which they intended to remove him from office. The friend petitioned to have the company wound up on the 'just and equitable' ground. The court held that the company had been formed and operated on a 'quasi-partnership' basis which required a degree of trust and confidence between the members. As Gannon J. stated:

> a limited company is more than a mere legal entity . . . behind it or amongst it there are individuals with rights, expectations and obligations *inter se* which are not necessarily submerged in the corporate structure.

---

36 [1972] 2 All ER 492.
37 [1979] ILRM 141.

As the trust and confidence had been destroyed by the acts of the brothers, an order for the compulsory winding up of the company was made.

Additional rights of Shareholders

The rights of shareholders vis à vis their 'section 25 contract' have already been described in Chapter 5. The Companies Acts also confer specific rights on shareholders, many of which cannot be abridged by the articles of association, including *inter alia* the right:

(a) to receive a copy of the memorandum and articles of association;[38]
(b) to apply to the court for an injunction restraining the company from acting *ultras vires*;[39]
(c) to receive notice of general meetings;[40]
(d) to receive copies of the minutes of general meetings;[41]
(e) to exercise their pre-emption rights when applicable on the issue of new shares by the company;[42]
(f) to apply to the court for a disclosure order in relation to shareholdings in a private company;[43]
(g) to object to an alteration of the memorandum and articles of association;[44]
(h) to object to a reduction in capital by the company under section 72 of the Principal Act;
(i) to object to the giving of financial assistance by a company to purchase shares in the company under section 60 of the Principal Act;
(j) to petition the court to have an examiner appointed;[45] and
(k) to apply to the court to have an inspector appointed to investigate the affairs of a company.[46]

---

38 Section 29 of the Principal Act.
39 Section 8(2) of the Principal Act.
40 Sections 131–133 of the Principal Act.
41 Section 143 of the Principal Act.
42 Section 23 of the Companies (Amendment) Act 1983.
43 Section 98 of the Companies Act 1990.
44 See Chapter 4 and Chapter 5.
45 Section 3 of the Companies (Amendment) Act 1990.
46 Section 7(1)(a)and (b) of the Companies Act 1990.

CHAPTER SIXTEEN

DIRECTORS AND SECRETARIES

Introduction

Companies, as artificial persons, cannot manage themselves. Therefore, the articles of association usually provide for the delegation of the management powers to a board of directors. Directors, as agents of the company, can bind the company without incurring personal liability. They also have extensive power in relation to the day-to-day control of the company's business undertaking and its assets. The potential for abuse is obvious. The means of preventing this abuse are more complicated. Equitable principles, common law rules and statutory obligations are interwoven to form an intricate legal framework within which directors must operate. These are considered further in the next chapter.

Section 174 of the Principal Act requires every company to have at least two directors, who together with the secretary of the company are its officers. Although there is no comprehensive definition, the Principal Act describes a director as 'any person who occupies the position of director by whatever name called'.[1] It is therefore the function rather than the title which will determine whether or not a person is in fact a director. Accordingly, persons who are not formally appointed as directors may be deemed directors. These 'shadow directors' are subject to the same rigours of the law as apply to every director.

Shadow Directors

The legal responsibilities of company directors are burdensome and in certain circumstances directors can be held responsible for the debts of the company. In the past, persons tried to avoid these responsibilities, and the potential for liability, by acting as directors without accepting formal appointment. The Companies Act 1990 defines these shadow directors as: 'the persons in accordance with whose directions and instructions the directors of a company are accustomed to act, other than in a professional capacity.'[2] The Companies Act 1990 imposes the same legal responsibilities on shadow directors as are imposed on directors. In *Re Gasco Ltd*[3] the restriction provisions of Part VII of the Companies Act were applied to a person who, although effectively running the company, was not formally a director of the company.

---

1 Section 2 of the Principal Act.
2 Section 27 of the Companies Act 1990.
3 Unreported, High Court, McCrachen J. 5 February 2001.

1. Directors' Qualifications

No formal qualifications attach to the position of director. However, the Companies Acts restrict the following persons from becoming directors:

(a) a body corporate;[4]
(b) an undischarged bankrupt;[5]
(c) an auditor appointed to that company, its holding company or subsidiary;[6]
(d) a person who is restricted under the Companies Act 1990, unless the company of which he is to be a director meets certain capital requirements; and
(e) a person disqualified under the Companies Act 1990.

Section 43 of the Companies (Amendment) (No.2) Act 1999 introduces a new restriction in relation to the parties who may act as a director of a company by requiring that at least one director must be resident in the state. This provision was introduced to avoid the possibility that non-resident directors could avoid any sanctions imposed upon them for breaches of the Companies Acts. A company does not have to comply with this requirement if it satisfies one of two conditions. First, the company may enter into a £20,000 (€25,395) bond securing the payment of any fine that could be imposed by the Companies Acts or certain Tax Acts. Second, it can obtain a certificate from the registrar of companies stating that a company has a real and continuous link with one or more economic activities that are being carried on in the State.[7]

Section 45(1) of the Companies (Amendment) (No.2) Act 1999 stipulates that a person cannot, at a particular time, be a director (including shadow director) of more than twenty-five companies. An appointment as a director of a company in breach of the maximum directorships provisions shall be void. If a person becomes or remains a director or shadow director of one or more companies, he or she shall be guilty of an offence.[8] The Registrar may prosecute summarily for this offence.

Directors are not required to be members of the company unless the articles of association provide otherwise.[9] Where the articles require directors to hold a minimum number of qualifying shares, section 80 of the Principal Act provides as follows:

(a) the share qualification must be obtained within two months after the director's appointment, or such shorter time as may be fixed by the articles;

---

4 Section 176 of the Principal Act.
5 Section 183 of the Principal Act.
6 Section 162(5) of the Principal Act. as amended by section 6 of the Companies (Amendment) Act 1982.
7 Section 44 Companies (Amendment)(No.2) Act 1999.
8 Section 45 (8) ibid.
9 Table A does not require directors to hold qualification shares.

(b) if the share qualification is not obtained within the specified time, or the director ceases to hold his qualification, his must vacate his office immediately;

(c) in the event that the office is vacated because of failure to obtain or hold the necessary qualification shares, that person cannot be re-appointed as director of the same company until the qualification shares have been obtained.

Generally speaking, all business letters on which the company's name appears and which are sent by the company to any person, must state in legible characters the following particulars in relation to each director:

(a) his present Christian name, or the initials thereof, and present surname; and
(b) any former Christian names and surnames; and
(c) his nationality, if not Irish.

Default in complying with these obligations, renders every officer in default liable on summary conviction for each offence to a fine not exceeding £125 (€159).

2. Appointment

The first directors of the company are those named in the documents delivered to the Registrar before incorporation. All subsequent appointments are governed by the articles of association. The usual method of appointment is by the company in general meeting. Where non-directors are proposing the appointment of a person as a director, other than a retiring director, Table A requires that notice should be sent to the company's registered office between twenty-one and three days before the meeting. When the appointment of directors is proposed at a general meeting a separate resolution should be proposed for the election of each director, unless the members unanimously agree to waive this rule.[10]

3. Alternate Directors

The articles of a private company may permit a director to assign or transfer his office to another person, subject to the approval of a special resolution of the general meeting. Where the articles permit retiring directors to nominate replacements, no such approval is required. Casual vacancies may arise due to the death or resignation of a director. Where this occurs, Table A empowers the board of directors to fill such vacancies and appoint additional directors, provided the maximum number specified in the articles is not exceeded. Persons appointed in this manner by the board hold office until the next Annual General Meeting, at which time they will be eligible for re-election.

---

10 Section 181 of the Principal Act.

4. *Vacation of and Removal from Office*

Table A sets out the rules relating to the retirement and rotation of directors as follows:

(a) at the first AGM all directors must retire and thereafter on an annual basis one-third of the directors must retire;
(b) those retiring shall be those longest in office since the last election — retiring directors are eligible for re-election;
(c) a director offering himself for re-election shall be deemed to be re-elected unless the meeting decides otherwise;
(d) directors co-opted by the board of directors must stand for re-election at the next AGM — such persons do not count in determining the one-third to retire for rotation;
(e) managing directors are not subject to retirement by rotation and do not count in the determination of the one-third to retire by rotation.

A director may vacate his office by resignation or by not offering himself for re-election.

Section 182 of the Principal Act gives the members the power to dismiss or remove a director by passing an ordinary resolution. Directors of private limited companies, appointed for life by the memorandum and articles of association, can only be removed if the correct procedure for the alteration of the constitutional documents is followed. In *Coubrough v. James Panton & Co. Ltd*,[11] the removal of a director by the passing of an ordinary resolution was declared invalid, because the articles had required the passing of a special resolution for such an action. Where a resolution to remove a director is proposed, the Principal Act requires the following procedures to be followed:

(a) extended notice of twenty-eight days must be given to all members, and on receipt of such a notice the company must send a copy to the director concerned;
(b) on receipt of written representations, relating to the proposed resolution, by the director, the company must, unless the court otherwise orders, notify members of such representations;
(c) if the company fails to notify the members of such representations, either because they were received too late or because of the company's default, the director may require that the representations be read at the meeting — in any case, the director may speak on the resolution at the meeting.

The company may be deterred from exercising its power to remove a director for various reasons. First, section 182(7) of the Principal Act provides that a director who is removed under the section, will not be deprived of compensation or

---

11 [1965] IR 272.

damages to which he is entitled. Such an entitlement may exist where a director has a separate contract of employment. In *Carvill v. Irish Industrial Bank*,[12] a managing director was held to be entitled to one year's notice, and having been removed without notice he was awarded damages in lieu thereof. Second, where the articles provide weighted voting rights to members, the company may be precluded from generating sufficient support for a resolution to remove a director, as occurred in *Bushell v. Faith* (considered already in Chapter 5). Finally, any attempt to remove a director for improper reasons may give rise to an action by a director who is also a member of the company, and may result in the court making an order for the winding up of the company under section 213(f) of the Principal Act.[13]

5. Remuneration

Table A provides that the company in general meeting shall determine the remuneration and expenses of the directors. Directors, particularly executive directors, who do not have a substantial interest in the company, would be advised to negotiate a separate contract for services or contract of employment with the company. In some circumstances the courts have inferred the existence of such a contract.[14]

In any case, contracts of employment entered into between a company and a director for a term exceeding five years and which cannot be terminated by notice, or which can only be terminated in specific circumstances, must be approved by the shareholders in general meeting.[15] A written memorandum of the agreement including the term specifying its length must be available for inspection by the members at the registered office for a period of not less than fifteen days prior to the meeting and at the meeting itself.

The company must keep a register of directors' contracts of service or, where the contract is not in writing, a memorandum of the details.[16] The requirement to keep records of directors' service contracts does not apply in the following circumstances:

(a) where the director concerned is working outside the State; and
(b) where the contract will expire in less than three years; and
(c) where the contract can be terminated within three years without payment of compensation.

---

12 [1968] IR 325.

13 *Re Murph's Restaurant* [1979] ILRM 141. See Chapter 15.

14 *Carvill v. Irish Industrial Bank Ltd* [1968] IR 325. Cf. *Read v. Astoria Garage Streatham Ltd* [1952] Ch 637.

15 Section 28 of the Companies Act 1990.

16 Section 50 of the Companies Act 1990.

6. Restriction

Prior to the introduction of Part VII of the Companies Act 1990, the practice whereby directors of insolvent companies could re-emerge with a similar business, but under a new corporate identity, went unregulated for the most part.[17] However, Chapter 1 of Part VII of the Companies Act 1990 introduced new provisions designed to restrict such directors' further use of the statutory privileges of incorporation.

A director of an insolvent company in liquidation or receivership,[18] who fails to satisfy the court as to his honesty and responsibility, will be restricted for a period of five years. An application can be made to have a person restricted by a liquidator, receiver or the Director of Corporate Enforcement. A liquidiser is obliged to make an application for a restriction order unless the Director of Corporate Enforcement has relieved the liquidator of such an obligation. Such a restriction will operate to prevent him from being a director or secretary or being involved in the formation or promotion of any company except where it is adequately capitalised. In the case of private companies, this capital requirement is £50,000 (€63,487) in allotted paid-up share capital, and for public companies the greater amount of £250,000 (€317,435) is required. Additionally, such companies will not enjoy the benefit of many of the capital maintenance exemptions under the Companies Acts. The restrictions will also apply to shadow directors and persons who were directors of the company within the twelve months prior to winding up. The restriction will not be imposed if the court is satisfied that the person concerned:

(a) acted honestly and responsibly in relation to the conduct of the affairs of the company and no other just and equitable reason exists for imposing the restriction;[19] or
(b) is a nominee of an institution providing credit facilities to the company, provided that personal guarantees from the directors have not been obtained for such facilities; or
(c) is a nominee of a venture capital company which has purchased or subscribed for shares in the company.

The nominees of the financial institution or the venture capital company described above will not avoid a restriction order if it is proven that they did not act honestly and responsibly. In *Re Squash Ireland Ltd*,[20] the Supreme Court

---

17 Section 184 of the Principal Act gave the court the power, on the application of the Attorney General, to restrain certain persons from acting as directors of or managing companies.
18 Section 154 of the Companies Act 1990.
19 In this regard it has been stated that a person who permitted or facilitated conduct which was irresponsible should not be acquitted of blame: see judgment of Murphy J. in *Business Communications Ltd v. Baxter*, High Court, 21 July 1995 .
20 [2001] 8(3) CLP 72.

considered what irresponsible conduct might entail. The court endorsed the criteria of Shanley J. in *La Moselle Clothing Ltd*[21] which were as follows:

(a) the extent to which the director has complied with the obligations imposed by the Companies Acts;
(b) the extent to which his conduct would be regarded as so incompetent as to amount to irresponsible;
(c) the extent of the director's responsibility for the company's insolvency or net deficiency in the company's assets at the time of its winding-up; and
(d) the extent to which, in his conduct of the affairs of the company, the director displayed a lack of commercial probity or want of proper standards.

The court may lift the restriction on the application of a restricted person, who may within a year apply for such relief.

On notification by the court, the Registrar will keep a register of the particulars of all restrictions and orders made under Part VII of the Companies Act 1990.

7. Disqualification

Chapter 2 of Part VII of the Companies Act 1990 widens considerably the grounds whereby a person may be disqualified by the court from acting as a director. An application for the making of a disqualification order can be made by the Director of Corporate Enforcement, the DPP, a member, creditor, officer, employee, receiver, liquidator or examiner of the company. Disqualification will be automatic in the following circumstances:

(a) where a person is convicted on indictment of any indictable offence in relation to the company or one involving fraud or dishonesty; or
(b) is convicted of acting while restricted except in the circumstances permitted by the Companies Act 1990; or
(c) is convicted of acting as auditor, officer, liquidator or examiner of, or in the formation, promotion or management of, any company while an undischarged bankrupt; or
(d) where a person is a director of a company and there has been a failure to notify the Registrar, either at the time the memorandum and articles were being registered or when there was a change in the register of directors, that the person was disqualified in another jurisdiction, and details of same.

The effect of a disqualification order is that the person concerned is disqualified from acting as a director, auditor, officer, receiver, liquidator or examiner, or from being involved in the promotion, formation or management, of a company for a period of five years or such other period as the court may direct.

The court may also, at its own discretion and either on its own motion or on application, disqualify a person for such period as it deems fit where that person,

---

21 [1998] 2 ILRM 345.

while in the position of promoter, auditor, officer, receiver, liquidator or examiner of the company, has been guilty of any of the following:

(a) a fraud in relation to the company, its members or creditors;
(b) a breach of his duty in relation to the company;
(c) conduct which makes him unfit to be concerned in the management of a company;
(d) conduct which, according to a report made by an inspector appointed by the court or the Director of Corporate Enforcement, makes him unfit; or
(e) fraudulent or reckless trading which resulted in a declaration of personal liability for some or all of the debts of a company; or
(f) default in complying with the filing, notice and the making of returns to the Registrar of Companies. Such a default is deemed conclusive where the person has been adjudged guilty of three or more defaults in the five years prior to the application; or
(g) two or more offences in respect of failure to keep proper books of account under section 202 of the Companies Act 1990.

In addition to the above, the court may also disqualify a person where he or she is a director of a company which has been struck off the register for failing to submit one or more annual returns. The court will not make a disqualification order in such a case if it can be shown to the court that the company had no liabilities at the time its name was struck off or that if there were any liabilities that they were discharged.

The court may also disqualify a person who is disqualified in another jurisdiction where it would have been proper to disqualify that person in this State had the conduct of that person, which gave rise to the disqualification, occurred or arisen in this State.

The court may, where it adjudges that disqualification is not justified, instead make an order restricting the person under section 150.

A person who acts while disqualified faces the following consequences:

(a) being guilty of a criminal offence; and
(b) having the period of disqualification extended for a further period of ten years; and
(c) incurring personal liability for the debts of the company if it becomes insolvent during, or within a period of twelve months of, the disqualification order.

The court shall cause the Registrar of Companies to be furnished with particulars of all orders prescribed under section 160. The Registrar shall keep a register of such particulars.

8. *Directors' Meetings*

General

Unless otherwise provided in the articles, directors' powers are conferred collectively. In order to exercise these powers, there must be agreement among the directors. The formal manner of achieving such agreement is by a resolution of a properly constituted board meeting. However, Table A recognises the validity of decisions made informally, provided that an appropriate resolution is signed by all the directors.

The courts have accepted that board meetings may be held on an informal basis, but the directors must at least appreciate that they are in fact attending a meeting. In *Re Aston Colour Print Ltd,*[22] a meeting took place of some of the company's shareholders, two of its directors and the company's accountant to assess the failing fortunes of the company. The meeting was chaired by a non-director. The discussions focused on the option of appointing an examiner, but no formal resolution was put to the meeting in this regard. Following the meeting the accountant, who believed a decision had been made, initiated the petition process which culminated in an interim examiner being appointed. Later, it transpired that not everyone in attendance believed such a decision had been made, including one of the directors whose name appeared on the petition. The question arose as to whether a meeting had been held and whether a resolution to petition for the appointment of an examiner had been passed. The court concluded that a board meeting had not been validly held for the following reasons:

(a) the directors did not appreciate that they were attending a board meeting;
(b) despite the presence of two directors, the meeting was chaired by a shareholder;
(c) the chairman was unsure as to the nature of the meeting because he believed he was presiding over a general meeting of the shareholders which had subsequently become a board meeting.

With respect to the validity of the 'informal resolution', the court made it clear that where the solemn and important decision is being taken to petition the court to appoint an examiner, every care must be taken to ensure that the will of the board is clear. As it was not clear from the circumstances, the court held that no such decision had been made.

Proceedings at Directors' Meetings

The articles usually govern the proceedings of directors' meetings. Table A makes the following provisions in this regard.

(a) Questions arising shall be decided by a majority of votes. Where there is an equal vote, the chairman shall have a second or casting vote.

---

22 High Court, 21 February 1997 (Kelly J.).

(b) A director may requisition a meeting of the directors and the secretary must then summon such a meeting.

(c) Directors must be given advance notice of meetings. Although the model articles are silent as to the amount of notice required, it has been held that such notice must be reasonable.[23]

(d) If the directors so resolve, it shall not be necessary to give notice of a meeting to any director normally resident in the State, but for the time being absent from the State.

(e) Unless otherwise agreed by the directors, the quorum necessary for the transaction of the business of the meeting is two. In the event that the number of directors falls below the quorum required by the articles, the continuing director may act only for the purpose of increasing the number of directors to satisfy the quorum or for the purpose of summoning a general meeting.

(f) The directors may elect a chairman of their meetings. If no such chairman is elected or if the chairman is absent from any meeting, the directors may choose an alternative chairman.

(g) The director may not generally vote in respect of any contract in which he is an interested party.

Section 145 of the Principal Act requires minutes to be kept of the proceedings of board meetings. When signed by the chairman, those minutes are *prima facie* evidence of the proceedings.

The Company Secretary

Every company must have a secretary, who may be one of the directors of the company.[24] Although there are no requisite qualifications for appointment of a person as secretary to a private limited company, section 236 of the Companies Act 1990 imposes a duty on directors of a public limited company to take all reasonable steps to ensure that the secretary has the necessary knowledge and experience to discharge the functions of secretary and who is qualified by reason of:

(a) being secretary to the company at the time of coming into force of the section; or

(b) having been a secretary of a company for three of the five years prior to appointment; or

(c) being a member of a relevant professional body recognised by the appropriate Minister; or

(d) being a person who by reason of his having held any other position or having been a member of any other body appears to the directors to be capable of discharging the functions of the secretary.

---

23 *Per* Murphy J. in *Holland v. McGill*, High Court, 16 March 1990.
24 Section 175 of the Principal Act.

Persons restricted or disqualified under the Companies Act 1990 cannot act as a secretary of a company except in limited circumstances.[25]

1. Functions and Duties

The function of the company secretary is mostly administrative. Such a role is reflected by the Companies Acts, which impose very few duties that are exclusive to the secretary. These duties include signing the annual return, completing application forms to the Registrar where a company is converting to another type of company and compiling a statement of affairs on the appointment of a receiver or liquidator. The remaining administrative functions are allocated to the company itself, but are generally carried out by either the secretary or a director. These include maintaining the statutory registers, calling meetings of the board of directors and keeping records of their minutes, and arranging for the filing of various returns and notifications to the Registrar of Companies.

2. The Secretary's Power

The traditional view of the company secretary's role was described by Esher MR in *Barnett Hoares v. South London Tramways*,[26] when he observed that

> A secretary is a mere servant; his position is to do what he is told, and no person can assume that he has any authority to represent anything at all.

The imposition by statute of more onerous administrative functions on the company, which are often delegated to the company secretary, has been met by a corresponding recognition by the judiciary of the importance of the company secretary. As the chief administrative officer of the company, it is apposite that the secretary has apparent authority to make contracts, relating to his functions, on behalf of the company. This position was accepted in *Panorama Developments (Guildford) Ltd v. Fidelis Furnishing Fabrics*.[27] There a company secretary had hired cars, representing that they were for company purposes. The cars were then used for his personal use. The company refused to pay, claiming that the secretary did not have the authority to enter into such a contract. The court rejected this argument and held that the secretary did have apparent authority to make contracts relating to the administrative side of the business, which included contracts of this type. Lord Denning MR declared:

> Times have changed. A company secretary is a much more important person nowadays than he was in 1887. He is an officer of the company with extensive duties and responsibilities . . . He is certainly entitled to sign contracts connected with the administrative side of the company's affairs.

---

25 Restricted persons may act as a secretary of an adequately capitalised company as described in section 150(3) of the Companies Act 1990.

26 (1887) 18 QBD 815.

27 [1971] 2 QB 711.

However, the court did suggest that had the contract related to the commercial side of the business, it might not treat the secretary as having such authority to bind the company. Therefore, the secretary has apparent authority to bind the company in administrative matters, but has no such authority in matters of an executive nature. However, it may be possible, if the articles do not provide otherwise, for the board expressly to delegate an executive function to the secretary and give him actual authority.

Register of Directors and Secretaries

Section 195 of the Principal Act requires every company to keep at its registered office a register of its directors and secretary which must contain the following details relating to each director:

(a) the forename, surname and any other names;
(b) the date of birth;
(c) the usual residential address;
(d) nationality;
(e) business occupation, if any;
(f) particulars of other directorships of other corporate bodies.

In relation to the secretary, the register must contain the following details:

(a) in the case of an individual, his name, former names and his usual residential address;
(b) in the case of a body corporate, its name and registered address.

Any change in the details contained in the register must be notified to the Registrar of Companies within fourteen days of the change. Section 195 also imposes a duty on the directors and secretary to give information to the company in writing in order that it may comply with its requirements under the Act.

The register must be kept open for inspection for not less than two hours per working day.

CHAPTER SEVENTEEN

DIRECTORS' POWERS AND AUTHORITY

Actual Authority of Directors

The actual authority of an agent is the authority which the principal, either expressly or impliedly, agrees he shall have. In the case of company directors, their express authority will be determined primarily by the articles of association. While the authority of the company is, in the first instance, vested in the members, Article 80 of Table A provides that the business of the Company shall be managed by the directors. The power to manage is conferred upon the board of directors acting collectively and not on individual directors. While Article 80 may seem to give directors very wide powers, the law confers many duties upon them in order to limit the abuse of those powers. These limitations are discussed in Chapter 18. Of course, a company does not have to adopt Article 80 and may accordingly limit the authority of directors. However, where the company adopts the model articles, the members cannot thereafter interfere with the director's power to manage the company without first altering the articles of association.[1]

In addition to the general power of management, Table A also contains articles delegating specific powers to the directors including *inter alia* the following:

(a) the power to borrow money and give security for such borrowings (Article 79);
(b) to allot un-issued shares (Article 5);
(c) to make calls on shares (Article 15);
(d) to decline to register share transfers (Article 3 Part II);
(e) to convene an EGM whenever they think fit (Article 50).

Article 110 Table A provides that the board can appoint a managing director from amongst their number and, under Article 112, they many confer on him any of the powers exercisable by them together. Where a company has adopted Articles 80, 110 and 112, the potential actual authority of the managing director is as extensive as that of the board of directors itself.

The express authority of individual directors and the company secretary is minimal under Table A. However, where a director is an 'executive director' or employed by the company, their actual authority may be greatly increased by the terms of their contract of employment. As Article 81 Table A allows the directors to delegate their powers, the individual directors may be conferred with additional powers by the board itself. However, even if no actual authority exists,

---

1 *Re Gramaphone & Typewriter Ltd v Stanley* [1904] 2KB 89 CA.

the company may still be bound where the director, as agent for the company, acts within his implied or apparent authority.

Implied actual authority is based on the idea that if the principal appoints an agent to act in a particular capacity, then the agent has the implied authority to do what is necessary to achieve those acts. Where, for example, a director is given the express authority to hire employees, then it is assumed, unless the contrary is expressly provided, that he has the implied authority to advertise for vacancies and interview the candidates.

Ostensible Authority of Directors

The ostensible authority of an agent is that authority which his principal represents, to the party dealing with the agent, that he has given to the agent. If a company holds out a person as having a certain authority, when in fact he does not so have, the company will be estopped from denying this authority. The leading case is *Freeman Lockyer v. Buckhurst Park Properties (Mangal) Ltd.*[2] The defendant company carried on the business of property developers. The articles of association provided that the directors could appoint a managing director, but this was never done. One of the directors, to the knowledge of the board, but without its express authority, acted as if he were managing director in relation to finding a purchaser for an estate of land and in engaging a firm of architects and surveyors to prepare plans, draw up boundaries and apply for planning permission for the estate. The company later refused to pay the fee of the architects and surveyors on the grounds that the director did not have the authority to enter into the contract. The court held that the company was liable to pay the fees because the board had by its acquiescence represented that he was the managing director who had, by virtue of the usual authority of a managing director, the power to bind the company. In considering whether a contract could be enforced against a company on the basis of the ostensible authority of the company's agent, Diplock LJ. laid down four conditions, all of which must be proved by the claimant:

(a) a representation was made to him that the agent had the authority to enter into a contract, of the kind sought to be enforced, on behalf of the company;
(b) the representation was made to him by a person or persons who had 'actual' authority to manage the business of the company;
(c) he was induced to enter into the contract by such representations; and
(d) there is nothing in the company's memorandum or articles which deprived the company of the capacity to enter into that contract or to delegate the authority to enter into that contract to the agent.

The representation need not have been expressly made by the person with authority. Rather, the courts will infer from the conduct of that person whether or

---

2 [1964] QB 480.

not in fact a representation was impliedly made. In *Hely-Hutchinson v. Brayhead Ltd*,[3] the chairman of the board acted as the managing director of the company. Although the articles permitted the appointment of a managing director, the board never in fact appointed anyone to the position. As part of a complicated series of transactions between the defendant company and the plaintiff's company, the chairman of the defendant company purported, on the company's behalf, to indemnify the plaintiff against personal guarantees he had given to, and in respect of, the obligations of the plaintiff's company. When the company became insolvent, the plaintiff honoured his commitments under the guarantee. Later, the defendant company refused to indemnify him on the grounds that the chairman did not have the authority to sign the letters of indemnity on the company's behalf. The Court of Appeal held that the chairman had the appropriate authority and, accordingly, the company was bound by the letters of indemnity.

The conditions laid down by Diplock LJ. in *Freeman* were applied by Laffoy J. in the recent case of *Ulster Factors Ltd v. Entoglen (in liquidation) and Moloney*.[4] The plaintiff company had entered into a debt-factoring agreement whereby the debts of the defendant company were assigned to the plaintiff which, having deducted a factoring fee, would make the balance available for 'draw-down' by the defendant. The agreement stipulated that the defendant would advise the plaintiff as to which of its officers could authorise a draw-down instruction. The agreement further provided that the funds would, on draw-down by the defendant, be payable to the defendant company or the third parties specified by the defendant company. No formal notification of the authorised signatories was made to the company, although it was agreed verbally that draw-down instructions would be authorised by either a director or secretary of the company. All but three draw-downs involved payments to the company itself and were authorised by one officer. The other three draw-downs were effected by payments to third parties. Two of those draw-downs were authorised by two officers of the defendant company in line with a decision of the board to that effect. The board's decision had not been notified to the company. The remaining draw-down instruction, the subject of the dispute, to pay a firm of solicitors £37,000 was signed by only one officer. The board, on being informed of the payment, did not query it until six months later. When the defendant company later became insolvent, the liquidator claimed that the payment to the firm of solicitors was unauthorised and that £37,000 should be deducted from the amount owed by the defendant to the plaintiff. The plaintiff successfully invoked the doctrine of ostensible authority. The court was satisfied that:

(a) there was a tacit representation that an individual director had the authority to draw down funds to both the company and third parties;

---

3 [1968] 1 QBD 549.
4 High Court, 21 February 1997 (Laffoy J.).

(b) the board had the authority to make the representation as it had been given the powers to manage the company by the articles of association;

(c) the plaintiff relied on the representations; and

(d) the company had not been deprived by the memorandum or articles of association from requesting funds to be paid to third parties.

In each of the above cases, the person making the representation had the capacity to 'hold out' the agent as having the relevant authority. This capacity is determined by the articles of association. Even if the outsider is not aware of the contents of the articles, under the doctrine of constructive notice he is deemed to be so aware. Therefore, if the representative has not the authority to 'hold out' the agent, the outsider cannot satisfy the conditions laid down in the *Freeman* case. However, the effect of the doctrine of constructive notice has been mitigated by the rule in the *Turquand* case and Article 6 of the European Communities (Companies) Regulations 1973.[5]

The Rule in Turquand's Case

The articles of association may reserve to the company in general meeting or to the board of directors itself the power to impose restrictions on directors. Under the rule in *Turquand*'s case the outsider is entitled to assume that the internal requirements have been complied with. In *Royal British Bank v. Turquand*,[6] the company's articles provided that directors could only borrow amounts authorised by the company in general meeting. Although a resolution was passed, it did not specify the amount. Unaware of the defect, the directors borrowed £2,000 and issued a bond as security. When the bearer of the bond later sought to enforce the bond, the company argued that the bank was deemed to be aware of the articles' requirement that borrowings must be sanctioned by the general meeting. The court rejected this argument and held that although the bank was deemed to be aware of the contents of the articles, it was entitled to infer that the internal formalities had been completed. The rationale for the rule in *Turquand*'s case is straightforward. The act which satisfies the requirements imposed by the articles may not be a matter of public record and therefore the outsider cannot be deemed to be aware that the internal requirements have or have not been satisfied.

The rule in *Turquand*'s case was applied in the Irish case of *Allied Irish Banks Ltd v. Ardmore Studios International*.[7] There, a bank had notice of the company's articles of association which required a quorum of two directors. The bank received a copy of a board resolution signed by two of the three directors authorising the loan from the bank. However, the resolution was defective because the third director had not been given notice of the meeting. The High

---

5 SI 163/1973: see Chapter 6.

6 [1843–60] All ER 435.

7 Unreported, High Court, 30 May 1973 (Finlay J.).

Court held that the invalid procedure was an irregularity in the internal management of the company. Applying the rule in the *Turquand* case, the bank was entitled to assume that internal procedures were complied with and the company was bound by the loan agreement.

The rule in the *Turquand* case will not apply where the outsider is actually aware that the director has no authority. In *Howard v. Patent Ivory Manufacturing Co.*,[8] the directors required the authority of the general meeting in order to borrow amounts over £1,000. Without this authority the directors borrowed £3,500 secured by debentures. As the bank was aware that the general meeting had not authorised the borrowing, the court held that the company was only liable to the extent of the authorised borrowings of £1,000.

The rule will not protect outsiders where the authorising act is one which must be filed in the companies registry office.[9] This is because the outsider, in such a case, is deemed to have notice of all public documents which have been filed. In *Irvine v. Union Bank of Australia*,[10] the company's articles required a special resolution of the members to authorise borrowings in excess of a specified amount. In breach of this requirement, the directors borrowed money from the bank. It was held that the bank could not recover the unauthorised amount because it had constructive notice that a special resolution had not been passed. This was so because it had not been filed in the companies registry office.

In addition to the memorandum and articles and special resolutions, outsiders are deemed to be aware of the following documents:

(a) certificate of incorporation and certificate of change of name;
(b) alterations to the memorandum and articles of association;
(c) returns relating to directors and changes in directors;
(d) any decision which authorises non-board members to enter into transactions on behalf of the company;
(e) annual returns;
(f) notice of the registered office;
(g) winding-up orders;
(h) orders for the dissolution of the company;
(i) returns by the liquidator relating to the final meeting on winding up.[11]

Notice of the delivery of the above documents to the Registrar of Companies must be published in *Iris Oifigiúil* within six weeks of the relevant delivery. A person is deemed to have notice of the documents from the sixteenth day after the date of publication in *Iris Oifigiúil*. Where the notice of delivery has not been published, an outsider will not be deemed to be aware of their contents unless the

---

8 [1883] 3 Ch D 156.
9 For example, a special resolution.
10 (1877) 2 App Cas 366, Privy Council.
11 Regulation 4(1) of the 1973 Regulations.

evidence shows that they were actually aware. Therefore, the filing itself with the Registrar of Companies will not be sufficient to put a person on notice.

Even where an outsider is not actually aware or deemed to be aware of the irregularity he may be obliged, where the circumstances suggest, to make such further enquiries as to satisfy himself that the purported agent has the power which he represents himself as having. In *A & L Underwood Ltd v. Bank of Liverpool and Martins Ltd*,[12] the bank paid cheques into the account of the director. The cheques were payable to the company but endorsed on behalf of the company by the same director. The bank was held liable to the receiver of the company. It could not rely on the rule in *Turquand*'s case as the circumstances were so suspicious that the bank should have made further enquiries with respect to the director's actions. Similarly, in *Houghton & Co. v. Northard Lowe & Wills Ltd*,[13] the defendant company's director purported to assign to the plaintiffs the right to receive and sell goods owned by the company as security for a loan. It was held that the transaction was so unusual that the plaintiff was put on enquiry and was not entitled to assume that the director had authority. As he made no such enquiry, the company was not bound by the contract.

Finally, the rule in *Turquand*'s case will not apply where the 'outsider' is also an 'insider', such as a director or other officer of the company. In *Morris v. Kanssen*,[14] K and C were first directors of a company. A dispute arose between them as C forged an entry in the board minutes to record the appointment of S as a director. C and S later co-opted M on to the board and the three of them purported to allot shares to themselves. M was aware of a dispute between C and K concerning the legality of certain transactions, but made no further enquiry. K later claimed that the allotment was invalid as S and M were not directors and had no power to allot shares. It was held that S could not rely on *Turquand*'s case because his 'appointment', on foot of a forgery, was no appointment at all. M could not rely on the rule because as an insider with access to the records he could have made further enquiries.

However, where outsiders are dealing with persons purporting to act as directors they may assume that, if those persons are capable of being appointed as directors, they have in fact been so appointed. In *Mahoney v. East Holyford Mining Co.*,[15] a bank had received a board resolution from a person describing himself as the company secretary, which instructed the bank to honour company cheques signed by any two directors and the secretary. The bank paid on foot of a number of these cheques. It was later discovered that the persons acting as the secretary and directors were not formally appointed to those positions. However, they were the original subscribers to the memorandum and articles and could have appointed themselves, and indeed had intended to. It was held that as the

---

12 [1924] All ER 230.
13 [1927] All ER 97.
14 [1946] AC 459.
15 (1875) LR 7 HL 869.

bank had no means of discovering the non-appointment they could assume that proper appointments had been made.

Section 178 of the Principal Act protects outsiders who deal with directors even where their appointment is defective. However, the statutory protection has no application where there has been no appointment at all.

The 1973 Regulations

Regulation 6 of the European Communities (Companies) Regulations 1973 modifies the doctrine of constructive notice by increasing the protection afforded to outsiders who deal with limited liability companies. The regulation provides that all transactions are deemed to be within the capacity of the company, the board or the authorised person where the outsider was acting in good faith. Furthermore, Regulation 6(2) provides that a person will be presumed to have acted in good faith unless otherwise proven. As a result of the regulation, the rule in *Turquand*'s case is no longer of direct relevance where the outsider is dealing with the board or an authorised person. It remains relevant, however, where an outsider is dealing with an officer or an agent not authorised by the board. (See Chapter 7.)

CHAPTER EIGHTEEN

DIRECTORS' DUTIES AND LIABILITIES

Introduction

Table A provides that the directors may exercise all the powers of the company which are not otherwise required, either by the articles or the Companies Acts, to be exercised by the general meeting. This day-to-day control of the company's assets creates a potential for the abuse of directors' powers. In an attempt to curb such abuse, the law has developed a number of duties and procedural rules which must be followed by directors. Legislative provisions, particularly under the 1990 Act, have significantly widened these duties, originally found in principles of common law and equity. For the purposes of this chapter, these duties will be considered under the following categories:

1. fiduciary duties;
2. duty of care and competence; and
3. statutory duties.

Fiduciary Duties

First and foremost, a director is in a fiduciary position. Fiduciaries are those who have been 'entrusted with powers for the benefit of others, but who in the exercise of those powers are not subject to the direct and immediate control of those others'.[1] Directors are fiduciaries because, as agents of the company, they are in control of the assets and business undertaking of the company. As fiduciaries, directors must exercise their powers *bona fide* in what they honestly believe to be the best interests of the company.[2] The test is multifaceted. A claim of honesty will not be sufficient in defending the propriety of a director's decision, if the best interests of the company were not considered. In *Re W & M Roith Ltd*[3] the controlling shareholder and director of the company wished to make provision for his wife in the event of his death. He entered into a service agreement with the company whereby if he died his wife would receive a widow's pension for life. When the company ultimately failed, the administrators of his estate sought to prove for the amount owing under the pension. It was held that the agreement was for the benefit of the widow and as no thought was given to the interests of the company, the agreement was not binding on the company.[4]

---

1 Finn, *Fiduciary Obligations,* Sydney: Law Book Co. (1977) 3.
2 *Re Smith & Fawcett Ltd* [1942] 1 All ER 452.
3 [1967] WLR 432.
4 The decision followed *Re Lee, Behrens & Co.* [1932] 2 Ch 46.

It is for those who claim that directors have exercised their powers in bad faith to produce evidence of this fact. As Lord Greene MR stated in *Re Smith & Fawcett Ltd*, directors 'must exercise their discretion bona fide in what they consider not what the court may consider to be in the best interests of the company . . .'.[5] The test is therefore a subjective one and the court will not substitute its own view for that of the directors. The burden of proving the *male fides* of a director is particularly difficult given that directors are not required to give any reasons for their decisions. As Meredith MR observed in *Re Dublin North City Milling Co. Ltd*:

> I think the law is wise in refusing to compel directors to disclose their reasons . . . the law allows the directors to hold their tongues. It allows them to say that everything was done honestly and *bona fide* in the interests of their company . . . and according to my view I have no power to make them say more.[6]

Although directors cannot be compelled to give reasons for their decisions, their silence may lead to an inference of bad faith. In *Clark v. Workman*[7] Ross J. held that on the basis of the director's failure to refute the allegations of impropriety made by the plaintiff, an inference of bad faith could be made. In determining the fiduciary duties of directors the courts have developed a number of principles:

(a) directors must exercise their powers for a proper purpose; and
(b) directors must not fetter their discretion when deciding how to act; and
(c) directors must not put themselves in a position whereby their own personal interests and those of the company conflict.

1. The Duty to Use Their Powers for a Proper Purpose

Directors are conferred with a number of discretionary powers, the use of which can have far-reaching effect. The powers must be exercised not only in furtherance of the company's objects, but also for a proper purpose. In ascertaining the purpose of a particular transaction, a difficulty may arise where multiple consequences arise. In such a case, it is the substantial purpose of the transaction that will determine whether the powers have been exercised properly. If the directors can establish that they honestly believed the action was for the greater good of the company, they will have fulfilled their duty even though the outcome may be beneficial or indeed detrimental to some shareholders. Most litigation concerning the misuse of directors' powers arises in relation to their

---

5 [1942] 1 All ER 452.
6 [1909] 1 IR 179 at 184. See similar comments made by Black J. in *Re Hafner, Olhausen v. Powderley* [1943] IR 426.
7 [1920] 1 IR 107.

power to allot shares.[8] In *Hogg v. Cramphorn*[9] the directors, in order to prevent a take-over bid which they believed would be detrimental to the interests of the company, issued shares to the trustees of the employees' pension fund. The shares were paid for by a loan advanced by the company to the trustees. Although the court recognised that the directors were acting *bona fide*, the issue of shares to forestall a take-over bid was in breach of the directors' fiduciary duties and the allotment was thus invalid. Similarly, in *Nash v. Lancegaye Safety Glass (Ireland) Ltd*,[10] an allotment of preference shares, which was made to ensure that the company would be controlled by a director's family, was set aside on the grounds that it was an improper use of the directors' powers.

In *Howard Smith Ltd v. Ampol Petroleum Ltd*,[11] the majority shareholders intended to reject a take-over bid for the company. The directors honestly believed that the proposed take-over was in the company's best interest because the bidder was expected to inject additional capital into the company. The directors allotted new shares to the bidder, which had the effect of diluting the existing majority's stake, and ensuring the take-over would succeed. Although the directors were not motivated by self-interest, the decision to allot the additional shares was successfully challenged. The court held that its primary purpose was to reduce the majority to a minority position and that this was an improper exercise of their powers. Interestingly, the court rejected the argument that the only proper purpose for which the power to allot shares could be exercised was to raise new capital when the company required it. Accordingly, it has been accepted that the issue of shares to a larger company to secure the financial stability of the company and to ensure its future trading activities was a proper exercise of the directors' power, even though the effect was to frustrate a take-over bid.[12] The issue of shares, as part of a joint-venture agreement relating to the exploitation of mineral rights owned by the company, has also been upheld, despite the fact that the issue had the effect of reducing a majority to a minority position.[13]

Even if the directors themselves benefit from a transaction, this will not automatically give rise to an inference of improper motives. In *Re Jermyn Turkish Baths Ltd*,[14] an allotment of shares to a director which gave her a majority stake in the company was upheld because it formed part of rescue proposals for the failing

---

8 It should be noted that the directors' power to allot shares has been restricted by section 20 of the Companies (Amendment) Act 1983. However, where they are authorised to allot shares under the articles or by the general meeting, the principle that their powers must be exercised for a proper purpose continues to apply.
9 [1966] 3 All ER 420.
10 (1958) 92 ILTR 11.
11 [1974] AC 403, HL.
12 *Harlowe's Nominees Pty Ltd v. Woodside Oil Co.* (1968) 121 CLR 483, Aust. HC.
13 *Teck Corporation Ltd v. Millar* (1972) 33 DLR (3d) 288, BC Sup. Ct.
14 [1971] 1 WLR 1042.

company, and was therefore in its best interests. In *Mills v. Mills* [15] the company's board decided to capitalise profits by way of a bonus issue of shares rather than distributing them by way of dividend. The decision, which had the incidental effect of increasing the managing director's voting power, survived judicial scrutiny because the dominant purpose was to retain the profits for the company's business. Speaking for the Australian High Court, Latham CJ. suggested that directors:

> are not required by law to live in an unreal region of detached altruism and to act in a vague mood of ideal abstraction from obvious facts which must be present to the mind of any honest and intelligent man when he exercises his power as a director. [16]

The rules governing minority protection may overlap with cases concerning directors' abuse of power. In *Clemens v. Clemens Bros Ltd* [17] it was held that an allotment of shares for the purpose of reducing a member's stake might constitute oppression. This would entitle the member to bring an action against the directors under section 205 of the Principal Act. (See Chapter 15.)

2. The Duty not to Fetter Their Discretion

Directors must keep their discretion unfettered by outside influences, notwithstanding the *bona fides* of their intentions. They cannot therefore, as a general rule, contract with third parties as to how they will vote at board meetings. The case of *Clark v. Workman* [18] illustrates this point. The chairman of the board of directors had promised an outsider that he would use his influence to obtain approval from the board for the transfer of company shares from a majority shareholder to the outsider. The chairman then used his casting vote to secure board approval for the transfer. The plaintiff shareholders argued that the board did not have sufficient time to consider the matter and that the director was in breach of his duty by fettering his discretion to act in the best interests of the company. The court held that the actions of the director were such as to disqualify him from acting *bona fide* in the interests of the company. However, if directors have entered into a contract in the best interests of the company, and have committed themselves to take further action at a board meeting to give effect to that contract, this is not regarded as an improper fetter on their discretion. In *Thorby v. Goldberg,* [19] the directors of a company agreed with third parties, as part of a reorganisation of the company, to alter the articles of association to provide for the issue of new shares. The argument that such an agreement was illegal as a fetter on the directors' discretion was rejected by the Australian High Court. As Kitto J. observed:

---

15 (1938) 60 CLR 150.
16 Ibid. at 164.
17 [1976] 2 All ER 268.
18 [1920] 1 IR 107.
19 (1964) 112 CLR 597.

There are many kinds of transaction in which the proper time for the exercise of the directors' discretion is the time of the negotiation of a contract and not the time at which the contract is to be performed . . . If at the former time they are *bona fide* of the opinion that it is in the best interests of the company that the transaction should be entered into and carried into effect, I can see no reason in law why they should not bind themselves to do whatever under the transaction is to be done by the board.[20]

A similar view was taken in the Scottish case of *Dawson International plc v. Coats Paton plc*.[21] Here, the plaintiff company had made a take-over bid for the defendant company. The directors of both companies entered into an agreement whereby the directors of the defendant company agreed not to co-operate with any other bidder and to recommend the plaintiff's bid to the general meeting. The defendant subsequently announced that it would be taken over by a rival bidder. The court held that the agreement between the plaintiff and the defendant was enforceable, because it was made in the best interests of the company. In the recent case of *Fulham Football Club Ltd v. Cabra Estates plc*[22] the English Court of Appeal endorsed the principle that provided the fetter on the discretion of the directors is not improper, it will not necessarily amount to a breach of their fiduciary duties.

There may be circumstances whereby a director is appointed to serve the interests of someone other than the company. Sometimes directors are appointed purely to represent a shareholder or creditor of the company. The terms of appointment of these directors, referred to as nominee directors, will usually determine the way in which they will cast their votes. In *Scottish Co-operative Wholesale Society Ltd v. Meyer*[23] it was suggested that nominees are not totally absolved from their duties to act in the best interests of the company even though this may place them in an impossible position. However, in the Australian case of *Levin v. Clark*[24] commercial reality prevailed. The court held that the company, in accepting the appointment of a nominee to protect the interests of a financial institution, had waived its right to the loyalty of that nominee.

3. *The Duty to Avoid a Conflict of Interest*

Directors, as agents for the company, must not put themselves into a position whereby their personal interests and those of the company are in conflict. One of the leading cases concerning a director's duty to avoid a conflict of interest situation is *Regal (Hastings) Ltd v. Gulliver.*[25] The plaintiff company had

---

20 Ibid. at 605–606.
21 [1989] BCLC 233.
22 [1994] 1 BCLC 363.
23 [1959] AC 324.
24 [1962] NSWR 686.
25 [1942] 1 All ER 378. See also *Dawson International plc v. Coats Paton plc* [1989] BCLC 233.

established a subsidiary company to acquire the lease of two cinemas. The subsidiary company had an authorised share capital of 5,000 £1 ordinary shares. The owner of the cinemas agreed to grant the lease on condition that the 5,000 shares in the subsidiary company were subscribed for. The plaintiff company lacked the resources to acquire all the shares, so it was agreed that the company's directors would purchase 3,000 shares. When the plaintiff company and the subsidiary were subsequently sold, the directors made a substantial profit from their holdings in the subsidiary. The new owners of the plaintiff company caused the company to bring an action against the ex-directors to account for the profit they made from their office. The court held that the liability of a fiduciary 'in no way depends on fraud, or absence of *bona fides*'.[26] Despite the absence of *male fides* on the directors' part, they had made a profit from their position and were therefore obliged to account to the company.

The decision in *Regal* seems harsh when one considers that the directors were acting honestly and for the benefit of the company. However, the fact that they benefited personally from the transaction resulted in a conflict of interest. In holding that the directors were in breach of their fiduciary duty, the court endorsed the strict rule of equity that a person in a position of trust cannot benefit from that position, even if he acts honestly for the benefit of the company. It was, however, suggested in *Regal* that had the shareholders, either prospectively or retrospectively, ratified the directors' breach of duty, the outcome would have been different.[27]

The courts have imposed liability on directors to account to the company for profits they made from personally obtained information, if the company itself could have used that information. In *Industrial Development Consultants Ltd v. Cooley*,[28] the defendant was the managing director of the plaintiff company which was in the construction consulting business. He tried, unsuccessfully as it transpired, to obtain on behalf of the company a contract with the Gas Board. However, because of his own extensive experience in the gas industry, the Gas Board did offer him the contract in his personal capacity. He accepted, and resigned from the plaintiff company on the grounds that he was ill. Fearing the onset of a breakdown, the chairman released him immediately. The company later sought to make him account for the profit he had made. The defendant argued that the information concerning the contract had come to him in his personal capacity and not as a director of the company. In response to this Roskill J. stated:

> The defendant had one capacity and one capacity only in which he was carrying on business at the time. That capacity was as managing director of the plaintiffs.

---

26 *Per* Lord Russell of Killowen [1967] 2 AC 134n at 144.
27 *Per* Lord Russell of Killowen [1967] 2 AC 134n at 150.
28 [1972] 2 All ER 162.

Information which came to him . . . was information which it was his duty to pass on . . . because between himself and the plaintiffs a fiduciary relationship existed . . .[29]

Given the absence of good faith in the manner in which the defendant resigned, and having failed in his duty to disclose the relevant information to the company, he was in breach of his fiduciary duty and had to account for his profits.

It has been suggested that the courts are now developing a more benign approach towards directors' liability to account for profits made.[30] In *Peso Silver Mines Ltd v. Cropper*,[31] the defendant was managing director of the plaintiff company. An opportunity to acquire prospecting claims had been presented to the company's board but was declined, mainly due to lack of finances. The defendant, together with two other directors, formed a syndicate and acquired the claims. The plaintiff company was later acquired and proceedings were instituted against the director to account for the profits he had made. The Supreme Court of Canada rejected the claim and held that where the board of directors rejects a business opportunity, individual directors are thereafter free to take up the opportunity and retain any resulting profits.

4. Ratifying Directors' Breaches

The general meeting may in certain circumstances ratify breaches of directors' duties. In *Hogg v. Cramphorn*,[32] Buckley J. held that, despite the improper use by the directors of their power to allot shares, the directors' actions could have been endorsed by the general meeting. He allowed the matter to stand until the general meeting was given an opportunity to consider the matter, at which point the breach was ultimately ratified. In *Regal Hastings*[33] Lord Russell suggested that had the directors sought the approval of the general meeting, either prospectively or retrospectively, they could have retained their profits. In a recent decision by the Supreme Court concerning misfeasance proceedings taken by a liquidator against the directors, it was made clear that a company can only ratify transactions involving the directors where the company itself benefited from the transaction.[34]

5. To Whom are the Duties Owed?

The fiduciary duties of directors are owed to the company as a whole and not to the individual shareholders. The case of *Percival v. Wright*[35] aptly supports this viewpoint. The plaintiffs offered to sell their shares to the defendants, who were

---

29 [1972] 2 All ER 162 at 173.
30 MacCann (1991) ILT 104 at 105.
31 (1966) 58 DLR (2d) 1.
32 [1966] 3 All ER 420.
33 [1942] 1 All ER 378.
34 *Re Greendale Developments Ltd (in Liquidation)*, Supreme Court [1998] 1 IR 8.
35 [1902] Ch 421.

directors of the company. The offer was accepted and the directors purchased the shares at £12.50. Unknown to the plaintiffs, the directors had also been in discussions with a third party concerning the sale of the company for a price representing an amount greater than that paid to the plaintiffs. Although the take-over did not proceed, the plaintiffs claimed that the defendants had breached their fiduciary duty in not disclosing this information, and sought to have the transfer set aside. The court, rejecting the plaintiffs' submission, held that the directors owed a fiduciary duty to the company alone and not to any individual member. Although this decision has been subjected to much criticism,[36] it can be defended on the basis that it was the plaintiffs who had in fact approached the directors. In any case, if similar circumstances arose today the directors' actions would likely fall foul of the insider dealing provisions of the 1990 Act.[37] While it is clear that the duties are owed to the company, those duties may be extended in certain circumstances to include:

(a) individual shareholders;
(b) employees; and
(c) creditors.

Individual Shareholders

Although directors' duties are owed to the company and not to the individual shareholders, each case turns on its own facts, and if directors put themselves in a position whereby they have undertaken to act on behalf of the shareholders, the courts will impute a fiduciary relationship. Such was the position taken in the New Zealand case of *Coleman v. Myers*.[38] The defendants, a father and son, were directors and shareholders of a small family company. Using another company which they controlled, they successfully made a bid for a sufficient number of shares in the 'family' company which enabled them to force a compulsory acquisition of the remaining shares. Because the other shareholders had at all times looked to them for business advice and the defendants had suppressed information regarding the true value of the shares, the court held that the directors did owe a fiduciary duty to the plaintiffs, as shareholders.

The decision in *Coleman* echoes the view expressed by the Judicial Committee of the Privy Council in the earlier case of *Allen v. Hyatt*.[39] There, the appellants, who were the directors of the company, were in the process of negotiating a merger with another company. They obtained options to purchase the shares of the respondents at par value, by representing that the options were

---

36 The Reports of the Cohen Committee Cmnd 6659 and Jenkins Committee Cmnd 1749.
37 See Chapter 21, Insider Dealing.
38 [1977] 2 NZLR 225.
39 (1914) 30 TLR 444.

needed to enable the directors to negotiate on behalf of the shareholders. They did not disclose that when the merger was finalised the shares could be sold at 7 per cent above par. The directors exercised their options and resold the shares at a profit. It was held that the appellants had become the agents of the respondents on making the representations and were therefore obliged to account for the profit they had made. It would appear from *obiter* remarks made in one Irish decision that a similar approach may be adopted in this jurisdiction, particularly where insufficient or inaccurate information concerning a proposed take-over is given to shareholders.[40]

It should be noted that section 205 of the Principal Act gives a statutory remedy to shareholders where the affairs of the company are being conducted in a manner oppressive to them.[41]

Employees

It has long been accepted that directors do not owe a fiduciary duty to employees.[42] This was made clear in *Parke v. The Daily News Ltd*,[43] where an agreement by the company to make *ex gratia* payments to employees was struck down by the court on the ground that it did not confer any financial benefit on the company. However, section 52 of the Companies Act 1990 requires directors to have regard to the interests of employees when considering the interests of the company. While this provision gives greater flexibility to directors when considering the interests of employees, it remains the position that the duty is owed to the company and therefore enforceable only by an action of the company.

Creditors

It is settled law that directors do not owe a fiduciary duty to creditors when the company is solvent.[44] However, recent decisions of the Irish courts have endorsed the view taken in other jurisdictions[45] that, where the company is insolvent, the members' interests are subordinated to the interests of debenture holders and other creditors. In *Kinsella v. Russell Kinsella Property Ltd*, Street CJ. observed that:

> . . . where a company is insolvent the interests of the creditors intrude. They become prospectively entitled through the mechanism of liquidation, to displace the power of shareholders and the directors to deal with the company's assets.[46]

---

40 McWilliam J. in *Securities Trust Ltd v. Associated Properties Ltd*, High Court, 19 November 1980.
41 See Chapter 15.
42 See *Hutton v. West Cork Railway Company* [1883] 23 Ch D 654.
43 [1962] 2 All ER 929. See also *Re W. & M. Roith Ltd* [1967] WLR 432.
44 See Barrett (1977) 40 MLR 226.
45 Most notably in Australia and New Zealand.
46 [1986] 4 NSWLR 722 at 730.

This passage was cited with approval by Blayney J. in the Irish case of *Parkes v. Hong Kong & Shanghai Banking Corporation*.[47] There, it was held that the disposition of company assets by a director of an insolvent company was a breach of the director's duty to the creditors of the company. In the more recent case of *Re Frederick Inns Ltd*,[48] a similar line of reasoning was adopted by both the High Court and the Supreme Court.[49]

There are a number of statutory provisions designed to protect the creditors of companies which are insolvent or on the verge of insolvency. Furthermore, directors who do not consider the interests of creditors while the company is insolvent may face an action for fraudulent or reckless trading (considered later). Indeed directors may be obliged to place an insolvent company in liquidation.

Transactions between Directors and the Company

In an attempt to prevent directors from abusing their position and to create some level of transparency in relation to transactions between the company and its directors, a number of statutory provisions have been introduced by the Companies Act 1990 to strengthen the fiduciary duties of directors. Some of these provisions have the effect of amending previous statutory requirements while others create new obligations.

1. Interest and Dealings in Shares

The Companies Act 1990 significantly increases the obligations both on directors, who must disclose their interests and dealings in company securities, and on companies, which must maintain a register of such interests. Section 53 requires directors, shadow directors and the company secretary to disclose any legal and beneficial interests in the company's securities, held either by themselves or their families. On becoming a director or secretary the existence of any such interest must be notified within four days of becoming aware of it. Where a director or secretary ceases to be interested in the company's securities, he must notify the company within five days.

As with all individuals, if a director or secretary acquires or disposes of shares which brings his interest in the company above or below 5 per cent in nominal value of the 'relevant nominal capital'[50] of a public limited company, he must disclose this fact to the company.[51]

---

47 [1990] ILRM 341.
48 [1991] ILRM 582 (High Court) and [1994] 1 ILRM 387 (Supreme Court).
49 See also *Truck and Machinery Sales Ltd v. Marubeni Komatsu Ltd* [1996] 1 IR 12.
50 'Relevant nominal capital' means the issued share capital of a class carrying voting rights at general meetings.
51 Where the public limited company is listed on the Stock Exchange, supplemental notification is required: section 91 of the Companies Act 1990.

Section 59 of the Companies Act 1990 requires a company, on receipt of the relevant information, to keep a register of those interests and any changes thereto, all of which must be entered within three days.[52] The register must be maintained at the same place as the register of members.[53]

Section 30(1) makes it an offence for a director who deals in options to buy or sell certain shares in, or debentures of, the company or associated companies. This provision does not prevent directors acquiring a right to shares in a company pursuant to a scheme approved by the Revenue Commissioners.[54]

2. Substantial Property Transactions

Section 194(1) of the Principal Act[55] imposes a statutory duty on directors to disclose to the board of directors the fact and the nature of any interest, whether directly or indirectly, in a contract or proposed contract with the company. Where a contract is made between the company and a 'connected person', the director is deemed to be interested in that contract. A person is a connected person if, but only if, he is:

(a) that director's spouse, parent, brother, sister or child;
(b) a person acting in his capacity as the trustee of any trust, the principal beneficiaries of which are the director, his spouse, or any of his children or any body corporate which he controls;
(c) a partner of that director; or[56]
(d) a company controlled by that director.

The disclosure must be made to the board at the meeting at which the question of entering into the contract is first proposed or at the next meeting of the directors held after the director became interested. Failure to comply with the requirements of section 194 renders a director liable to a fine.

3. Acquisition of Non-Cash Assets

In addition to the disclosure requirements described above, the Companies Acts impose restrictions on the kinds of transactions which may be entered into between the company and its directors. Section 29 of the Companies Act 1990 provides that a company shall not enter into any arrangement:

(a) whereby a director of the company or its holding company or a person connected with such a director acquires or is to acquire one or more non-cash assets of the requisite value from the company; or

---

52 Section 60(2) of the Companies Act 1990.
53 Section 60(5) of the Companies Act 1990.
54 Section 30 (3A) of the Companies Act 1990.
55 As amended by section 47 of the Companies Act 1990.
56 Section 26 of the Companies Act 1990.

    (b) whereby the company acquires or is to acquire one or more non-cash assets of requisite value from such a director or a person so connected;

unless the arrangement is first approved by a resolution of the company in general meeting and, if the director or connected person is a director of its holding company or a person connected with such a director, by a resolution of that holding company.

A non-cash asset of a requisite value is one whose value is greater than £50,000 (€63,487) or whose value is more than 10 per cent of the company's net assets, whichever is the lesser. In any case the provisions do not apply to an amount less than £1,000 (€1,269).

Section 29(3) broadly provides that where a company enters into a transaction in contravention of the section, the arrangement is voidable at the instance of the company unless:

(a) restitution of any money or assets, the subject of the arrangement, is no longer possible;
(b) rights acquired *bona fide* and for value by innocent third parties who are not a party to the arrangement would be affected by the avoidance of the transaction; and
(c) the arrangement is, within a reasonable period of time, affirmed by the company in general meeting.

Where the arrangement is entered into in breach of the provisions, the director involved is liable to account to the company for any gain he makes on the transaction, and to indemnify it against any loss.

4. Prohibited Transactions

Section 31(1) of the Companies Act 1990 provides that, subject to certain exceptions, a company is prohibited from entering into any transactions for the provision of:

(a) loans or quasi-loans [57] to a director of the company or its holding company or to a person connected with such a director;
(b) credit transactions [58] as creditor for such a director or a person so prohibited;

---

57 A quasi-loan is defined by section 25(2)(a) as a transaction whereby one party agrees to pay a sum for another or agrees to reimburse expenditure incurred by another person on terms that the borrower will reimburse the creditor or in circumstances giving rise to a liability on the borrower to reimburse the creditor.

58 Section 25(3) defines a credit transaction as one where the creditor supplies any goods or sells any land under a hire-purchase agreement or conditional sale agreement; or leases or licenses the use of land or hires goods in return for periodical payments; or otherwise disposes of land or supplies goods or services on the undertaking that payment is deferred.

(c) guarantees or other security in connection with a loan, quasi-loan or credit transaction made by any other person for such a director or a person so connected.

Where the directors of a company become aware, or ought reasonably to become aware, that there exists a section 31 situation, it shall be the duty of the company, its directors and any persons for whom the arrangements were made, to amend, within two months, the terms of the arrangements concerned, so that the total amount outstanding falls within the permitted levels.

The Act provides for exemptions to the general prohibition in the following circumstances.

(a) where the value of the arrangement and aggregate arrangements entered into by the company is less than 10 per cent of the company's relevant assets. For the purposes of the section, 'relevant assets' is defined as the value of the net assets of the company with reference to the accounts, which have been prepared and laid in accordance with the requirements of section 148 of the principal Act, in respect of the last preceding financial year when such accounts were laid. Where no accounts have been prepared and laid under that section, the relevant assets will be the amount of the company's called-up share capital.[59] It should be noted that this exemption only applies to loans, quasi-loans and credit transactions and has no application to guarantees or the provision of security; or

(b) where, in the case of a guarantee or the giving of security in connection with a loan, quasi-loan or credit transaction by a person for a director of the company or holding company, the transaction is made under the authority of a special resolution of the company, passed not more than twelve months previously, before which the company has forwarded, with each notice of the meeting at which the special resolution is to be considered, a statutory declaration by the directors in the prescribed form accompanied by an independent report, by a person qualified to be an auditor of the company, stating that the statutory declaration is reasonable; or

(c) where a company makes a loan or quasi-loan to, or gives a guarantee or other security on behalf of, or enters into a credit transaction as creditor for, any company which is its holding company, subsidiary or a subsidiary of its holding company; or

(d) where a company provides any of its directors with funds to meet vouched expenditure properly incurred, or to be incurred, by them for the purposes of the company or to enable them to properly perform their duties as officers of the company, or doing anything to enable any of its directors to avoid incurring such expenditure. Where a company enters into such a transaction, any liability falling on any person from such a transaction must be

---

59 Section 32 of the Companies Act 1990.

discharged by him within six months. Failing this the person shall be guilty of an offence;[60]

(e) where such loans, quasi-loans and credit transactions are entered into in the ordinary course of the company's business and the value of the transaction, and the terms on which it is entered into, is not greater than that which the company ordinarily offers, or is reasonable to expect the company to have offered.

Transactions falling within section 31 are deemed to be transaction in which a director is interested and are subject to the section 194 disclosure rules.

Where a prohibited transaction is entered into, it is voidable at the instance of the company provided that rescission is possible, the company has been indemnified against any loss and innocent third party rights are not affected.[61] Any officer of the company who authorises a prohibited transaction may be guilty of a criminal offence where they know, or have reasonable cause to believe, that the company was contravening section 31.[62]

5. *Other Contracts*

Section 41 of the Companies Act 1990 provides that all loan and loan type transactions between the company and its directors, shadow directors and connected persons must be disclosed in the company accounts.[63] Section 41 further requires all companies to disclose in their annual accounts contracts, transactions and arrangements in which any director, or director of a holding company, has a material interest.[64]

Duties of Care and Competence

The fiduciary duties imposed on directors prevent them from diverting company resources for their own personal gain. Otherwise, relatively few legal restraints are placed on directors' freedom to manage the assets and undertaking of the company. While directors may be held negligent for corporate mismanagement, the reported cases are few, leading one American commentator to suggest that:

> the search for cases in which directors have been held liable for negligence uncomplicated by self-dealing is a search for a very small number of needles in a very large haystack.[65]

---

60 Section 37 of the Companies Act 1990.

61 Section 38(1) of the Companies Act 1990.

62 Section 40 of the Companies Act 1990.

63 Exemptions are available in the case of licensed banks and their holding companies or where the loan or loan type transaction, or the aggregate thereof, is for an amount not greater than £2,500 (€3,174) and represents an amount less than 10 per cent of the company's relevant assets.

64 Certain transactions are not required to be disclosed: section 41(7) of the Companies Act 1990.

65 Bishop (1968) 77 Yale LJ 1078 at 1099.

The reasons why negligence actions are not pursued against inept directors are understandable. First, the board of directors are unlikely to bring an action against one of their own. Second, liquidators are always mindful that the pool of assets available to creditors would be depleted by unsuccessful litigation — furthermore, even if the liquidator is successful, the courts can relieve a director from liability if he acted honestly and reasonably. Third, even if litigation was initiated, judges have traditionally shown a marked reluctance to condemn business decisions made without the benefit of hindsight. Finally, a problem arises in establishing a standard of care and skill for a range of persons who may have a common title but whose knowledge, experience and business acumen will vary significantly.

The leading authority on the duty of care owed by company directors is the judgment of Romer LJ. in *Re City Equitable Fire Insurance Co. Ltd.*[66] The chairman of an insurance company had misappropriated sums of company money. He concealed his dishonesty by juggling short-term investments at financial year-ends. The other directors left the investment business of the company in the hands of the chairman and never queried the accounts. Although concerned about certain long-term investments, they left this matter to the general manager, who was instructed by the chairman. The company ultimately failed as a result of the misapplication of investments. The liquidator sued the other directors for negligence. The directors were held to be negligent but escaped liability because the company's articles of association exonerated directors from liability for negligence unless it was wilful. The case is important because of the three propositions put forward by Romer LJ. concerning the care, skill and diligence to be exercised by directors. These propositions can be summarised as follows.

1. Skill

A director, while owing a duty of care to the company, need not exhibit in the performance of his duties a greater degree of skill than may reasonably be expected from a person of his knowledge and experience. The test is largely subjective, in that the reasonable man will be judged on the basis of that particular individual's knowledge and expertise. The formulation of the director's duty in these terms would seem to impose little or no duty on the unskilled and unqualified director, who can make business decisions, however ill advised, safe in the knowledge that ignorance is bliss. In these cases it would seem that only acts of gross negligence will give rise to liability. On the other hand, the director who has, or purports to have, a particular skill will be required to use that skill. Failure to do so may render the director, whether executive or non-executive, liable for negligence. In *Dorchester Finance Co. Ltd v.*

---

66 [1925] Ch 407.

Stebbing,[67] the three defendants were all directors of a licensed moneylending company. Stebbing was an executive director and the remaining two were non-executive directors. Each of them had either an accountancy qualification or extensive accounting experience. No board meetings were ever held, and the non-executive directors left the management of the company's affairs to Stebbing, often leaving blank cheques for Stebbing to complete at a later date. Stebbing used some of these cheques for transactions outside the terms of the moneylending licence, which subsequently proved to be irrecoverable. The company issued proceedings against all three directors for negligence. The court held that had the directors exercised their skills the loss in question would not have arisen. Furthermore, these skills must be exercised by all directors, not just executive directors. Accordingly, all three were held liable.

2. Diligence

The second proposition put forward by Romer LJ. relates to the degree of diligence that is required by directors. He suggested that a director is:

> . . . not bound to give continuous attention to the affairs of his company. His duties are of an intermittent nature to be performed at periodical board meetings, and at meetings of any committee of the board upon which he happens to be placed. He is not, however, bound to attend all such meetings, though he ought to attend, whenever, in the circumstances, he is reasonably able to do so.

What will constitute reasonable attendance is not clear from the above passage. What is clear, however, is that failure to attend meetings, having been put on notice of irregular decision-making, may render a director liable in negligence. In *Jackson v. Munster Bank Ltd ex parte Dease*,[68] Dease was a director of a bank with branches in Cork and Dublin. He regularly attended Dublin board meetings which concerned the Dublin branch, but rarely attended the Cork board meetings. In his absence, the Cork directors approved unauthorised loans to themselves, many of which were irrecoverable. Although Dease was advised of these irregular dealings in February 1883, he took no action to investigate them. He was successfully sued for breach of duty. The court accepted that Dease could be excused from attending all the Cork meetings because of his heavy schedule in Dublin. However, once he was put on notice of the fraudulent misappropriation of the property of the bank, it was his duty to attend those meetings and enquire into the matter. Because he had not done so, he was held liable for the losses incurred by the bank as a result of the improper loans made after February 1883.

The mere attendance at meetings is not enough to discharge the duty of care and diligence. Directors who attend but fall asleep or allow themselves to be distracted cannot escape liability by claiming that they took no part in or were

---

67 (1989) BCLC 498.
68 (1885) 15 LR Ir 356.

unaware of the decisions being made at that meeting.[69] Similarly, the director who rubber-stamps a recommendation by the chairman is in a riskier position than the person who does not attend at all.[70]

3. Delegation

The third proposition of Romer LJ. related to the delegation by directors of their duties. He stated:

> In respect of all duties that, having regard to the exigencies of business and the articles of association, may properly be left to some other official, a director is, in the absence of grounds for suspicion, justified in trusting that official to perform such duties honestly.

While delegation is permissible, and advisable in certain circumstances, directors should not abdicate all management responsibilities, as *Dorchester v. Stebbing*, considered above, demonstrates. They may delegate to a fellow director who is skilled or competent in the manner required and whose previous conduct has given no grounds for suspicion. As Lord Halsbury LC stated in *Dovey v. Cory*:[71]

> I cannot think that it can be expected of a director that he should be watching the inferior officers . . . the business of life could not go on if people could not trust those who are put into a position of trust for the express purpose of attending to details of management.

The delegation of responsibilities should not be confused with the abdication of responsibilities, as the case of *Re Hunting Lodges Ltd* demonstrates.[72] Here, the wife of the executive director was appointed as the other director of the company, probably just to meet the minimum statutory requirements. The evidence showed that she had acted merely as a non-executive director and played no real role in the day-to-day management of the company. In an attempt to resist liability for fraudulent trading, she claimed that any business she did undertake was based on instructions from her husband. In holding her liable, Carroll J. held that a person who 'abdicates all responsibility is not to be lightly excused'.

It should be noted that the directors in *City Equitable* escaped liability by virtue of the company's articles of association. Section 200 of the Principal Act renders void any provisions in the company's articles which exempt company officers from liability.

---

69 *Land Credit Co. of Ireland v. Lord Fermoy* (1870) LR 5 Ch App 763.
70 *Selanger United Rubber Estates Ltd v. Cradock* (No. 3) [1968] 2 All ER 567.
71 [1901] 1 Ch 477.
72 [1985] ILRM 75.

Statutory Duties

In the foregoing paragraphs and previous chapters, mention has been made of many of the statutory duties owed by directors and the sanctions which may be imposed if these duties are breached. These duties may be described as positive, whereby the directors are required to carry out a particular task, or negative, where the directors are prohibited from doing certain things. Either way, these duties are prescribed to limit the potential for abuse by directors. In the remaining and subsequent chapters specific statutory duties and liabilities will be outlined in detail including:

(a) the duty to keep proper books of account;[73]
(b) the laying before the annual general meeting of the annual accounts;[74]
(c) the prohibition on directors using 'inside' information which could, if made publicly available, affect the value of shares;[75]
(d) the duty to the creditors of an insolvent company, provided for by the imposition of statutory liability for fraudulent and reckless trading;[76]
(e) the duty to co-operate in investigation, examinership, receivership and liquidation procedures under the Companies Acts;
(f) the duty to co-operate with the Director of Corporate Enforcement.

When a company becomes insolvent, the normal day-to-day activities and duties, while continuing, are displaced to some degree by the duty owed to the company's creditors. That this is the case is reflected by several statutory provisions, in particular those dealing with:

1. fraudulent trading;
2. reckless trading; and
3. misfeasance.

1. Fraudulent Trading

Under section 297 of the Principal Act, as amended, a person is trading fraudulently if he is knowingly a party to the carrying on of the business of the company with intent to defraud creditors of the company or creditors of any other person or for any fraudulent purpose. The sanctions are both civil and criminal.[77] On summary conviction the penalty is imprisonment for twelve months or a fine not exceeding £1,000 (€1,269), or both. On indictment, the penalty is a term of imprisonment not exceeding seven years or a fine not exceeding £50,000

---

73 Section 202 CA 90.
74 Section 148 of the Principal Act.
75 Part VII of the Companies Act 1990.
76 Section 297 of the Principal Act.
77 Section 297 imposes criminal liability for fraudulent trading whereas section 297A(1) imposes civil liability.

(€63,487), or both. If the civil sanction is imposed the person may be held personally responsible for the debts of the company. The section is not restricted to directors or officers of the company but can apply to any person who is party to the fraudulent activities.[78]

Before a person can be found guilty of fraudulent trading it must be proved that the person was knowingly a party to the fraudulent carrying on of the company's business and did so with intent. The use of the double-subjective test of 'knowingly' and 'with intent' makes the standard a difficult one for a liquidator to prove. In *Re Kelly's Carpetdrome Ltd*,[79] the first Irish case to deal with section 297, debts were incurred by the company at a time when it failed to keep proper books of account. The evidence also showed that some of the company's records were actually destroyed. Certain of the company's assets were transferred to other connected companies in an attempt to hive off the company's only valuable assets. On the basis of the evidence before him, Costello J. ordered that personal liability for the debts of the company should be imposed on the defendants. In *Re Aluminium Fabricators Ltd*,[80] two sets of books of account were maintained by the company. One was for the benefit of the controllers of the company and the other for the benefit of the Revenue Commissioners. The intention and effect of this was to allow the controllers to siphon off company assets for their own benefit. Obviously such activities do not impinge on creditors provided they continue to be paid. However, once the company went into insolvent winding up, it was clear that such actions had a detrimental effect on the creditors. O'Hanlon J. in the High Court held those responsible to be personally liable for the debts of the company.

It is not necessary that the fraudulent trading continues over a period of time. In *Re Hunting Lodges Ltd*,[81] a single act was held to constitute fraudulent trading. The act involved the sale at an undervalue of the 'Durty Nellies' public house which was the company's principal asset. The company sold the pub but disguised the true price of the sale by paying a substantial part of the consideration in an under-the-counter payment to one of the directors. In addition, £160,000 was paid by the purchaser to the controllers. This single fraudulent act was held to constitute the carrying on of the company's business in a fraudulent manner. Interestingly, in this case it was not only the directors and shareholders but also the purchaser that were held liable, as the purchaser had received a 'kickback' of some of his purchase price for co-operating with the fraudulent transaction.

Because of the difficulties involved in proving that a person acted knowingly and with intent, it was only in the most blatant cases of fraud that an action would

---

78 *Re Hunting Lodges Ltd* [1985] ILRM 75 and *Re Gerald Cooper Chemicals* [1978] 2 All ER 49.

79 High Court, 1 July 1983 (Costello J.).

80 [1984] ILRM 399.

81 [1985] ILRM 75.

be taken by a liquidator, who would be conscious of the legal costs involved in any unsuccessful litigation. Accordingly, it was recognised that there was an obvious need for the introduction of a new measure which would not impose such a burden on liquidators. The legislative response to this need came in the form of the reckless trading provisions of the Companies Act 1990.

2. Reckless Trading

In 1990 the concept of 'reckless trading' was introduced for the first time into Irish law. Originally introduced by section 33 of the Companies (Amendment) Act of that year, it has since been repealed by section 138 of the Companies Act 1990, which inserted a new section 297A into the Principal Act.

Section 297A provides that if, in the course of a winding up of a company or in the course of proceedings under the Companies (Amendment) Act 1990, it appears that any person while an officer of the company is 'knowingly' a party to the carrying on of business in a reckless manner, the court may, on the application of the receiver, examiner or liquidator or any other creditor or contributory of the company,[82] declare that such person shall be personally liable without limitation of liability for some or all of the debts of the company.

Even where it cannot be shown that a person was 'knowingly' a party — the difficult subjective test — to the carrying on of business in a reckless manner, he may be deemed to have acted recklessly. Section 297A(2) provides that a person is deemed to have been knowingly a party to reckless trading if either of two circumstances arise. First, that the person was party to the carrying on of such business which, in his experience and given his knowledge and skill, he ought to have known would cause loss to the creditors. This introduces an objective test based on the experience, knowledge and skill of the officer.

Second, the person is deemed to have traded recklessly if he was a party to the contracting of a debt by the company and did not honestly believe, on reasonable grounds, that the company would be able to pay the debt when it fell due for payment as well as all its other debts. If this circumstance arises the court must take into account whether the creditor in question was, at the time the debt was incurred, aware of the company's financial state of affairs and, being so aware, assented to the incurring of the debt.[83]

Liability will only be imposed under section 297A if the requirements of section 214 of the Principal Act have been satisfied.[84] These requirements are that:

---

82 A creditor or contributory of the company can only make an application under the section if he suffered loss or damage as a result of the director carrying on business in a reckless manner.
83 Section 297A(4) of the Principal Act.
84 Section 297A(3)(a) of the Principal Act.

(a) the company is unable to pay its debts within twenty-one days of a demand;
(b) an execution on the company has been returned unsatisfied; or
(c) it is proved to the court that the company is unable to pay its debts.

It should be observed that the section, unlike the fraudulent trading provision, only applies to officers of the company and not to other persons. An officer who acted honestly and responsibly in relation to the conduct of the affairs of the company may be relieved from liability on such terms as the court thinks fit.[85] This defence was successfully invoked in *Re Heffernan Kearns (No. 2)*.[86]

3. Misfeasance

Section 298(1) of the Principal Act, as amended,[87] provides that where, in the course of a winding up or on an application under section 251 of the Companies Act 1990, it appears that any person who has taken part in the formation or promotion of the company, or any past or present officer, liquidator, receiver or examiner of the company, has misapplied or retained or become liable or accountable for any money or property of the company or has been guilty of any misfeasance or other breach of duty or trust in relation to the company, the court may compel that person:

(a) to repay or restore the money or property; or
(b) to contribute such sums to the assets of the company by way of compensation in respect of the misapplication, retainer, misfeasance or other breach of duty or trust as the court thinks just.

What constitutes misfeasance is a matter for the court. It has been held that an act of negligence or an error of judgment will not necessarily amount to a misfeasance.[88]

Securing the Assets of Directors

The court may on the application of a Company director, member, liquidator, receiver, creditor or the Director of Corporate Enforcement order a director not to remove his assets from the State if the court is satisfied that the applicant has a substantive civil cause of action or the right to seek a declaration of personal liability or claim for damages against a director and there are grounds for believing that the respondent may remove those assets.[89]

---

85 Section 297A(6) of the Principal Act.
86 [1993] 3 IR 191.
87 By section 142 of the Companies Act 1990.
88 See *Re Mont Clare Hotels Ltd*, High Court, 2 December 1986 (Costello J.).
89 Section 55 CLEA 2001.

CHAPTER NINETEEN

Accounts and Returns

Introduction

The Companies Acts 1963–1990 require companies to prepare and maintain the following sets of financial information:

1. proper books of account which give a true and fair view of the state of affairs of the company and explain its transactions;
2. annual accounts which must be laid before the AGM and annexed to the annual return filed in the Companies Registry Office.

Books of Account

Section 202 of the 1990 Companies Act requires a company to keep proper books of account. The books of account must be maintained on a 'continuous and consistent basis' and in such a manner that will enable the financial position of the company to be determined, at any time, with reasonable accuracy. They must also enable the directors to produce the statutory accounts and the auditors to audit the accounts accurately. The directors and auditors have a statutory right to inspect the books at all reasonable times, and although the members have no statutory right of inspection, the articles may provide otherwise.

1. Content of the Books

Section 202(3) of the Act requires the books of account to contain the following:

(a) day-to-day entries of all monies received and expended and the matters in respect of which the receipt and expenditure takes place;
(b) a record of the assets and liabilities of the company;
(c) where the company's business involves dealing in goods, a record of all goods purchased and sold (except those sold for cash by way of ordinary retail trade) in such form as will identify the goods, the sellers, the buyers and the invoice relating thereto together with a statement of stock held by the company at the end of each financial year and any records of stock-taking from which any such statement of stock has been or is to be prepared;
(d) if the company's business involves the provision of services, a record of the services provided and the invoices relating thereto.

2. Maintenance of the Books

The books of account must be kept for a period of six years from the date to which they relate, at either the company's registered office or such other place as the directors think fit. Where the books of account are kept at a place outside the State, accounts and returns relating to the business dealt with in the books of account must be sent to a place in the State at intervals not exceeding six months. These accounts and reports must be available for inspection by the directors at reasonable times and must be maintained in such a manner to enable the company's balance sheet and profit and loss account to be prepared.

3. *Criminal and Civil Sanctions*

Failure to comply with the statutory requirement to maintain proper books of account may give rise to both criminal and civil liability.

Section 202(10) of the Act makes it an offence for a company to contravene the requirements. It is also a criminal offence for a director to fail to take all reasonable steps to secure compliance by the company, or, by his own wilful acts, to cause the company to be in default. An offence is punishable on summary conviction by a fine not exceeding £1,000 (€1,269) or imprisonment for a term not exceeding twelve months, or both. Conviction on indictment is punishable by a fine not exceeding £10,000 (€12,697) or imprisonment for a term not exceeding three years, or both. A director may not be sentenced to imprisonment unless the court is satisfied that the offence was committed wilfully.

Under section 203, if a company, which is being wound up and is unable to pay its debts, is shown to have failed in its obligation to keep proper books, every officer in default may be guilty of an offence if the court considers that the contravention contributed to or resulted in any of the following:

(a) the inability of the company to pay all its debts;
(b) a substantial uncertainty as to the assets and liabilities of the company;
(c) an impediment to the orderly winding up of the company.

This offence is punishable in a similar manner to an offence under section 202(10). However, on indictment the prison sentence may be for the greater term of five years.

Where the circumstances that are described in section 203 exist, section 204 provides that a court may, on the application of the liquidator or any creditor or contributory of the company, declare that any one or more of the officers and former officers in default are personally liable for some or all of the debts of the company. In *Mehigan v. Duignan*,[1] Shanley J. stated that before an officer could be held liable under section 204 the court had to be satisfied that the company had committed a criminal offence under section 202.

It is a defence for every officer involved in proceedings under both section 203 and section 204 to prove:

---

1 [1997] 1 IR 340.

(a) that he took all reasonable steps to secure compliance with the statutory requirements; or

(b) that he had reasonable grounds for believing, and he did believe, that a competent and reliable person, acting under the control and supervision of a director allocated with such responsibility, was charged with the duty to ensure that the section was complied with and was in a position to discharge that duty.

Any officer who is responsible for the destruction, hiding, concealment, mutilation or falsification of or the fraudulent parting with, alteration of or making of an omission in any book or document affecting or relating to the property or affairs of the company shall be guilty of an offence. The offence is punishable on summary conviction by a fine not exceeding £1,000 (€1,269) or by imprisonment for a term not exceeding twelve months, or both. Conviction on indictment is punishable by a fine not exceeding £10,000 (€12,697) or imprisonment for a term not exceeding five years, or both.

4. Investigation by Auditors

The auditors are obliged, as part of their statutory duty, to investigate whether the company is keeping proper books of account. Where the books are not being kept in the manner required by the Act, and the contravention is neither minor nor immaterial in nature, the auditors must serve a notice on the company stating their opinion to this effect. Furthermore, they must, within seven days of serving this notice, notify the Registrar of Companies of the default. The Registrar must notify the Director of Corporate Enforcement. Where the directors rectify the situation the auditors do not have to proceed with notification to the Registrar.[2]

The Annual Accounts

Section 148 of the Principal Act requires the company directors to lay before the AGM of the company a balance sheet and profit and loss account ('the annual accounts'), to which there must be annexed a copy of the directors' and auditors' reports (where applicable). The annual accounts must be signed by at least two directors and laid before the members in general meeting.[3] A resolution is normally proposed for the purpose of adopting or approving the accounts.

1. Form of Annual Accounts

The format and contents of the annual accounts are set out in the Schedule to the Companies (Amendment) Act 1986. The Schedule further requires that certain accounting principles be adhered to in the preparation of the accounts. In any case the accounts must show a 'true and fair view' of the state of affairs of the

---

2 Section 194 of the Companies Act 1990.
3 Section 156 of the Principal Act.

company even if this requires a departure from the Schedule's requirements or the provision of additional information by way of notes to the accounts.[4] Where a departure from the requirements of the Schedule is made, the directors must attach a note to the accounts giving details of and the reasons for the departures and their effect on the accounts. Certain companies are fully excluded from these requirements, and others are partially excluded.[5]

2. Exemptions for Small and Medium Private Companies

Although small and medium-sized private companies are not exempt from the 1986 requirements, they have been afforded some concessions. Small private companies may lay before the AGM a short version of the profit and loss account and an abridged balance sheet. To qualify as a small company for the purpose of the concessions, at least two of the following three conditions must be satisfied in the relevant financial year:

(a) the balance sheet total does not exceed £1,500,000 (€1,900,000);
(b) the turnover does not exceed £3,000,000 (€3,810,000);
(c) the average number of employees does not exceed fifty.[6]

Medium-sized companies must lay before the AGM a full balance sheet, but they are permitted to lay before the AGM a short version of the profit and loss account. To qualify as a medium company, at least two of the following three conditions must be satisfied in the relevant financial year:

(a) the balance sheet total does not exceed £6,000,000 (€7,620,000);
(b) the turnover does not exceed £12,000,000 (€15,240,000);
(c) the average number of employees does not exceed 250.

It is important to note that the concessions granted to small and medium private companies are subject to the overriding requirement that the accounts must give a 'true and fair view' of the state of affairs of the company.

3. Group Accounts

The legislative provisions governing group accounts are regulated by sections 150–155 of the Principal Act and by European Communities (Companies: Group Accounts) Regulations 1992. Under the Principal Act, holding companies, other than private companies, are required to prepare group accounts in addition to their own accounts. These group accounts will comprise of a consolidated

---

4 Section 3(1)(b) and section 4 of the Companies (Amendment) Act 1986.
5 Section 2 of the Companies (Amendment) Act 1986 fully exempts companies not trading for a profit and charitable companies from the requirements. Licensed banks, insurance and assurance companies are partially excluded.
6 Section 8 of the Companies (Amendment) Act 1986 as amended by Regulation 4 of the European Communities (Accounts) Regulations 1993: SI 396 of 1993.

balance sheet and consolidated profit and loss account which must be in the form prescribed. Generally speaking, these group accounts must be laid before the annual general meeting of the company and must give a fair view of the state of affairs, and the profit and loss, of the company and its subsidiaries. A holding company's directors shall secure that, unless there is good reason against it, the financial year of each of its subsidiaries shall coincide with the company's own financial year. The Minister may even permit the postponement of the submission of the accounts of a holding company or its subsidiary to the annual general meeting, or may permit an extension of the annual return date, to allow the accounts or the annual return date of the holding company and its subsidiaries to coincide with each other.

The 1992 Regulations require parent undertakings, which include, *inter alia,* that both private and public limited companies prepare and lay before the annual general meeting audited group accounts detailing the state of affairs of the group. The required form, format and content of the accounts are specified in the regulations. However, exemptions are granted to small and medium sized-private companies[7] and certain subsidiary undertakings of an EC undertaking.

4. Single-Member Companies

The requirement to lay the profit and loss account, balance sheet, directors' report and auditors' report before the AGM is deemed to be satisfied where these are sent to the sole member of the company.[8]

Directors' Reports

A report by the directors on the state of the company's affairs must be annexed to the accounts laid before the AGM.[9] The directors' report must contain the following information:

(a) the amount, if any, which the directors recommend by way of dividend;
(b) the amount, if any, which they propose to carry to reserves;
(c) details of any change in the nature of the company's business;
(d) a list of the company's subsidiaries and companies in which it has a beneficial shareholding of more than 20 per cent of the voting shares;
(e) a fair review of the development of the business of the company during the relevant financial year;
(f) particulars of any important events which have occurred since the end of the financial year affecting the company and its subsidiaries;

---

7 The exemptions specifically apply to medium-sized companies but as small companies will also satisfy the criteria which apply to medium-sized companies, the exemptions also apply thereto.

8 This is because a single-member company is not required to hold an AGM.

9 Section 158 of the Principal Act, as amended by sections 13 and 14 of the Companies (Amendment) Act 1986.

(g) an indication of the likely future development, if any, in the business of the company and its subsidiaries;
(h) an indication of any research and development activities of the company;
(i) an indication of the existence of branches of the company or its subsidiaries;
(j) details of the company's own shares acquired, and where acquired, details of those which were disposed of or cancelled, during the relevant financial year, together with particulars of such transactions;
(k) an evaluation of the extent to which the policy set out in a safety statement was fulfilled;
(l) details of directors' and secretaries' interests in the shares and debentures of the company, its subsidiaries, its holding company or subsidiaries of its holding company, provided that such information is not already given in the notes to the accounts;
(m) a statement of the measures taken by directors to secure compliance with the requirements of section 202 of the Companies Act 1990, with regard to the keeping of proper books of account and the exact location of those books; and
(n) particulars of all donations exceeding £4,000 (€5,079) to political parties.

The directors' report must be signed on behalf of the directors by two of the company's directors.

Failure to comply with the statutory requirements in respect of the annual accounts and the directors' report renders the directors liable for an offence punishable on summary conviction by a fine not exceeding £500 (€634) or imprisonment for a term not exceeding six months, or both. It is, however, a defence for a director to prove that he had reasonable grounds to believe, and he did believe, that a competent and reliable person was charged with the duty of seeing that the requirements were complied with and was in a position to discharge that duty. Furthermore, a sentence of imprisonment will not be imposed unless the court is of the opinion that the offence was committed wilfully.

The Auditors' Report

Section 193 of the Principal Act requires the auditors to make a report to the members on the accounts examined by them, and on every balance sheet and profit and loss account, and all group accounts, laid before the company in general meeting. The auditors' report must be read at the AGM of the company and must be open to inspection by any member. The report must include a statement as to the following:

(a) whether the auditors have obtained all the information and explanations which, to the best of their knowledge and belief, are necessary for the purposes of their audit;
(b) whether, in their opinion, proper books of account have been kept by the company;

(c) whether, in their opinion, proper returns adequate for their audit have been received from branches of the company not visited by them;

(d) whether the company's balance sheet and profit and loss account are in agreement with the books of account and returns;

(e) whether, in their opinion, the company's balance sheet and profit and loss account and, in the case of a holding company, the group accounts, have been prepared in accordance with the provisions of the Companies Acts and give a true and fair view of the company's or group's, whichever the case may be, state of affairs and profit and loss.

(f) whether, in their opinion, there existed at the balance sheet date a financial situation which under section 40(1) of the Companies Amendment Act 1983 would require the convening of an EGM;

(g) particulars of any transactions involving directors which have not been disclosed in the notes to the accounts;

(h) whether, in their opinion, the information given in the directors' report is consistent with the accounts prepared for that year.

(i) whether they are satisfied that a medium-sized or small company seeking to rely on filing concessions is entitled to file those accounts and that the said accounts are properly prepared.

Exemptions for small private companies

In certain circumstances, small private companies are exempt from the requirement to have their accounts audited.[10] To qualify, a company must comply with sections 31–33 of the Companies (Amendment) (No.2) Act 1999 and meet the following criteria:

(a) its turnover does not exceed £250,000 (€317,434);

(b) its balance sheet total does not exceed £1,500,000 (€1,903,881);

(c) the average number of employees does not exceed 50;

(d) the company is not one specified in the Second Schedule of the 1999 Act;

(e) the company is not a parent or subsidiary company within the meaning of the European Communities (Companies: Group Accounts) Regulations 1992 (see Chapter 2, Companies in General);

(f) the company is not the holder of a banking licence; and

(g) the company is a not an insurance company.

Before relying on any audit exemption, the directors must be of the opinion, and resolve formally, that the company satisfies the necessary criteria and will avail of the exemption.[11] The company cannot avail of the exemption if members holding at least 10 per cent of the voting rights request the company not to.[12]

---

10 Part 111 of the Companies (Amendment) (No. 2) Act 1999.
11 Section 33 of the Companies (Amendment) (No. 2) Act 1999.
12 Section 33 ibid.

Where the company avails of the exemption, its balance sheet must include a directors' statement to this effect confirming also that the conditions for exemption have been satisfied, that no notice of objection has been received by members and that the obligations of the company to keep proper books of accounts has been satisfied. The statement must be immediately above the directors' signatures.[13]

Section 34 requires that the removal of an auditor, in a situation whereby the company is availing of the exemption, should be accompanied by a notice from the auditor to the company stating that there are no circumstances connected with the removal which should be brought to the attention of the members or creditors of the company. Where there are such circumstances, a statement of the same nature should be sent to the company which must forward it to all members and creditors who are entitled to receive it. The Registrar must be given a copy of the auditor's notice. Where the criteria for exemption can no longer be satisfied, the directors must appoint an auditor as soon as is practicable.[14]

The Annual Return

With the exception of certain investment companies, all companies having a share capital are obliged, by virtue of section 125 of the Principal Act, to file a return on an annual basis with the Registrar of Companies. The matters to be included in the annual return are as follows:

(a) the address of the registered office of the company;
(b) the address of the place where the register of members is kept, if it is not kept at the registered office;
(c) details of all shares issued for cash and other consideration, any calls made, received or unpaid, any commissions paid or discounts given on shares or debentures and any shares forfeited;
(d) particulars of the total amount of indebtedness of the company which is secured by mortgages or charges which are required to be registered;
(e) a list of all persons, including their names and addresses, who on the fourteenth day after the company's AGM are members of the company, and of persons who have ceased to be members since the date of the last return. If the names are not in alphabetical order, it must be accompanied by an index which will enable the name of any person contained therein to be easily found;
(f) details of the shares held by each of the existing members specifying the shares transferred since the date of the last return by existing members and persons who ceased to be members on the date of registration of the transfers;

---

13 Section 33(4) and (5) ibid.
14 Section 35 ibid.

(g) particulars of the directors and secretary that are required to be entered in the company's register of directors and secretary;

(h) details of all political donations made by the company which exceed £4,000 (€5,079); and

(i) the registered number of the company.

In addition, the annual return must state the registered number of the company. The following documents must be annexed to the annual return:

(a) a copy of the balance sheet;

(b) a copy of the profit and loss account;

(c) a copy of the directors' report;

(d) a copy of the auditors' report (where applicable).[15]

Small and medium-sized private companies are exempt from some of the requirements in respect of the annual return. Small companies are permitted to file an abridged balance sheet and are not required to annex copies of the profit and loss account and directors' report. Medium-sized companies are permitted to annex an abridged balance sheet (but the permitted omissions are fewer than in the case of small private companies) and a short form profit and loss account. Where small and medium-sized companies avail of these concessions, a special auditors' report must be annexed to the return. This report will contain the usual requirements of an auditors' report together with a statement that in the auditors' opinion, the directors are entitled to annex abridged accounts and such accounts have been properly prepared.

Under section 127 of the Principal Act, the return shall be made up to a date which is not later than the company's annual return date[16] and delivered to the Registrar of Companies not later than twenty-eight days after the annual return date.[17] The court, or Minister, may in certain circumstances extend the time for delivery.[18]

Breach of either sections 125 and 127 renders the company, and every officer in default, guilty of an offence which may be prosecuted by the Registrar of Companies. Furthermore, the Registrar may strike off the company if it fails in any one year to file an annual return.

---

15 Section 7 of the Companies (Amendment) Act 1986.

16 Section 127(1) of the Principal Act.

17 Section 127(2) of the Principal Act.

18 Section 127(3) and section 153(2) of the Principal Act.

CHAPTER TWENTY

AUDITORS

Appointment

The first auditors of the company may be appointed by the directors or, failing this, the company in general meeting. Thereafter, the company in general meeting must appoint an auditor to hold office from the conclusion of that meeting until the conclusion of the next such meeting.[1] A retiring auditor will automatically be reappointed at the AGM without the need for an authorising resolution unless any of the following occur:

(a he is not qualified for appointment;
(b) a resolution has been passed at that meeting appointing somebody instead of him or providing expressly that he shall not be reappointed;
(c) he has given notice in writing of his unwillingness to be reappointed;
(d) notice of a resolution to appoint a replacement has been given, but the proposed resolution cannot be passed by reason of the death, incapacity or disqualification of the replacement.

Casual vacancies in the office of auditor may be filled by the directors or by the company in general meeting.

Where the AGM fails to appoint an auditor, the company must notify the Minister, within one week, of that fact.[2] The Minister may then appoint a person to fill the vacancy. Failure to notify the Minister renders the company and every officer in default liable to a fine not exceeding £1,000 (€1,270).

The Companies Acts recognise the practice of appointing more than one person as auditor of a company. Section 160(9) of the Principal Act provides that where a firm is appointed as the auditors of a company, the partners for the time being of that firm, who are qualified to be auditors of a company, are deemed to be the company's auditors. Accordingly, any change in the partners of that firm during the relevant period will not constitute a change of auditors.

Qualifications for Appointment

Section 187(1) of the 1990 Act sets out a list of persons who are qualified to be company auditors. These persons must be members of an accountancy body recognised by the Minister. The bodies currently recognised are as follows:

---

1 Section 160(1) of the Principal Act.
2 Section 160(5A) of the Principal Act, as inserted by section 183 of the Companies Act 1990.

(a) the Institute of Chartered Accountants in Ireland, England, Wales and Scotland;
(b) the Institute of Certified Public Accountants in Ireland; and
(c) the Chartered Association of Certified Accountants.
(d) the Institute of Incorporated Public Accountants Ltd.

A person qualified to act as an auditor by virtue of his membership of a recognised body must hold a valid practising certificate from the body in question. The Director of Corporate Enforcement may also enquire as to a person's qualifications to act as an auditor and, where that person is not qualified, can facilitate prosecution.

Section 187(2) provides that none of the following persons shall be qualified for appointment as auditor of a company:

(a) an officer or servant of the company;
(b) a person who was an officer or servant of the company;
(c) a parent, spouse, brother, sister or child of an officer of the company;
(d) a person who is a partner of or in the employment of an officer of the company;
(e) a person who is disqualified, for any of the above reasons, for appointment as an auditor of any other body corporate which is a subsidiary or holding company of the company or is a subsidiary of the company's holding company, whether or not that body corporate is a company;
(f) a person who is disqualified, for any of the above reasons, for appointment as an auditor of any industrial or provident society which is a subsidiary or holding company of the company or a subsidiary of the company's holding company;
(g) a body corporate.

Furthermore, a person is prohibited from acting as an auditor of any company if he has been subject to a disqualification order by the court under Part VII of the 1990 Act. A person who acts as an auditor, or gives directions or instructions in relation to the conduct of an audit or works in any capacity in the conduct of an audit, while the subject of a disqualification order, will be guilty of an offence.

Auditors' Duties

1. Statutory Duties

The principal statutory duties of an auditor are as follows:

(a) to make a report to the members and to ensure that such a report complies with the provisions of section 193(4) of the 1990 Act;
(b) to report any failure to keep proper books of accounts;[3]
(c) to carry out the audit with professional integrity;[4]

---

3 Section 194 of the Companies Act 1990.
4 Section 193(6) of the Companies Act 1990.

(d) to disclose all directors' emoluments if they are not already disclosed in the accounts;[5]

(e) to inform a designated officer of the company on becoming aware that the company is defrauding the Revenue Commissioners and to require the company to rectify the situation. Where an auditor is not satisfied that remedial action has taken place to rectify the situation within six months, he must resign by giving notice to the designated officer of the company, and he must not act for the company for a period of three years. Failure to comply with this requirement renders the auditor liable on summary conviction to a fine not exceeding £1,000 (€1,270) and on indictment to a fine not exceeding £5,000 (€6,349) or two years' imprisonment, or to both;

(f) to make themselves familiar with the companies articles of association;

(g) to notify the Director where the auditors form the opinion that there are reasonable grounds for believing that an indictable offence under the Companies Acts has been committed; and

(h) to co-operate with the Director of Corporate Entertainment.

2. Duty of Care and Skill

In addition to the statutory duties, auditors are under a common law duty to act honestly and with reasonable care and skill. The mere verification of the numerical accuracy of the accounts does not discharge this duty. The auditor must also ensure that omissions and untruths are not made and irregularities are investigated.[6] In *Re Thomas Gerrard & Sons Ltd*,[7] the managing director falsified accounts by including non-existent stock. As a result of the overstated profits, additional taxes were paid by the company and dividends were declared which otherwise would not have been. The auditors became suspicious when they discovered that invoices relating to the stock had been altered. Rather than investigate the matter they accepted the managing director's explanation. The auditors were held liable to the company for the amounts paid by way of dividends and excess taxes. In deciding whether an auditor has failed in his duties, the courts will take into account the standard statement of accountancy practices and auditing guidelines for the profession.[8]

To Whom is the Duty Owed?

Because auditors have a contractual relationship with the company, a duty of care is owed to the company. However, since the decision in *Hedley Byrne & Co. Ltd v. Heller Partners*,[9] it is clear that a person may also be liable for financial loss resulting

---

5 Section 191(8) of the Companies Act 1990.

6 *Fomento (Sterling Area) Ltd v. Selsdon Fountain Pen Co.* [1958] 1 All ER 11.

7 [1967] 2 All ER 525.

8 *Kelly v. Haughey, Boland & Co.* unreported, High Court, 30 July 1985.

9 [1964] AC 465.

from a negligent statement, even if there is no contractual relationship between the person making the statement and the person who relied upon it. In the absence of a contractual or statutory relationship, the plaintiff must demonstrate the following:

1. there was a sufficient degree of proximity between the defendant and the plaintiff;
2. the person who made the statement did so in a professional capacity which makes it reasonably foreseeable that the plaintiff will rely on what he says;
3. the plaintiff does rely on what was said and in doing so suffered a loss which was reasonably foreseeable.[10]

The principles laid down in *Hedley Byrne* are significant because in practice shareholders and prospective investors often rely on the audited accounts and auditors' statement. In *JEB Fasteners Ltd v. Marks, Bloom & Co.*,[11] the defendant firm had prepared an audited set of accounts which showed an over-inflated stock valuation. The auditors knew that the company, which was in financial difficulty, was seeking capital investments. The plaintiffs were shown the accounts and, although they were suspicious of the stock valuation, proceeded to purchase the company. When their investment subsequently failed they sued the auditors of the company for negligent misstatement. In applying the test laid down in *Hedley Byrne*, the court held that the defendants were negligent in preparing the accounts, and that they owed the plaintiffs a duty of care as they ought to have foreseen that outside investors would rely on the accounts. However, the court concluded that the plaintiffs would not have acted any differently had they known the true position of the accounts, because they were only interested in buying the company to obtain the services of two of its directors.

The judgment in *JEB Fasteners* was followed in the Irish case of *Kelly v. Haughey Boland & Co.*[12] There, the plaintiffs planned to purchase the company to which the defendants were auditors. On this basis they were given a series of the company's audited accounts and, at a number of subsequent meetings, the company's auditors explained these accounts to them. Following the purchase the plaintiffs discovered a number of inaccuracies in the accounts and sued the auditors for negligent misstatement. It was held that the auditors were in breach of their duty of care to the plaintiffs. However, as the plaintiffs could not show a direct link between the negligence of the auditors and the loss they suffered, the action failed.

A much more restrictive approach was followed by the House of Lords in *Caparo Industries plc v. Dickman*.[13] In March 1984, the plaintiffs had purchased a number of Fidelity shares in the open market. When the accounts of Fidelity, published

---

10 *Hedley Byrne & Co. Ltd v. Heller & Partners*, ibid. note 9.
11 [1981] 3 All ER 289.
12 Unreported, High Court, 30 July 1985.
13 [1990] 2 AC 605.

in June of that year, revealed substantial profits the plaintiffs purchased further shares. By October they had purchased or received acceptances on enough of the issued shares to acquire the balance by way of compulsory purchase. The plaintiffs later claimed that their reliance on the 1984 accounts, which were inaccurate, had caused them a loss. The House of Lords decided that the relationship between a potential investor and the auditor of the company was not sufficiently proximate to satisfy the *Hedley Byrne* test, particularly as the auditors did not know of the plaintiffs' take-over plans for the company. The court also dismissed the plaintiffs' claim that the auditors owed a duty to existing shareholders who wished to buy more shares in the company. The auditors did not fare as well in *Morgan Crucible Co. plc v Hill Samuel Co. Ltd.*[14] Here, during the course of a take-over bid, a profits forecast, that was supported by a letter from the auditors, was issued. As the auditors were aware of the proposed take-over and the purpose of the profits forecast, they were held to have owed a duty of care.

Rights of Auditors

In order to fulfil their statutory duties, auditors are conferred with the following rights.

(a) The right of access to the books, accounts and vouchers of the company.[15]
(b) The right to require from the officers and employees of the company such information and explanations as the auditors think necessary for the performance of these duties. Any person who fails to give such information, within two days of the request, or any person who knowingly or recklessly gives false information, will be guilty of an offence. However, it will be a defence to show that the request was complied with within a reasonable time.
(c) The right to request information and explanations from either any of the company's subsidiary companies incorporated in the state or their auditors. If the subsidiary is incorporated outside the state, it is the duty of the holding company to obtain such information from the subsidiary. Failure to comply within five days with any such request for information renders the company or its auditor liable on summary conviction to a fine not exceeding £1,000 (€1,270) or on indictment to a fine not exceeding £10,000 (€12,697). It will be a defence to show that the request was complied with as soon as was reasonably possible.
(d) The right to attend any general meeting and to receive the same notices and communications relating to such meetings as the members. Auditors also have the right to be heard at such meetings on any matter which concerns them as auditors. In the case of a single-member company, the auditor may even requisition an AGM.

---

14 [1991] Ch 295.
15 Section 193(3) of the Companies Act 1990.

Removal of Auditors

An auditor, other than the first auditor of the company, may be removed by an ordinary resolution of the company in general meeting.[16] Where a resolution proposes to remove or replace an auditor or fill a casual vacancy in the office of auditor, extended notice of the proposed resolution is required.[17] The auditor concerned must be sent a copy of the proposed resolution and must be given the right to make representations to the company and to request that such representations be notified to the members.[18] Where a request is made, the company must, unless it is too late to do so, circulate the members with a copy of the representations. Where the representations have not been circulated, the auditor may require them to be read out at the meeting at which it is proposed that he be removed. An application may be made to the court to prevent the auditor's right to make representations being abused. The court may order that the representations need not be circulated or read out if it is satisfied that to do so would secure needless publicity for defamatory matters.

An auditor is also conferred with the following rights in the event that his removal or replacement is proposed:

(a) to attend the AGM at which, but for his removal, his term of office would have expired;
(b) to attend the general meeting at which it is proposed to fill the vacancy caused by his removal;
(c) to receive all notices and communications relating to the above meetings which a member is entitled to receive;
(d) to be heard at such a meeting on any part of the business of the meeting which concerns him as former auditor of the company.

Resignation of Auditors

An auditor is permitted to resign before the expiry of his term of appointment.[19] To effect such a resignation, the auditor must serve a notice in writing on the company which contains a statement of the circumstances, if any, connected with his resignation, which he considers should be brought to the attention of members and creditors. Failure on the part of the auditor to state those circumstances, if any, constitutes an offence. Where a statement of such circumstances has been notified to the company, it must, within fourteen days of the notices being served, send a copy of the notice to every person entitled to

---

16 Section 160(5) of the Principal Act as amended by section 163 of the Companies Act 1990.
17 Section 161(1)(a) and (b) of the Principal Act as amended by section 184 of the Companies Act 1990.
18 Section 161(3) of the Principal Act.
19 Section 185(1) of the Companies Act 1990.

receive copies of the annual accounts. Failure by the company to circulate the notice constitutes an offence.

Where those circumstances have been notified to the company, the auditor is also entitled to requisition a general meeting of the company for the purpose of considering these circumstances.[20] Where such a requisition has been made, the directors must convene a general meeting for a day not later than twenty-eight days after being served the resignation notice. The auditor is entitled to attend and be heard at such a meeting.

An auditor who has resigned is also entitled to attend and be heard at the AGM at which, but for his resignation, his term of office would have expired, and at any meeting at which it is proposed to fill the vacancy caused by his resignation. The Registrar of Companies must be notified of any resignation by the company's auditors within fourteen days of the notice to resign being served on the company.

Remuneration of Auditors

The remuneration and expenses of an auditor appointed by the directors or by the Minister is fixed by the person who appointed him.[21] Where the auditors are appointed by members, it is the AGM that fixes the remuneration or determines the manner in which it is to be fixed. In practice, the AGM usually delegates this power to the directors.

Current Legislative Developments

In light of recent high-profile scandals that centre upon poor and, in some instances, grossly negligent accountancy practices,[22] much attention has turned towards the role of auditors in the overall context of good corporate governance principles. In Ireland, the report of the Review Group on Auditing was published in 2000. The report made recommendations in relation to the following:

(a) the role of auditors in ensuring compliance with statutory provisions;
(b) the auditing of financial institutions;
(c) the regulation of the auditing and accountancy profession (an interim Irish Auditing and Accounting Supervisory Authority (IASSA) Board was established in 2001); and
(d) the creation of internal audit committees akin to the system which exists in the United States.

---

20 Section 186 of the Companies Act 1990.
21 Section 160(8) of the Principal Act.
22 The collapse of Enron in the United States and the subsequent successful prosecution of Enron's auditors has prompted a major world-wide focus on accountancy practices and auditors' duties.

Many of the recommendations are now contained in the draft scheme of the Company Law (Audit and Accountancy) (Amendment) Bill, approved by the government in December 2001, which is expected to progress during the term of the next Dáil.

CHAPTER TWENTY-ONE

INSIDER DEALING

Introduction

Economic analysis of publicly quoted companies rests largely on the hypothesis that the market for shares and securities is efficient. This hypothesis, referred to as the 'efficient market hypothesis', suggests that share prices correctly reflect all public information available about those shares. According to the theory, it is only unforeseen new information that affects share prices. If information is the key to turning a profit or avoiding a loss, then clearly those with undisclosed price-sensitive information can use it to their advantage when buying or selling shares. Company directors and officers are in an ideal position to acquire knowledge about their company's affairs before it becomes publicly available and to use this information to make a personal profit.

The law recognises this potential abuse by imposing a fiduciary duty on directors, which prohibits their using company information to make a personal gain. More importantly, as the wrong is done to the company, it is given a cause of action to reclaim any profits made by directors in such circumstances. Furthermore, the statutory obligations imposed on companies to maintain a register of directors' interests in company securities enables other members to ascertain the true extent of the directors' involvement in the company.

Equity's insistence that directors ought not use their position to further their personal interests has been considered in Chapter 18. However, the available remedies are rarely invoked, for a number of reasons. First, the members have ordinarily no right against the directors whose duties are owed to the company,[1] although in exceptional cases a duty to the shareholders may be said to exist, where directors have put themselves in a special position *vis-à-vis* their dealings with them.[2] Accordingly, any action against the directors must be taken by the company which, as the beneficiary of the duty, is the only proper claimant for the available relief.[3] The difficulty lies in the fact that such a decision must be taken by the board of directors, which is unlikely to cause the company to sue one of their own.[4] Therefore it is only in the most unusual circumstances, such as when a company is taken over or wound up, that it will take action against the errant directors.

---

1 *Percival v. Wright* [1902] 2 Ch 421.
2 *Coleman v. Meyers* [1977] 2 NZLR 225, considered in Chapter 18.
3 Unless an exception to the rule in *Foss v. Harbottle* applies: see Chapter 15.
4 Cf. *Industrial Developments Ltd v. Cooley* [1972] 2 All ER 162.

Insider dealing is objectionable not just because of the potential wrong done to the company itself, but also because it affects the integrity of the securities market. As Bingham CJ. observed in *R v. Staines*:[5]

> The integrity of the market depends on equality of knowledge, since fair operation of the market is jeopardised if those who are 'in the know' (often called 'market insiders') can exploit information for their personal advantage which they have obtained in the course of their professional activities when such information is unavailable to others.

This consequence of insider trading has finally been given legislative recognition by the enactment of Part V of the Companies Act 1990, which tackles insider dealing head-on for the first time in this jurisdiction.[6]

Part V of the 1990 Act

1. General Prohibition

Section 108(1) makes it unlawful for a person, who is, or at any time in the preceding six months was, connected with a company to deal in its securities if that person is in possession of price-sensitive information which is not generally available. Furthermore, the prohibition applies only where the purpose of the transaction is to secure a profit or gain for the person involved.

The prohibition applies to 'dealing', which is defined in section 107 as the

> acquiring, disposing of, subscribing for or underwriting the securities; or making or offering to make, or inducing or attempting to induce a person to make or offer to make, an agreement —
> (a) for or relating to acquiring, disposing of, subscribing for or underwriting the securities; or
> (b) the purpose or purported purpose of which is to secure a profit or gain to a person who acquires, disposes of, subscribes for or underwrites the securities or to any of the parties to the agreement in relation to the securities.

For the purposes of Part V of the Act 'securities' means:

> (a) shares, debentures or other debt securities, issued or proposed to be issued . . . whether in the state or otherwise[7] and for which dealing facilities are, or are to be, provided by a recognised Stock Exchange; and
> (b) any right, option or obligation in respect of any such shares, debentures or other debt securities referred to in paragraph (a); and

---

5 [1997] 2 CR App Rep 426.
6 The Companies Act 1990 incorporates most of the provisions of the 1989 EEC Directive on Co-ordinating Regulations on Insider Dealings: 89/592/EEC.
7 Part V of the Companies Act 1990 originally included dealings in securities outside the state. However, the Companies Act 1990 (Insider Dealing) Regulations 1992 (SI 131 of 1992) excludes the application of section 108 to such dealings.

(c) any right, option or obligation in respect of any index relating to any such shares, debentures, or other debt securities referred to in paragraph (a); or

(d) such interests as may be prescribed.

Although the provisions refer only to those securities which are quoted or will be quoted on the Stock Exchange, they leave open the possibility of the Minister extending their scope to such interests as he may prescribe, which could encompass shares or securities in unquoted companies.

Section 108(2) extends the basic prohibition on insider dealing to prevent a person who is, or at any time in the preceding six months has been, connected with the company from dealing in securities of any other company, if the information relates to a transaction between the two companies. This prohibition applies even where the transactions were, but are no longer, contemplated. A person is connected if he is:

(a) an officer, which includes directors (and shadow directors), secretaries, employees, liquidators, examiners, auditors and receivers, of that company or a related company;

(b) a shareholder in that company or in a related company; or

(c) occupying a position which may reasonably be expected to give him access to inside information by virtue of his professional, business or other relationship with the company or a related company or by his being an officer of a substantial shareholder in that company or a related company.

2. *Prohibition Imposed on 'Tippees'*

Section 108(3) makes it unlawful for a person to deal in securities if he has received price-sensitive information from another person, often referred to as a 'tipper', and is, or ought reasonably to be, aware of the facts and circumstances which preclude the tipper from dealing in those securities. Where a person is prohibited from dealing in securities in any of the above mentioned ways, it is also unlawful for him to cause or procure any other person to deal in those securities.[8] Indeed, the mere communication of price-sensitive information is unlawful if that person knows or ought reasonably to know that the recipient will use it for the purpose of dealing or causing or procuring another person to deal in those securities. It would appear to be irrelevant that the information communicated does not identify the individual company whose securities are the subject of the insider dealing. What is relevant is the fact that the information is sufficient to enable the recipient to identify the company whose securities are involved, even where further investigation is necessary to discover that identification.[9]

---

8 Section 108(4).

9 *R v. Staines, R v. Morrisey* [1997] 2 CR App Rep 426.

3. Dealing by Companies

A company is generally prohibited from dealing in securities when one of its officers is so prohibited.[10] However, the prohibition will not apply where a decision to deal is taken, on the company's behalf, by a person other than the officer concerned. To secure this derogation, the company must have written arrangements in place, referred to in the financial services industry as 'Chinese walls', which ensure that no information or advice relating to the transaction is given to that person and no information or advice was in fact given. Supposing a financial services company had both a dealing division and a mergers and acquisitions division. If the latter is aware of price-sensitive information relating to a particular company's securities, such as a proposed merger, the dealing division can still deal in those securities, provided that a formal system is in place which ensures that the price-sensitive information remains within the mergers division.

A company is further exempted in circumstances where the price-sensitive information is itself the fact that the company proposes to deal in the securities in question.[11]

Section 108(10) provides an additional exemption where notice is given to the Stock Exchange of the person's intention to deal and the Stock Exchange publishes this notice. However, in such a circumstance, the dealing must take place within a specified 'window period' beginning seven days after the publication of the company's interim or final results, as the case may be, and ending fourteen days after the relevant publication.

4. Exemption for Stabilising Activities

Section 108 will not be regarded as contravened where stabilising activity takes place in conformity with the Stabilisation Rules set out in the Schedule to the Companies (Amendment) Act 1999.

5. Dealing by Others

Dealing on behalf of another person, where the dealer has reasonable cause to believe or to conclude that the deal is contrary to section 108, is prohibited and a person found guilty of dealing in this manner shall be guilty of an offence.[12]

6. Exemptions from the Prohibition

Section 110 sets out what could be regarded as further exemptions from the provisions contained in section 108. The prohibition will not apply to persons who:

 (i) acquire securities under a will or on the intestacy of another person; or

---

10 Section 108(6).
11 Section 108(8).
12 Section 113.

(ii) acquire securities in a company pursuant to an employee profit-share scheme, provided that all the employees of the company are offered the opportunity to acquire the securities on the same terms, the company has approved the terms of the scheme in general meeting, and the approval of the Revenue Commissioners is obtained;

(iii) acquire a right to shares in a company under a scheme approved by the Revenue Commissioners for the purposes of the Tax Acts and the Capital Gain Tax Acts;

(iv) enter into, in good faith, any of the following transactions —

    (a) the acquisition by a director of a share qualification under section 180 of the Principal Act;

    (b) a transaction pursuant to obligations in an underwriting agreement;

    (c) a transaction by a personal representative of a deceased person, a trustee, or liquidator, receiver or examiner in the performance of the functions of his office; or

    (d) a transaction by way of or arising out of a security interest taken over the securities or the documents of title to securities.

Nor will the prohibition apply to transactions entered into in pursuit of monetary, exchange rate, national debt management or foreign exchange reserve policies by any Government Minister, the Central Bank or by any person on their behalf.

7. *Civil Liability for Unlawful Dealing*

Civil liability for insider dealing is imposed by section 109. The liability is twofold. First, the person is liable to compensate any other party to the transaction who sustained a loss.[13] The compensation will be the difference between the price of the securities at the time of the transaction and the price at which they would have been dealt in if the information had been generally available. Because of the difficulty in matching up sales and purchases, it will not be an easy task to prove a loss, particularly where the transaction involved securities bought or sold through stockbrokers. Second, the person is liable to account to the company, whose securities were unlawfully dealt, for any profit which accrued to him.

8. *Criminal Liability for Unlawful Dealing*

A person who deals, on his own or on some other person's behalf, in securities when prohibited from so doing shall be guilty of an offence. The guilty person is liable on summary conviction to a term of imprisonment not exceeding twelve months or a fine not exceeding £10,000 (€12,697), or to both, and on indictment to imprisonment for a term of imprisonment not exceeding ten years or a fine not

---

13 Subject to a two year limitation period: section 109(4).

exceeding £200,000 (€253,948), or to both.[14] Furthermore, a person convicted of an offence is prohibited from any dealing for twelve months from the date of conviction.[15] In this regard, transactions which were commenced before the conviction can be completed if the Stock Exchange indicates in writing to the parties to the transaction, its satisfaction that:

(a) the transaction was initiated but not completed before the date of the conviction; and
(b) if the transaction is not concluded, the rights of an innocent third party would be prejudiced; and
(c) the transaction would not be unlawful under any other provision of Part V of the Act.

9. Enforcement of the Provisions

The duty of policing the Act rests with the Stock Exchange. Where it appears to the Stock Exchange or any of its members that an offence has been committed, the Director of Corporate Enforcement (Director) must be notified. The Director must also be furnished with such information and be given access to such facilities for inspecting and taking copies of any documents in the possession of, or under the control of, the Stock Exchange, as he so requires. If it appears to a court that an offence has been committed which has not been reported to the Director, the court may direct the Stock Exchange to make such a report.[16] If the Director, on receipt of a report, has reasonable grounds for believing that an offence has been committed and he either initiates proceedings in respect of that offence or refers the matter to the Director of Public Prosecutions (DPP) who himself institutes proceedings in respect of that offence, the Stock Exchange and every officer of the company whose securities are concerned, or such other person as may have relevant information, must give all assistance in connection with the proceedings as can reasonably be given.

If it appears to the Director, following a complaint to the Stock Exchange that the Stock Exchange ought to have exercised its powers or reported a matter to the Director but has not done so, he may direct the relevant authority to exercise its powers or make a report.

Section 116 imposes a duty on the Stock Exchange to exercise its powers under the Act when requested to do so by a similar authority in another Member State of the European Union. The Stock Exchange must notify the Director of such a request and the Director may direct it not to co-operate if specific statutory grounds apply.

Section 117 confers on the Stock Exchange a statutory power to appoint

---

14 Section 114.
15 Section 112.
16 Section 115(3).

authorised persons to investigate suspicious cases. Where an alleged offence is being investigated by an authorised person, the Stock Exchange must ensure that potential conflicts of interest are avoided on the part of the authorised person. Where an authorised person has reasonable cause to believe that any person has dealt with securities in a manner prohibited by the Act, or has information about such dealings, he may require that person:

(a) to produce to him such information as is reasonably necessary to carry out his investigation; and

(b) to give him access to, and facilities for, inspecting and taking copies of any documents relating to the matter as he reasonably requires.

Information obtained by the Stock Exchange or by an authorised person shall not be disclosed except in accordance with the law.[17] Persons in breach of this confidentiality requirement shall be guilty of an offence.

10.Annual Report of the Stock Exchange

The Stock Exchange must present an annual report to the Minister detailing the number of written complaints received, the number of reports made to the DPP and the number of instances in which the powers of investigation were exercised by its authorised persons but were not made to the DPP. In its 2000 Report the Stock Exchange stated that:

(a) Four written complaints were received in relation to alleged breaches of the Insider Dealing provisions of the Companies Acts;

(b) No reports were made to the DPP;

(c) Authorised persons exercised their statutory rights in relation to seven investigations into suspected breaches of Insider Dealing rules.

---

17 Section 118.

CHAPTER TWENTY-TWO

INVESTIGATION OF COMPANIES

Introduction

Under sections 165–173 of the Principal Act, the responsibility of appointing inspectors to investigate the affairs of companies was vested in the Minister. In practice, the power was seldom invoked due to both a reluctance on the part of successive Ministers to exercise their powers and to the limited circumstances in which the powers could be exercised. Part II of the Companies Act 1990 repealed and replaced the 1963 provisions, and the power to order investigations was transferred to the High Court. The Minister was still given unilateral powers to appoint inspectors to investigate the *membership* of a company and the present incumbent has exercised this power in a number of high-profile cases. Since the introduction of the Company Law Enforcement Act 2001, the Minister's powers in this regard have now been transferred to the Director of Corporate Enforcement (the Director).

Types of Investigations and Inquiries

1. Court Investigations

Under section 7(1) of the Companies Act the High Court may appoint one or more inspectors to investigate the affairs of a company and to report thereon in a manner directed by the court. The order may be made on the application of any of the following:

(a) in the case of a company having a share capital, either at least 100 members, or members holding at least one-tenth of the paid-up share capital of the company;
(b) in the case of a company not having a share capital, not less than one-fifth in number of the members;
(c) the company itself;
(d) a director of a company;
(e) a creditor of a company.

An application to the High Court must be supported by such evidence as the court may require or as may be prescribed by way of ministerial regulation.[1] The court may also require applicants to put up security for the costs of the investigation which must not be less than £5,000 (€6,349) and must not exceed £250,000 (€317,435).[2] This security requirement may prove a deterrent for applicants with genuine grievances as well as vexatious applicants.

---

1 Section 7(2) (no such regulations have been introduced by the Minister in relation to company investigations).
2 Section 7(3).

Section 8(1) further empowers the court to order an investigation into the company's affairs on the application of the Director. However, the court must be satisfied that there are circumstances suggesting —

(a) that its affairs are being or have been conducted with the intent to defraud its creditors or the creditors of any other person or otherwise for a fraudulent or unlawful purpose or in an unlawful manner which is unfairly prejudicial to some part of its members, or that any actual or proposed act or omission of the company (including an act or omission on its behalf) is or would be so prejudicial, or that it was formed for a fraudulent or unlawful purpose; or

(b) that persons connected with its formation or the management of its affairs have in connection therewith been guilty of fraud, misfeasance or other misconduct towards it or towards its members; or

(c) that its members have not been given all the information relating to its affairs which they might reasonably expect.

The Director may request that one of his officers be appointed as Inspector. A number of points arise in relation to (a) above. First, the reference to 'members' has, by virtue of section 8(2)(b), been extended to include not only those whose names appear on the register of members, but also those who acquired shares by operation of law, but who have not yet been registered or who have been refused registration as members. Accordingly, an apparent defect in previous legislation has been remedied by equating such persons with registered members for the purpose of the provision. Secondly, the importation of the English standard of conduct which is 'unfairly prejudicial' is unusual as it departs from the long-established statutory standard of 'oppressive' conduct which has heretofore been used in Ireland.[3] The manner in which the Irish courts will construe this new terminology remains to be seen.

It should be noted that the power to order an investigation under section 8 is exercisable with respect to a company notwithstanding that it is in the course of being wound up.[4]

The scope of an inspector's investigation and subsequent report on 'the affairs of the company' is a matter for the court. However, section 9 gives the inspector the power, subject to court approval, to extend his investigation into the affairs of a related company, where he considers it necessary for the purpose of his investigation.The definition of 'related company' has been extended beyond the normal statutory meaning (see Chapter 2) to include a company with which the investigated company has a 'commercial relationship'.

---

3 See Chapter 15.
4 Section 8(2)(a).

2. Section 14 Investigations by the Director

The Director may, under section 14 of the Act, appoint an inspector to investigate and report on the membership of any company for the purpose of determining the true persons who are or have been financially interested in the success or failure of the company, or who control or materially influence the policy of the company.

Grounds for a Section 14 Appointment

Before the Director can appoint an inspector, section 14(2) provides that he must be of the opinion that there are circumstances suggesting that the appointment is necessary:

(a) for the effective administration of the law relating to companies; or
(b) for the effective discharge by the Director of his functions under any enactment; or
(c) in the public interest.

Scope of a Section 14 Investigation

The scope of an investigation ordered by the Director is determined by the appointment itself,[5] and may include the investigation of any circumstances that suggest the existence of an arrangement or understanding which, though not legally binding, is, was or is likely to be observed in practice.[6] The far-reaching nature of the section 14 investigation can be seen in *Lyons, Kelehan and Murphy v. Curran.*[7] An inspector had been appointed to investigate and report on a number of companies involved in the highly publicised 'Greencore affair'. One of the companies named in the warrant of appointment was Gladebrook, which had purchased shares in a company called Sugar Distributors Holdings Ltd and at a substantial profit had resold them to Siuicre Éireann cpt. Gladebrook was partially owned by a foreign registered company, Talmino, and the inspector included this company in his investigation. The inspector's report later revealed that a director of Siuicre Éireann was the beneficial owner of Talmino. The applicants sought an order of *certiorari* quashing the report, on the grounds, *inter alia*, that:

(a) Talmino was not named in the warrant of appointment and therefore the inspector had no power to investigate its ownership;
(b) the inspector had not sought prior approval under section 9 to investigate a related company; and
(c) if the investigation of Talmino could proceed without the section 9 approval, this would render section 9 a superfluous provision in the Act.

Blayney J. rejected the applicants' contentions. He said that the purpose of the section 14 investigation was to establish the 'true persons' financially interested

---

5 Section 14(3).
6 Section 14(4).
7 [1993] ILRM 375.

in the success or failure of the company. This would necessarily involve ascertaining the persons who were 'entitled to the shares of a corporate member'. On this basis, the inspector did not require prior approval under section 9. As to the continued relevance of section 9, Blayney J. went on to say that prior approval under the section would still be required where the inspector 'thinks' but does not 'know' that it is necessary for the purpose of his investigations to investigate also the membership of another body corporate. Whether this analysis will bear further judicial scrutiny remains to be seen.

3. Section 15 Inquiry by the Director

In certain circumstances the Director may inquire into the ownership of any shares or debentures of a company, without the appointment of inspectors. The grounds for ordering such an inquiry are the same as those for ordering an investigation under section 14. A person who is requested and fails to provide, or knowingly or recklessly provides false information to the Director in relation to any such inquiry is guilty of an offence.

4. Restrictions on Shares

Where, in connection with an investigation or enquiry under sections 14 and 15, it appears to the Director that there is difficulty in finding out the relevant facts about any shares, the Director may, by notice in writing, direct that the shares be subject to the following restrictions:

(a) any transfer of those shares is void;
(b) no voting rights are exercisable in respect of those shares;
(c) no rights issue can be made to the holders of those shares; and
(d) no payment can be made to the shareholders of any sums due on the shares.[8]

Where a transfer of shares takes place in breach of the above restrictions the transfer is void unless the Director lifts the restriction. Where a Director places a restriction on shares, the aggrieved person may apply to the court to have the restriction lifted. The court, or indeed the Director, may lift the restriction if satisfied that the relevant facts have been disclosed about the shares and the shares are being sold under a sale approved by either the court or the Director.

In any case the court may, on the application of the Director or the company, having given notice to the Director, order the 'restricted' shares to be sold. In granting an order for the sale of shares the court may lift the restrictions or continue them in so far as they relate to rights issue or payment entitlements acquired before the transfer. The court may also make such further orders relating to the sale of the shares as it thinks fit. Where the shares are sold on foot of a court order, the proceeds of sale shall be paid into court for the benefit of the

---

8 Section 16(1) and (2) of the Companies Act 1990.

persons beneficially interested in the shares, and those persons may apply to have the proceeds or a proportion thereof paid to them. Before ordering the payment to the interested person, the court may order that the costs of the application by the Director or the company shall be paid out of the proceeds of sale.

Any person who acts in breach of a restriction order or direction shall be guilty of an offence. Where shares are issued in contravention of the restriction, the company and any officer in default will also be guilty of an offence.

5. Section 19 Order

Section 19 also empowers the Director, or an officer authorised by the Director, to require the production of a company's books and papers for inspection. The Director may also take copies of or extracts from the books or documents and require any officer of the company to provide an explanation of them. The section 19 order may be invoked against all companies formed or registered under the Companies Acts, unregistered companies, foreign companies carrying on business within the State, and all insurance companies.

Grounds for a Section 19 Order

The Director may make such an order if he is of the opinion that there are circumstances suggesting that:

(a) it is necessary to examine the books and documents of the body with a view to determining whether an inspector should be appointed; or
(b) the affairs of the company are being or have been conducted with intent to defraud its creditors, the creditors of any other person, the members or for any other fraudulent purpose; or
(c) the affairs are being conducted in a manner which is unfairly prejudicial to some of the members; or
(d) any actual or proposed act or omission or series of acts or omissions would be unfairly prejudicial to some of the members; or
(e) any actual or proposed act or omission or series of acts or omissions are or are likely to be unlawful; or
(f) the body was formed for an unlawful or fraudulent purpose;
(g) the body may be in possession of books or documents containing information relating to the books or documents of a body which come within any of the above circumstances.

The Director may also order the production of books and documents other than those of the company concerned but which may contain information relating to that company's books.

Where the director orders the production of books and documents from a company or person he may also require that person or an officer, past officer or employee of that company provides an explanation of certain matters relating to those books or documents.

Failure to comply with any requirements under this section is an offence. Furthermore, it is an offence for any person who knows or suspects that a Director is investigating, or may investigate, an offence under the Companies Acts, to destroy or conceal any documentary evidence that may relate to that offence.

Powers of Inspectors

Section 10 confers a number of powers on the inspector in relation to the production of documents and evidence relevant to his investigation. Section 10(1) imposes a statutory duty on officers and agents of the company, under inspection or being investigated because of its related status, to produce books and documents of or relating to the company, or those of a related company which is being investigated, which are in their custody or power.[9] A document is within the power of a person if he has an enforceable legal right to obtain sight of it from the person who holds the document.[10] Furthermore, they are required to attend before inspectors when requested to do so, to be examined under oath and to give inspectors all reasonable assistance in connection with the investigation. In this regard there is no obligation on the inspector to carry out all such enquiries in public.[11] For the purposes of this section the term 'officers' includes past and present officers and the term 'agents' includes the company's bankers, solicitors and those persons employed as auditors of the company. Inspectors are given the same powers in relation to third parties that are considered to be in possession of information concerning the affairs of the company or a related company. Where a person fails to produce books, documents or information as requested, and attend before the inspectors and answer any questions, the inspector may certify the refusal to the court, and the court may thereupon enquire into the case and, after hearing any witnesses and any statement offered in defence, make any order or direction it thinks fit.[12]

It is no defence to argue that compliance with an inspector's request to produce books or documents will breach an existing contractual agreement. In *Glackin v. Trustee Savings Banks*[13] it was held that a bank may not refuse to co-operate on the basis that to do so would breach the bank's duty of

---

9 In *Chestvale Properties Ltd and Hoddle Investments Ltd v. Glackin* [1993] 3 IR 35, the court held that an inspector was entitled to demand documents even when their ownership was vested in other companies.

10 *Bula v. Tara Mines* [1994] 1 ILRM 111. See also *Quigley v. Burke*, unreported, Supreme Court, 7 November 1995.

11 *Re Redbreast Preserving Company (Ireland) Ltd*, 91 ILTR 12, and *Re Countyglen plc* [1995] 1 ILRM 213.

12 Section 10(6).

13 [1993] 3 IR 55.

confidentiality towards its customer. According to Costello J. any such contractual arrangements are 'overridden' by the statutory duties imposed. Similarly, it would appear to be the case that a person may not refuse to answer a question which would be self-incriminating.[14] This clearly has implications, particularly as section 18 states that an answer given to an inspector exercising his section 10 powers can later be used in evidence against the person who gave such an answer. Nor is it a defence to a refusal to give evidence on oath that the information had already been submitted to the inspector by way of statutory declaration.[15]

Inspectors appointed by the court are empowered to require directors and connected persons to give details of their private bank accounts, whether held solely or jointly, within or outside the State. This power may be invoked if the inspector reasonably believes that accounts are being maintained which contain amounts that have not been disclosed to the company (when required to be so disclosed) or which are connected with any misconduct on the part of a director towards the company.

If at any stage during the course of an investigation the inspector is required to make a determination which may be damaging to a party, the principles of natural justice must be applied. The inspector is required to act reasonably,[16] the party concerned must be given an opportunity of being heard and fair procedures must be followed.[17]

Inspector's Report

Court-appointed inspectors may, and if so directed by the court shall, make interim reports to the court and on the conclusion of the investigation shall make a final report to the court.[18] An inspector may also, during the course of his investigation, inform the court of matters which tend to show that an offence has been committed.[19] The court shall furnish a copy of the report to the Director and may forward at its discretion a copy to any of the following:

(a) the company's registered office;
(b) any member of the company or other body corporate which is the subject of the report;
(c) any person whose conduct is referred to in the report;

---

14 *Heaney v. Ireland* [1996] 1 IR 580, *Gilligan v. Criminal Assets Bureau* [1998] 3 IR 185, *R v. Harris* [1970] 2 All ER 746, but cf. *Saunders v. The United Kingdom* (43/1994/490/572).
15 *Probets v. Glackin* [1993] 3 IR 134.
16 *O'Keefe v. An Bord Pleanala* [1993] 1 IR 39.
17 *Re Pergamon Press Ltd* [1970] 3 All ER 589 and *Chestvale Properties Ltd v. Glackin* [1993] 3 IR 35.
18 Section 11(1).
19 Section 11(2).

(d) the auditors of that company or body corporate;

(e) the applicants for the investigation;

(f) any other person including an employee, creditor or other body corporate whose financial interests appear to the court to be affected by the matters dealt with in the report;

(g) the Central Bank, where the report relates to the affairs of a holder of a banking licence under section 9 of the Central Bank Act 1971.

(h) such other authorities as the court may direct.

The court may also cause the report to be printed and published but may direct that a part of the report be omitted from the printed or published form.

Having considered the inspector's report, the court may make such order as it deems fit, including:

(a) an order for the winding up of the company;

(b) an order for the purpose of remedying any disability suffered by any persons whose interests were adversely affected by the conduct of the affairs of the company, provided that when making such an order the court has regard for the interests of any other person who may be adversely affected by the order.[20]

Furthermore, the Director may, on the basis of the report, present a petition for the winding up of the company on the grounds that it is just and equitable to do so.[21]

Expenses of the Investigation

The expenses of an investigation ordered by the court will be defrayed in the first instance by the Minister for Justice, Equality and Law Reform. However, the court may direct that a body corporate dealt with in the report or the applicant for the investigation repay the Minister up to a maximum amount of £250,000 (€317,435). Similarly, any of the following parties may be ordered to repay all or part of the costs of the investigation:

(a) any person convicted of an indictable offence;

(b) any person ordered to pay damages or restore any property as a result of the investigation;

(c) any person who was awarded damages or to whom property was restored as a result of the investigation.

---

20 Section 12(1).
21 Section 12(2).

CHAPTER TWENTY-THREE

REORGANISATION OF COMPANIES

Introduction

In certain circumstances companies may wish or be forced to undergo fundamental changes. This may involve the reorganisation of the capital structure, ownership or assets of the company or it may involve drastic changes in relation to the company which can prove terminal, not only for the company but also its underlying business and undertaking.

Whichever is the case, the law sets out certain procedures that must be followed, usually with some degree of independent supervision. In Chapters 25 and 26 the most drastic form of change in relation to a company — its winding up — is described in detail. The reorganisation of an insolvent company by way of a compromise and scheme of arrangement is discussed in Chapter 27. The following methods of reorganisation are discussed in this chapter:

(a) schemes of arrangement under sections 201–203 of the Principal Act;
(b) scheme of reconstruction under section 260 or 271 of the Principal Act; and
(c) amalgamations.

Schemes of Arrangement under Sections 201–203

Sections 201–203 of the Principal Act attempt to deal with a process of structured reorganisation which would involve the company in an arrangement[1] or compromise with its creditors, members or any class of them. This process may be engaged when a restructuring of the company's share capital is required or it may arise as part of the winding-up process. There is no requirement that the company is insolvent before the procedure can be invoked.[2]

Where a compromise or scheme of arrangement is proposed an application may be made to the court to call a meeting of the various classes of creditors or members.[3] The application may be made by the company, a creditor or member or, in the case of a company being wound up, by the liquidator.

The application is made by way of Special Summons based on an affidavit, usually by a director, setting out in detail the terms of the scheme. On hearing the application the court is not concerned with the merits of, or giving its approval to, the scheme. Rather, if the court is satisfied that *prima facie* the proposal is

---

1 Section 201(7) of the Principal Act.
2 By contrast, a company must be insolvent before an examiner can be appointed and a scheme of arrangement put in place under the Companies (Amendment) Act 1990: see Chapter 27.
3 Section 201(1) of the Principal Act.

suitable for consideration as a scheme of arrangement, it may then direct that a meeting of the various classes of creditors and members be held.

Where an application is made the court may, on such terms as it thinks just, stay all proceedings or restrain further proceedings against the company.[4] The purpose of this provision is to prevent any individual creditor from pre-empting any possible arrangement by getting a judgment in his favour.

1. Class Meetings

It is up to the company to decide on the different classes of creditors and members. Once this has been done the various meetings must be summoned. The information that must be provided with the notice of the meeting is set out in section 202 as follows:

(a) a statement explaining the effect of the compromise or arrangement;
(b) details of any material interests of the directors and the effect thereon of the compromise and scheme in so far as it differs from the effect on the interests of other persons;
(c) a statement of the effect of the scheme on the rights of debenture holders.

Section 201(3) provides that a majority in number representing 75 per cent in value of the creditors or members or class of creditors or members present must vote in favour of the scheme before it will be sanctioned by the court. This means that each class must consent to the scheme. This aspect differs from the procedure for effecting a compromise or scheme of arrangement under the Companies (Amendment) Act 1990, which requires that only one class of creditor need approve the scheme. In that instance, classes of creditors or members may be forced to accept a scheme. The difficulty with the section 201 procedure is that a class can effectively veto any compromise or scheme. This has proved to be a main stumbling block for schemes of arrangement proposed for an insolvent company because the preferential or indeed the secured creditors are unlikely to approve a compromise to their claims when they enjoy a superior position in a liquidation situation.

It is up to the company to decide on the different classes of creditors or members. Great care should be taken in this regard, because if within one class of shareholders there are groups whose interests in the proposed scheme are clearly different, the court must be asked to order that separate meetings be called of each group. This is where the constitution of class meetings will differ from those held in the winding up of a company. Where a scheme does not distinguish each such group (to be consulted separately), the court will at the final decision stage withhold its approval on the ground that there has not been fair and proper consultation.

---

4 Section 201(2) of the Principal Act.

In *Re Hellenic and General Trust*,[5] a scheme of arrangement was agreed by the ordinary shareholders of Hellenic, the effect of which was that the shareholders would receive cash and ultimately the company would be taken over by a bank. When court approval for the scheme was sought, a minority shareholder objected on the grounds that the majority shareholder, who voted in favour of the scheme, was in fact a subsidiary of the company which would ultimately take control of Hellenic. If that majority shareholder had not constituted part of that class of shareholders, the dissentient shareholder would have had a sufficient shareholding to block the scheme. Despite the fact that all the shareholders belonged to the same class in terms of shares, the court refused to sanction the scheme. In rejecting the scheme the court concluded that where there are shareholders within the same shareholding class but who have different interests in the scheme being proposed then the class should be further divided and approval must be sought from the newly constituted classes. The case is important for a number of reasons. First, it is clear that the constitution of the class meetings will not necessarily follow those held during the winding up of the company or indeed those held where a variation of shareholders rights is being sought under section 78 of the Principal Act (See Chapter 8). The difference between the section 201 procedure and these others is that the former requires the classes to be constituted depending on their interests, including their interests in the proposals, whereas the latter require the classes to be constituted in terms of the similarity in rights attaching to each category of shares. Second, the case demonstrates that if class approval is not obtained in the correct manner then the entire scheme may be put in abeyance or indeed it may founder completely.

It is not sufficient to claim that a class member has an ulterior motive for approving the scheme. In *Re Pye Ireland Ltd*,[6] an unsecured creditor, voting for a scheme of arrangement to defer payment of the company's debts, happened also to hold 25 per cent of the shares in the company. This creditor had an extra interest in voting for the scheme because the breathing space being granted to the company was advantageous and enabled it to develop its assets which would ensure the benefit of the members as well as the creditors. The court held that inclusion of this creditor in the meeting did not render it improperly constituted in the absence of proof that the others had been prejudiced by the inclusion. The meeting was accordingly declared to be valid.

2. Powers of the Court

Section 203 gives wide powers to the court to make orders facilitating the compromise or scheme of arrangement which is proposed for the purposes of

---

5 [1976] 1 WLR 123.
6 Unreported, High Court, 12 November 1984.

reconstruction or amalgamation, but only where it is proposed to transfer all or any part of the company's undertaking or property to another company. In this regard the court may make provision for any of the following:

(a) the transfer of the whole or any part of the undertaking or property to the new company;
(b) the allotment or appropriation of any shares, debentures, policies or other interests by the transferee company to any person as provided in the scheme of arrangement;
(c) the continuation of any legal proceedings by or against the transferor company;
(d) the dissolution of the transferor company without winding up;
(e) the making of provision for any dissentients;
(f) any incidental, consequential and supplemental matters as are necessary to secure that the reconstruction or amalgamation shall be fully and effectively carried out.

The court has discretion to approve the scheme of arrangement or reject it. It will not sanction the scheme where the notices of the meetings contained insufficient information or where the authorising resolutions were improperly passed.[7] The court will also ensure that the scheme is one which an 'intelligent and honest man, a member of the class concerned and acting in respect of his interest, might reasonably approve'.[8] If the scheme is sanctioned by the court it will be binding on all creditors, members, liquidators or contributors once an official copy has been delivered to the Registrar of Companies.

Scheme of Reconstruction under Section 260 or Section 271

Section 260 of the Principal Act permits only one type of reconstruction by which a company in voluntary liquidation sells its undertaking for shares in another company. Section 271 of the Act extends section 260 to a creditors' voluntary winding up.

The procedure under section 260 is that when a company is proposed to be, or in the course of being, wound up voluntarily and the whole or part of its business or property is to be transferred to another company, the liquidator may, with the sanction of a special resolution, receive in compensation for the transfer, shares in the transferee company for distribution among the members of the transferor company.

Section 260(2) provides that such sale or arrangement is binding on the members of the transferor company, and there is no provision whereby dissenting members may object. However, section 260(3) does allow a dissenting member

---

7 *Re Dorman Long and Company Ltd* [1934] 1 Ch 635.
8 *Per* Maugham J., ibid. at 655.

to notify his dissent to the liquidator and request him either to abstain from carrying out the resolution or to purchase his interests. If the liquidator elects to purchase his shares, section 260(4) states that the purchase money must be paid before the company is dissolved and, unless otherwise provided for, shall be deemed to be part of the costs of the winding up.

The provisions of section 260 apply in exactly the same way in a creditors' winding up, except that section 271 prevents the liquidator from exercising his powers without the sanction of the court, or the committee of inspection.

Amalgamations

An amalgamation involves a reorganisation of a number of companies by which all transfer their assets to one company that may have been formed solely for that purpose. In consideration for this transfer, shares in the transferee company will be allotted to the members of transferor companies in proportion to their original holdings. An amalgamation can take place by following the section 201 procedure outlined above or it may take the form of a merger or take-over, whereby the companies are merged by consolidating their undertakings or by the acquisition of the controlling interests of both companies by a new company or by one company or the other company. The type of procedure followed may often depend on the relationship between the companies. Where, for example, an amalgamation is amicable, any method may be pursued. Where a proposed take-over is hostile, the acquiring company will first have to gain a controlling interest in the target company before it can pursue any further reorganisation. In practice, what occurs is that the acquiring company makes an offer to the shareholders of another company to buy their shares. Normally such an offer will be conditional on acceptance by a stated proportion of shareholders, usually those holding at least 80 per cent of the shares. By accepting the conditional offer the shareholders become bound to sell, but the offering company is not bound to buy until the condition is fulfilled. The reason for imposing the 80 per cent restriction is that once a company has acquired 80 per cent or more it can compulsorily purchase the remaining minority shareholders' interests under section 204 of the Principal Act.

1. Compulsory Purchase of Minorities — Section 204

Section 204 provides that where a company makes an offer for all the shares of a target company and receives binding acceptances in respect of at least 80 per cent of the shares, the acquiring company is entitled to acquire the remaining shares in that company. Section 204 is widely used in practice. The provision is designed to facilitate the take-over which has already been approved by the majority.

Section 204(1) provides that where the scheme, contract or offer involving the acquisition has become binding, or has been approved or accepted by the holders of 80 per cent of the relevant shares within four months after the publication of the scheme, contract or offer, the transferee company may, within six months following such publication, give notice to the dissenting shareholders that it intends to acquire their shares. When such notice is given the transferee company shall be entitled and bound to acquire those shares on the terms which under the scheme, contract or offer have become binding, approved and accepted. However, a dissenting shareholder may apply to the court within one month of the notice being issued and the court may make such order as it thinks fit. The court will not sanction the compulsory take-over if full particulars have not been given to the shareholders,[9] or if there is any evidence of *male fides* on the part of the acquiring company or the assenting shareholders.[10]

Section 204(1) is subject to 204(2), which provides that where the acquiring company is, at the date of publication of the offer, the beneficial owner of more than 20 per cent of the shares, the accepting shareholders must represent 75 per cent in number as well as 80 per cent value of the relevant shares.

The minority shareholder may also force the acquiring company to purchase his shares. Section 204(4) provides that if as a result of the scheme or offer the company holds 80 per cent of the target company's shares, then a dissenting holder may, within three months, require the transferee company to acquire his shares.

2. *General Rules Regarding Take-Overs and Mergers*

Where any one of the above mentioned methods of reorganisation is designed to effect a take-over or merger, a number of other legislative provisions will apply. Section 187 of the Principal Act requires that any payments of compensation for loss of office on the merger, takeover or amalgamation of the company must be approved by the company in general meeting. Furthermore, directors are under a duty to disclose payments to be made to them in connection with the transfer of shares, where the transfer involves an offer being made to the general body of shareholders.[11] In respect of mergers and divisions, the European Communities (Mergers and Divisions of Companies) Regulations 1987 impose requirements on directors of companies in relation to drafting terms of the merger or division, having those draft terms approved by a special resolution of the company and obtaining a court order confirming the draft terms. These Regulations apply in general to public limited companies only. The Mergers, Takeovers and Monopolies (Control) Act 1978 gives the Minister the right to refer a proposal for a large-scale take-over or merger to the Examiner of Restrictive Practices. On the report of the examiner the Minister may prohibit the take-over or merger or

---

9 *Securities Trust Ltd v. Associated Properties Ltd and Others*, High Court, 19 November 1980 (McWilliam J.).

10 *Re Bugle Press Ltd* [1960] 3 All ER 791.

11 Section 188 of the Principal Act.

approve it either unconditionally or conditionally.[12] The Competition Act 1991, as amended, also impacts on proposed take-overs or mergers which will be prohibited if they prevent or distort competition. Failure to comply with the provision of the Competition Act may give rise to criminal liability on the part of a company and its officers.[13] The most recent major development in the field of take-overs and mergers was the enactment of the Takeover Panel Act 1997.[14]This provides for the setting up of a take-over panel to monitor and supervise take-overs and mergers and to make rules and issue directions in respect of same. Schedule 1 of the Act sets out a number of principles in relation to the conduct of all take-overs and mergers, and these can be summarised as follows:

(a) all shareholders of the same class must be treated equally;
(b) no offer and no announcement of a proposed offer shall be made without careful and responsible consideration being taken by the offeror and only if the offeror is satisfied that the offer can, if accepted, be implemented;
(c) shareholders, to whom such an offer is made, shall be entitled to receive such accurate and adequate information and advice as will enable them to make an informed decision on the offer;
(d) it is the duty of all parties to a take-over to prevent the creation of a false market in the shares or debentures of the offeror or offeree and to refrain from any misleading statement or conduct;
(e) directors of the offeree must refrain from doing anything which might frustrate an offer or deprive the shareholders of the opportunity to consider the merits of the offer without the authority of the company in general meeting;
(f) directors must not fetter their discretion by entering into any commitment with an offeror which would restrict their freedom to advise shareholders of the offeree;
(g) directors of the offeree and the offeror must act in the interest of the shareholders as a whole and disregard their own personal interests when giving advice or furnishing information in relation to the offer;
(h) rights of control must be exercised in good faith and the oppression of a minority is not acceptable in any circumstances;
(i) an offeree must not be disrupted in the conduct of its affairs beyond a reasonable time by an offer for its securities;
(j) a substantial acquisition of securities shall take place at an acceptable speed and shall be subject to an adequate and timely disclosure.

---

12 See: The Proposed Merger or Take-Over Prohibition Order 1996 (SI 45 of 1996) which prohibited the proposed acquisition by Statoil (Ireland) Ltd of Conoco (Ireland) Ltd. This order was subsequently modified by a conditional approval (SI 214 of 1996) and the acquisition went ahead.
13 Sections 2–4 of the Competition (Amendment) Act 1996.
14 Which has been fully operational since 1 July 1997.

CHAPTER TWENTY-FOUR

RECEIVERS

Introduction

The most common way for a debenture holder to realise his security is by appointing a receiver. The receiver will take control over the charged assets and by selling them and applying the proceeds will discharge the debt owing to the debenture holder.

A receiver may be appointed under the terms of a fixed or floating charge. However, where a debenture is secured only by a fixed charge or mortgage, the debenture holder will usually have a right to sell the asset without going through the expense of appointing a receiver. In Ireland the normal practice of lending institutions is to take the all embracing fixed and floating charge over the entire assets and undertaking of the company. Where such a charge is being realised it will be necessary to appoint a receiver because the process may take quite a considerable period of time.

Appointment of a Receiver

A receiver can be appointed either by the debenture holder under the terms of the debenture or by the courts. The debenture or trust deed usually gives the debenture holders or their trustees the power to appoint a receiver in specified circumstances, usually described as events of default. Although a matter of negotiation between the company and the debenture holder, the debenture will usually incorporate the following events of default:

(a) the principal sum due has been unpaid for more than seven days;
(b) the company has failed to pay an instalment of the principal or interest;
(c) failure of any other covenant, condition, representation or warranty in the debenture;
(d) the levying of a distress or execution against the company;
(e) the appointment of a receiver over any of the company's assets;
(f) the disposal, without the sanction of the debenture holder, of a substantial part of the company's assets;
(g) the company is ceasing, has ceased to carry on business or is threatening to do so;
(h) there is a change in ownership of the company which is not acceptable to the debenture holder;
(i) there is a material adverse change in the business of the company, which in the opinion of the debenture holder would jeopardise the security.[1]

---

1 This 'catch-all' event of default has never been tested by the court, but is unlikely to survive judicial scrutiny unless it is exercised on reasonable grounds.

If an event of default occurs, the debenture holder will usually demand immediate repayment of the loan. If the company is not in a position to comply with the demand, the debenture holder will usually exercise his contractual right to appoint a receiver over the assets charged. However, the debenture holder cannot exercise his powers under the debenture if an examiner has been appointed under the Companies (Amendment) Act 1990.[2]

In the unlikely event that the debenture does not give adequate powers to the debenture holder to appoint a receiver, he may apply to the court to have a receiver appointed. Indeed, any creditor may apply to the court to have a receiver appointed. The usual grounds for such an application are that:

(a) the principal and/or interest are in arrears;
(b) the company has commenced winding up;
(c) the security is in jeopardy — this will occur where there is a threat to the assets charged or where the company has ceased or is about to cease trading.

Qualifications, Remuneration and Removal of Receivers

The Companies Acts do not prescribe any qualifications as a requisite for appointment as a receiver. However, the Acts prohibit the following persons from so acting:

(a) a body corporate;[3]
(b) an undischarged bankrupt;
(c) a person who is, or has been within twelve months of the commencement of the receivership, an officer (including secretary), auditor or servant of the company;
(d) a parent, spouse, brother, sister or child of an officer;
(e) a partner or employee of an officer or servant;
(f) anyone disqualified from acting as a receiver of the company's holding or subsidiary company or a subsidiary of its holding company.[4]

A person who becomes disqualified automatically vacates office and must notify the company, the Registrar of Companies, the debenture holder or court that he has vacated his office by reason of such disqualification.[5] Acting as a receiver while disqualified from doing so and failing to vacate the office when obliged to do so is a criminal offence punishable by a fine.[6]

Court-appointed receivers are officers of the court and as such have their remuneration fixed by the court. Where appointed by the debenture holder, the

---

2 See Chapter 27.
3 Section 314 of the Principal Act.
4 Section 315(1) of the Principal Act.
5 Section 315(2) of the Principal Act.
6 Section 315(5) of the Principal Act.

receiver's remuneration will ordinarily be fixed by the terms of the debenture. However, a liquidator, member or creditor of a company may apply to the court under section 318 of the Principal Act to fix the remuneration of a receiver, even if the document under which the receiver has been appointed purports to fix the remuneration.[7]

A receiver appointed under a debenture may resign provided he has given one month's notice to the holders of floating charges over all or part of the company, the company itself or its liquidator, and the holders of all fixed charges over all or part of the company.[8] When appointed by the court, a receiver can only resign with the consent of the court and subject to the terms laid down by the court.[9] Failure to comply with these notice provisions may cause the receiver to be liable to a fine of £1,000 (€1,269).

The court may also, on cause shown, remove a receiver and appoint another.[10] Notice of such proceedings must be served on the receiver and the person who appointed him not less than seven days before the hearing. The receiver and the person who appointed him must be given an opportunity to appear and be heard at such proceedings.[11]

Receiver's Status

A receiver appointed by the court is an officer of the court and takes his instructions from the court. Where a receiver is appointed by the debenture holder he will be the agent of the debenture holder unless the contrary is specifically stated in the debenture. However, in normal circumstances the debenture will provide that the receiver is an agent of the company. This will have the effect of making the company and not the debenture holder responsible for any wrongful act on the part of the receiver.

Although the company is the receiver's principal, the relationship between the receiver and the company does not follow the normal agency rules. This is because, as Costello J. stated in *Irish Oil and Cake Mills Ltd v. Donnelly*,[12] 'the agency here is of course very different from the ordinary agency arising every day in commercial transactions'. As the company's agent, the receiver may be bound by some of the company's obligations[13] and in other instances he may

---

7 *Re City Car Sales Ltd (in receivership & liquidation)* [1995] 1 ILRM 221.
8 Section 322C(1) of the Principal Act.
9 Section 322C(2) of the Principal Act.
10 Section 322A(1) of the Principal Act.
11 Section 322A(2) of the Principal Act.
12 Unreported, High Court, 27 March 1983.
13 In *Cretanor Maritime Co. Ltd v. Irish Marine Management Ltd* [1978] 3 All ER 164 it was held that the receiver was bound by a *Mareva* injunction which the plaintiff had obtained against the defendant company. See also *Kilgobbin Mink and Stud Farm Ltd v. National Credit Company Ltd* [1980] IR 175.

choose to repudiate those obligations.[14] The ability to repudiate existing contracts is considered further later in this chapter.

The difficulty in applying a strict agency relationship to the receiver and company lies in the fact that the receiver is appointed by the debenture holder and will always have the debenture holder's interests in mind. The company is not therefore in a position to instruct the receiver on the exercise of his powers and the carrying out of his duties, as would occur in a normal agency situation.[15] However, even where the debenture provides that the receiver is the agent of the company, the actions of the debenture holder may cause the court to infer an agency relationship between the debenture holder and the receiver. In *American Express International Banking v. Hurley*,[16] the facts of which are considered later in the chapter, the court held that the debenture holder, a bank, was liable in negligence to the guarantor of the company's debts because it had directed the receiver to sell the assets at an undervalue and thus had created a relationship of principal and agent between the bank and the receiver in this matter.

Effect of the Receiver's Appointment

The effect of the receiver's appointment is now considered under the following headings:

1. the company;
2. the directors;
3. the liquidator;
4. the examiner;
5. employees; and
6. publicity requirements.

1. The Company

The receiver must give notice of his appointment to the company although in reality the company will be aware that the receiver is appointed. The appointment of a receiver does not affect the legal status of the company. It continues its existence and its separate legal personality remains intact. However, once a receiver has been appointed, every invoice, order for goods or business letter issued by or on behalf of the company shall contain a statement that a receiver has been appointed.[17] Default by the company and any officer, liquidator or receiver of the company in complying with this provision may lead to a fine of £100 (€127).[18]

---

14 *Ardmore Studios (Ireland) Ltd v. Lynch* [1965] IR 1.
15 See Milman, *Receivers as Agents* 44 MLR 654.
16 [1986] BCLC 52.
17 Section 317(1) of the Principal Act.
18 Section 317(2) of the Principal Act.

Where the holder of a floating charge appoints a receiver over the entire undertaking and assets of the company, a statement as to the affairs of the company must be submitted to the receiver within fourteen days of his appointment.[19] By virtue of section 320 of the Principal Act, this duty is imposed on the directors and secretary of the company or such person as may be specified by the receiver. The statement must include the following:

(a) particulars of the company's assets, debts and liabilities at the date of appointment of the receiver;
(b) names and addresses of the company's creditors;
(c) the securities held by those creditors;
(d) the dates when the securities were respectively given.

The statement of affairs must be verified by affidavit if the receiver has been appointed by the court, or by a statutory declaration where the receiver is appointed under a debenture. Default in complying with the statutory requirements to submit the statement of affairs may give rise to a criminal offence.[20] Where a statement is not submitted the court may, on the application of the receiver or any creditor of the company, make such order as it deems fit, including an order compelling the submission of a statement of affairs.[21]

The appointment of a receiver is an event which causes floating charges to crystallise and become fixed. Once this occurs the company may no longer deal with the assets charged without the receiver's consent.

2. *The Directors*

On his appointment the receiver assumes control over the assets which are the subject of the charge. Accordingly, the directors' powers in respect of those assets are suspended during the receivership. However, the directors remain in office and can exercise such powers which have not passed to the receiver. If a receiver is appointed over a specific asset only, the directors will retain their powers over all remaining assets and the management of the company. Where a receiver is appointed over all the assets and undertaking of the company, the directors' powers are substantially curtailed. However, their position is not completely usurped by the receiver, as they retain residual decision-making powers. In *Newhart Developments v. Co-operative Commercial Bank*,[22] a bank appointed a receiver under a debenture. The debenture gave the receiver numerous management powers including, *inter alia*, the power to bring legal proceedings in the name of the company. The company directors claimed that the bank was in breach of contract, but the receiver refused to begin proceedings for

19 Section 319(1)(b) of the Principal Act.
20 Section 320(5) of the Principal Act.
21 Section 320A of the Principal Act.
22 [1978] QB 814.

the company against the bank. He also sought to restrain the directors from taking an action themselves against the bank. In holding that the directors could continue the proceedings, the court was very much persuaded by two particular points. First, although the receiver was an agent of the company he was appointed and paid by the debenture holder. Accordingly, it was unlikely that he would take an action against the bank himself. Second, the directors had provided a personal indemnity for the costs of the litigation in the event that the action was unsuccessful. This latter point is of particular importance as the court will only permit the directors to exercise their residual powers where they do not impinge upon the debenture holder's security. It was the absence of such an indemnity that prevented the directors from suing in the company's name in *Tudor Grange Holdings Ltd v. Citibank NA*.[23]

The Irish courts have accepted the view that directors retain their power to institute proceedings in an appropriate case. In *Wymes v. Crowley*,[24] the directors sought to institute proceedings in the name of the company, alleging negligence against the receiver. The receiver attempted to resist the claim. The court held that the directors retained residual powers even where a receiver was appointed as a manager-receiver. These residual powers included the power to initiate litigation on the company's behalf. However, the court accepted the UK line of reasoning that the exercise of those powers was subject to one important limitation — it must not deprive the debenture holders of their security.[25]

3. The Liquidator

A receiver can still be appointed even if a liquidator is already in place. If the company goes into liquidation when the receiver is already in office, he ceases to be the agent of the company if appointed in that capacity. However, he will retain his powers in relation to the assets comprised in the charge.[26] The liquidator is entitled to receive any surplus which remains after the receiver has discharged his duties, but otherwise he cannot interfere with the receiver's exercise of his powers. However, the liquidator in a compulsory or creditor's voluntary winding up may apply to the court for an order directing that the receiver shall cease to act or act only in relation to certain assets.[27] In any case, where the liquidator is appointed by the court the receiver should seek the approval of the court before disposing of any assets.

Where a receiver is appointed under a charge which is subsequently invalidated under section 286 of the Principal Act,[28] he must vacate his office and

---

23 [1991] 4 All ER 1.
24 High Court, 27 February 1987.
25 For a similar view see *Lascomme Ltd v. UDT* [1994] 1 ILRM 227.
26 *Sowman v. David Samuel Trust Ltd* [1978] 1 All ER 616.
27 Section 322B of the Principal Act.
28 See Chapter 26.

account to the liquidator forthwith. However, if the receiver has repaid the debenture holders before the charge is invalidated, the actions of the receiver cannot be retrospectively invalidated on that ground.

4. The Examiner

Where an examiner is appointed and a receiver is already in place, the court may make such order as it deems fit, including an order that:

(a) the receiver shall cease to act from the date specified by the court;
(b) the receiver act only in relation to certain assets as specified by the court;
(c) the receiver deliver to the examiner all books, papers and other records which are in his possession or control and which relate to the property or undertaking of the company;
(d) the receiver give to the examiner particulars of his dealings with the property or undertaking of the company.[29]

It should be noted that an examiner may not be appointed when a receiver stands appointed for more than three business days.[30] Furthermore, a receiver cannot be appointed if an examiner is already in place.[31]

5. Employees

The position of employees varies depending on the status of the receiver. At common law, the appointment of a receiver by the court operates to dismiss the employees automatically. However, the receiver may re-engage some or all of the employees if he considers it necessary. Where a receiver is appointed under a debenture there is no automatic dismissal and the position of employees will usually be a matter for the receiver. Where the debenture provides that the receiver is to be the agent of the company, all contracts of employment will usually remain in force. This is necessary in order to save the debenture holder the costs of redundancy payments which, as preferential payments, must be paid before the floating charge holder. However, there is nothing to prevent a receiver from dismissing employees where he considers it necessary, for example where the assets of the company are being sold on a piecemeal basis. Where the receiver decides to lay off workers, he is obliged to comply with many of the statutory requirements relating to labour law.[32]

6. Publicity

As soon as the receiver is appointed, the person who appointed him must cause to have a notice of his appointment published in *Iris Oifigiúil* and in at least one

---

29 Section 6 of the Companies (Amendment) Act 1990.
30 Section 3(6) of the Companies (Amendment) Act 1990.
31 Section 5(2)(b) of the Companies (Amendment) Act 1990.
32 *Bolands Ltd (in receivership) v. Ward & Others* [1988] ILRM 382.

daily newspaper circulating in the area where the registered office of the company is situated.[33] Notice of his appointment must also be sent to the Registrar of Companies in the prescribed form. The Registrar of Companies must then inform the Director of Corporate Enforcement of the appointment.

Functions and Duties of a Receiver

The primary function of the receiver is to receive and realise the assets which are the subject of the security for the purpose of discharging the debt owed to the debenture holder together with the receiver's own expenses. If the receiver is able to discharge these debts, he vacates his office and the directors resume full control. The general responsibility of the receiver is to the debenture holder rather than to the company, even if he is formally an agent of the company. However, in carrying out his function the receiver may be under a duty to the company and those who may be affected by his actions, such as the company's guarantors. These duties are considered under the following headings:

1. to exercise care in disposing of company property;
2. to apply the proceeds of sale in the manner fixed by law;
3. to satisfy the notification requirements laid down in the Principal Act;
4. report any misconduct; and
5. to co-operate with the Director of Corporate Environment.

1. To Exercise Care in Disposing of the Company's Assets

It has been established by a long line of case-law that a receiver must exercise all reasonable care to obtain the best possible price for assets which are realised.[34] Provided he acts *bona fide* without negligence in the proper exercise of his powers, the company cannot recover compensation from him for his actions, even though those actions may not be in its long-term interests. However, if he acts negligently or on the improper instructions of the debenture holder he may be held personally liable.

This duty to obtain the best price possible for company assets is owed not only to the company but also to third parties, such as guarantors, who may be affected by the receiver's actions. In *American Express International Banking v. Hurley*,[35] the company's liability to the bank was secured by a charge over equipment and by a personal guarantee of Hurley, a director of the company. The equipment had been independently valued at £193,000. When the bank appointed a receiver, he sold the equipment for £34,500. The bank then sued

33 Section 107 of the Principal Act.
34 *McGowan v. Gannon* [1983] 1LRM 516, *Holohan v. Friends Provident and Century Life Office* [1966] IR 1, *Casey v. Irish Intercontinental Bank* [1979] IR 364 and *Standard Chartered Bank v. Walker* [1982] 3 All ER 938.
35 [1986] BCLC 52.

Hurley, on foot of his guarantee, for the balance of the company's liability. Hurley claimed that both the receiver and the bank as his principal were negligent in selling the equipment at an undervalue. The court held that the receiver owed a duty to Hurley to take reasonable care to realise the true value of the asset. Because the asset was sold at an undervalue, the receiver was in breach of his duty and was accordingly negligent.

The duty of the receiver to act without negligence was placed on a statutory footing by section 172 of the 1990 Act which inserted a new section 316A into the Principal Act. This section provides that a receiver must, in selling the company's property, exercise reasonable care to obtain the best price reasonably obtainable for the property at the time of the sale. The section does not impose an obligation on the receiver to delay a sale in order to receive a better price, presumably because it is probably impossible to determine with foresight when would be the best time to sell. Indeed, both UK and Irish authorities have accepted that a receiver, in accepting the best price at the time of sale, is not obliged to delay for subsequent offers.[36]

In *Casey v. Irish Intercontinental Bank Ltd*,[37] an offer for assets, the subject matter of a floating charge, had been accepted by the mortgagee who considered that it was the best available price. After the contract for sale was completed, a further offer of a higher amount was made but rejected because of the original contract. An application was made to the court to have the original contract rescinded on the grounds that it did not obtain the best possible price. The Supreme Court rejected the application on the basis that a mortgagee who enters a contract for sale is only obliged to obtain the best price which all the circumstances and valuations show to be the best possible price at the date of the contract. That duty is discharged even where a higher price is offered at some time after the sale. However, where the mortgagee fails to consider alternative options which are available at the time, he will be in breach of his duty. In *Holohan v. Friends Provident and Century Life Office*,[38] the mortgagor successfully obtained an injunction restraining the mortgagee from selling a property without vacant possession, when he could have sold it for a higher price on the basis of vacant possession.

A receiver does not fulfil his statutory obligation to obtain the best possible price merely because he disposes of property at an auction. In *Tse Kwong Lam v. Wong Chit Sen*[39] a receiver was held liable to the mortgagor for disposing of the property to a sole bidder at an auction who also happened to be a major shareholder of the company. The court rejected the contention that a sale at a

---

36 *Bank of Cyprus (London) Ltd v. Gill* [1980] 2 Lloyd's Reports 51, but cf. the judgment of Carroll J. in *McGowan v. Gannon* [1983] ILRM 532.
37 [1979] IR 364.
38 [1966] IR 1.
39 [1983] 1 WLR 1349.

publicly advertised auction necessarily produces the best possible price. If a receiver has any doubt about the best price obtainable he should obtain an independent expert's opinion.[40] Indeed, the receiver may always apply to the court for directions in relation to any matter in connection with the performance of his duties.[41]

Where the receiver acts in breach of his obligations under section 316A, it will not be a defence to claim that he was acting as agent for the company.[42] Furthermore, where the receiver is in breach of his duty, he is not entitled to be indemnified by the company for any liability which may arise.[43] However, if a receiver acts in breach of section 316A, a bona fide purchaser for value of such property obtains a good title to it.[44]

The duty of care owed by a receiver to the company is generally limited to the duty to obtain the best price available when disposing of assets. Even when a receiver is appointed as a receiver-manager, the duty of care does not extend to a duty to keep the company appraised of how the business of the company is going. In *Irish Oil and Cake Mills Ltd v. Donnelly*,[45] the company applied for a mandatory injunction ordering the receiver-manager to furnish accounts and information to the company. The company claimed, *inter alia*, that the receiver–manager owed a duty of care to the company and that this duty included the giving of such information. The court rejected the contention that the duty of care owed to the company to obtain the best possible price included a duty that a receiver is also obliged to furnish information concerning his trading activities. However, Costello J. suggested that each case would turn on its own facts and that in certain circumstances the receiver may be obliged to account to the company whose affairs he is managing.[46]

Although the receiver may be obliged to provide information to the company regarding the sale of the company's assets, this obligation does not appear to extend to providing such information to other parties including those who may be personally affected by the receiver's decision. This was made clear in *McGowan v. Gannon*,[47] where it was held that the receiver does not owe a duty to provide information to a guarantor of the company's debts.

The 1990 Act also introduced a new provision relating to the disposal of certain assets by the receiver. Where a receiver proposes to sell by private

---

40 See *Lambert Jones Estates Ltd v. Donnelly*, High Court, 5 November 1982 (O'Hanlon J.).
41 Section 316 of the Principal Act as amended by section 171 of the Companies Act 1990.
42 Section 316A(2)(a) of the Principal Act.
43 Section 316A(2)(b) of the Principal Act.
44 *Re Ruby Property Co. Ltd et al. v Kilty & Another* [2000] 7 CLP 155.
45 High Court, 27 March 1983.
46 High Court, 27 March 1983 at 13 citing with approval *Smiths Ltd v. Middleton* [1979] 3 All ER 942.
47 [1983] ILRM 516.

contract a 'non-cash' asset [48] of the company to anyone who is, or was in the three years prior to the date of the receiver's appointment, an officer of the company, he must give at least fourteen days' notice of his intention to do so to all the creditors of the company who are known to him. [49]

2. *To Apply the Proceeds of Sale in the Manner Fixed by Law*

The receiver is primarily concerned with discharging the debts owed to the debenture holder. Where he obtains a surplus to those requirements he will pay those amounts to the company. However, where a receiver is appointed by a debenture holder and realises assets subject to a floating charge, section 98 of the Principal Act requires him to pay all preferential creditors before applying the proceeds to discharge the debts owed to the debenture holder. [50]

Section 98 has no application if a company is in the course of being wound up. However, the obligation to pay the preferential creditors continues if a liquidator is subsequently appointed before the receiver has complied with section 98. In *Re Eisc Teoranta* [51] a receiver had been appointed under a debenture, which was secured by a fixed charge over certain assets and a floating charge over other assets. The receiver realised all the assets charged and discharged the debts owing under the debenture out of the proceeds of the fixed charge. He was left in possession of the proceeds of the floating charge. Before he could apply those proceeds in payment of the preferential creditors, a liquidator was appointed. The liquidator requested that the receiver deliver the amounts realised under the floating charge. The receiver refused to comply with this request on the basis that he was under a statutory duty, by virtue of section 98, to discharge the preferential creditors out of the proceeds of the sale of the assets subject to the floating charge. The liquidator argued that section 98 did not apply once a liquidator was appointed. It was also argued that as no part of the assets subject to the floating charge had been used to discharge monies owed under the debenture, section 98 did not come into effect. Furthermore, once the surplus assets had been paid to the liquidator section 285 of the Principal Act would apply which gives priority to the preferential creditors in a liquidation. In reply to these arguments Lardner J. held as follows:

(a) the receiver's statutory duty to pay the preferential creditors out of the proceeds of the sale of assets subject to the floating charge was not terminated by the subsequent appointment of a liquidator;

---

48 Defined as one which is not less than £1,000 (€1,270) in value, but which exceeds either £50,000 (€63,487) in value or 10 per cent of the company's net assets. A 'non-cash asset' is defined in section 29 of the Companies Act 1990.
49 Section 316A(3)(a) of the Principal Act.
50 For order of application of assets, see Chapter 26.
51 [1991] ILRM 760.

(b) section 98 applied to a receiver once a claim for principal and interest had been made under a debenture – this claim existed at the time the receiver was appointed and it was irrelevant that the proceeds of the floating charge were surplus to requirements; and

(c) the fact that the preferential creditors would obtain a priority whether under section 98 or section 285 cannot be a factor in determining the statutory duty of a receiver.

The decision in *Re Eisc Teoranta* was approved in the High Court case of *Re Manning Furniture Ltd.*[52] Here the company had executed a debenture which was secured by a floating charge and other chattel mortgages in favour of ICC Bank plc. It had subsequently executed a legal charge in favour of the First National Building Society. A receiver was appointed and he discharged the bank's debt from the proceeds of the sale of the assets subject to the chattel mortgages. However, he also took into his possession the assets which were subject to the floating charge which gave him a surplus of £150,000. The receiver applied to the High Court for directions as to whether he was obliged to discharge the claims of the preferential creditors out of these surplus funds before paying the balance to the building society. The building society argued that the priority given by section 98 only applied in respect of debts due under the debenture and as no part of the assets which were subject to the floating charge were used in discharge of monies owed under the debenture, section 98 had no application. McCracken J. rejected this contention and held that the receiver must pay the preferential creditors out of any assets coming into his hands, irrespective of the fact that the proceeds of the floating charge were not used to discharge monies due under the debenture.

However, where a receiver does not realise or take into his possession the assets which are the subject of a floating charge and instead only realises the assets subject to a fixed charge it would seem that he is not obliged to pay the preferential creditors under section 98. In *United Bars Ltd v. Revenue Commissioners*[53] the receiver was appointed on foot of a debenture secured *inter alia* by a fixed and floating charge over certain of the company's asset. The receiver, having discharged the debenture holder's debt from the proceeds of assets which were subject to a fixed charge only, was left with a surplus. The question arose as to whether the receiver was obliged to pay that surplus to the preferential creditors or to the company. Murphy J., citing with approval the UK line of authority in this regard,[54] held that section 98 only applied to accounts coming into the hands of the receiver which were subject to a floating charge and not to assets which were the

---

52 [1996] I ILRM 13.

53 [1991] 1 IR 396.

54 *Re GL Saunders Ltd (in liquidation)* [1986] 1 WLR 215 and *Re Lewis Merthyr Consolidated Collieries* [1939] 1 Ch 498.

subject of a fixed charge. In his opinion, to interpret section 98 in such a way that the proceeds of the sale of assets subject to a fixed charge were to be made available to the preferential creditors, would confer on these creditors an unwarranted entitlement that they would not have in the event of a liquidation.[55] Section 98 may be disapplied if an examiner is, or may be, appointed and the court considers that an order disapplying section 98 would be likely to facilitate the survival of the company and the whole, or any part, of its undertaking as a going concern.[56]

3. Notification Requirements

Within two months from the receipt of the statement of affairs the receiver must send a copy of it, and any comments which he cares to make thereon, to:

(a) the Registrar of Companies;
(b) the company itself;
(c) the debenture holders or the trustees for the debenture holders;
(d) the court, where he is appointed by the court.[57]

Where a receiver of the whole, or substantially the whole, of the property of a company is appointed, he must also deliver to the Registrar of Companies the following information:

(a) an abstract showing the assets of the company of which he has taken possession since his appointment and their estimated value;
(b) the proceeds of sale of any such assets since his appointment;
(c) his receipts and payment during the period of six months from the date of his appointment; and
(d) an abstract at the end of every subsequent period of six months during which he continues to act as receiver.[58]

Where the receiver ceases to act as receiver of the property, the abstract shall be accompanied by a statement from the receiver declaring his opinion as to whether or not the company is solvent. The Registrar shall, on receiving the statement, forward a copy of it to the Director of Corporate Enforcement.

4. To Report Misconduct

If it appears to a receiver that any past or present officer or member of the company has been guilty of an offence in relation to the company, he must report the matter to the DPP together with any information relating to the matter.[59] Where a receiver refers such a matter to the Director of Public Prosecutions, he

---

55 [1991] 1 IR at 400.
56 Section 17 Companies (Amendment) (No.2) Act 1999.
57 Section 319 of the Principal Act.
58 Section 321 of the Principal Act.
59 Section 299 (2) of the Principal Act and section 179 of the Companies Act 1990.

must also furnish the same particulars to the Director of Corporate Enforcement. Where the DPP or Director consider that the case is one where a prosecution ought to be instituted, the receiver must give any assistance in connection with the prosecution that he is reasonably able to give.

5. *To Co-operate with the Director of Corporate Enforcement*

The director may, where he considers it necessary, request the production of a receiver's books for examination either in regard to a particular receivership or to all receiverships undertaken by the receiver. The receiver must furnish such books, answer any questions concerning the content of the books and the conduct of a particular receivership, and give all assistance as the receiver is reasonably able to give. If the receiver defaults in complying with this statutory duty he is guilty of an offence.[60]

Receiver's Powers

Where a receiver is appointed by the court, his authority is vested in him by the court. A person who attempts to obstruct the receiver in the exercise of his powers may be held in contempt of court. Where a receiver is appointed by the debenture holder his powers are contractually determined by the terms of the debenture. Where the debenture is secured by a fixed and floating charge over the entire assets and undertaking of the company, it is usual to confer on the receiver the power to carry on the business of the company. Although such a receiver–manager has the power to manage the business of the company, it should be noted that these powers are conferred on him for the sole purpose of realising the security and not for rescuing the company. As Richardson J. observed in *First City Corporation Ltd v. Downsview Nominees Ltd*:

> While in practice receiverships are sometimes used to achieve a moratorium and rehabilitation of the company's business, that is legitimate only where it is an incident of the receiver's proper role. The receiver is there to enforce the security and only for that purpose to trade. He is not a white knight.[61]

The debenture will usually confer on the receiver many of the powers of the board of directors including, *inter alia*:

(a) the power to dispose of the company's assets and do such things as are incidental to that power;

(b) the power to carry on the business of the company;

(c) the power to borrow money and give security where necessary;

(d) the power to institute proceedings on behalf of the company.

---

60 Section 323A of the Principal Act.
61 [1990] 3 NZLR 265.

It has already been noted that where a receiver is unsure about the exercise of a particular power, he may apply to the court for directions.[62] Furthermore, where a receiver is appointed by the debenture holder, section 316(1) of the Principal Act permits the following persons to apply to the court for directions as to the exercise of the receiver's powers:

(a) an officer of the company;
(b) a member of the company;
(c) employees comprising at least half of those persons employed in a full-time capacity;
(d) a liquidator; and
(e) any contributory.

Receiver's Liability

Before a receiver is appointed he should ensure that the charge appointing him is valid.[63] If the charge is invalid, the receiver's appointment will be invalid and he will be liable in respect of any acts or omissions. However, the court may relieve him from such liability provided his acts or omissions would have been within his power if the debenture had been valid.[64] Where such relief is granted the court will hold the debenture holder liable for everything for which, but for the grant of relief, the receiver would have been liable.

The receiver is personally liable on contacts entered into on behalf of the company unless the contract provides otherwise. However, he has a right of indemnity against the company in respect of any liability which he incurs.[65] Where a receiver is conferred with management powers under a charge over the entire assets and undertaking of the company, he may transfer the business to a new company of which he becomes managing director rather than a receiver. This practice, called 'hiving-down', is a common means of avoiding personal liability. However, the receiver may be bound by the previous contracts of employment of the company's employees.[66]

The receiver is not personally liable on any other contracts entered into by the company prior to his appointment.[67] In *Ardmore Studios (Ireland) Ltd v. Lynch*,[68]

---

62 Section 316(1) of the Principal Act.
63 A charge may be invalid for lack of registration under section 99 of the Principal Act. Similarly, a charge may be avoided in a liquidation as a fraudulent preference under section 288 of the Principal Act. A floating charge may be invalidated under section 286 of the Principal Act during a liquidation.
64 Section 316(3) of the Principal Act.
65 Section 316 of the Principal Act.
66 European Communities (Safeguarding of Employees' Rights on Transfer of Undertakings) Regulations 1980 (SI 303/1980).
67 *Re Johnson & Co. (Builders) Ltd* [1955] 2 All ER 775.
68 [1965] IR 1.

a receiver was held not bound to an agreement entered into between the company and a trade union prior to his appointment. In respect of pre-appointment contracts, the receiver may repudiate them or agree to perform them. In *Re Thames Ironworks Co. Ltd*,[69] the receiver, on his appointment, discovered that the company had partly built ships which were to be completed before delivery. The contracts were unprofitable and the company was not in a financial position to complete them. The court gave leave to the receiver to repudiate the contracts. In rescinding a contract the receiver must exercise his powers *bona fide* and must not, without leave of the court, repudiate a contract in such a manner that it will have the effect of destroying the goodwill of the company's business.[70]

In exercising his right to dispose of assets, the receiver must be certain that the company actually owns the assets which are in its possession. It is often the case that many of the non-fixed assets of the company are subject to retention of title clauses. The effect of these clauses is that while assets are in the possession of the company, their ownership or title has been retained by the person that supplied them.[71] If a receiver sells assets that are owned by someone else he may be liable for the tort of conversion, and will in any case be obliged to account to the true owner.

---

69 [1912] WN 66.
70 *Re Newdigate Colliery* (1912) 1 Ch 468.
71 *Aluminium Industrie Vaassen BV v. Romalpa Ltd* [1976] 2 All ER 552.

CHAPTER TWENTY-FIVE

THE LIQUIDATION PROCESS

Introduction

Liquidation is a winding up process which ultimately leads to the demise of the company as its property is distributed for the benefit of its creditors and members. However, the formal termination of the life of the company does not end until either the company has been struck off the register by the Registrar of Companies or the court has dissolved it under section 249 of the Principal Act. (See Chapter 3, Company Formation.) Until this time the corporate personality of the company remains intact. It should be noted that a liquidator cannot be appointed where an examiner stands appointed under the Companies (Amendment) Act 1990.[1]

Qualifications of a Liquidator

A liquidator is the person appointed to wind up the company. Although the Companies Acts do not prescribe specific qualifications for the position of liquidator, the following are prohibited from so acting:

(a) a body corporate;
(b) any person who is, or has been, an officer, servant or auditor of the company within the previous twelve months;
(c) any connected person, unless the court otherwise agrees;
(d) any partner of an officer or servant of the company;
(e) any person who has the above connections to any subsidiary of the company, the holding company and any subsidiary of the holding company;
(f) any person restricted or disqualified under the provisions of the 1990 Companies Act.[2]

Duties of a Liquidator

The principal duties of the liquidator can be summarised as follows:

(a) to take possession of the company's assets, including debtors, and to protect them;
(b) to arrange a list of creditors and contributories;[3]
(c) to resolve all disputed claims and where necessary request the court to adjudicate on them;

---

1 See Chapter 27.
2 Section 300 and 300A of the Principal Act.
3 A contributory is any person liable to contribute to the assets of the company in the event of its being wound up: section 208 of the Principal Act.

(d) to realise the assets of the company;

(e) to apply the proceeds in payment of the company's debts and liabilities in accordance with the rules governing the priorities of payments;

(f) to distribute the surplus, if any, among the shareholders in accordance with the provisions of the Companies Acts and the company's own articles of association;

(g) to investigate the conduct of the company's affairs;

(h) to fulfil the various filing and notification requirements required by the Companies Acts;

(i) to comply with a court direction, if any, to bring certain matters to the attention of the DPP or, in a voluntary winding-up, to bring matters directly to the DPP. In addition to the above duties the Director of Corporate Enforcement may on his own motion, or where a complaint is made to him by a member, contributory or creditor of the company, request the liquidator to produce to the Director the liquidator's books for examination. The liquidator must comply with such a request and answer any questions of the Director concerning the content of the books. The liquidator must also give to the Director such assistance as he is reasonably able to give. If a liquidator fails to comply with these requirements he is guilty of an offence.[4] A liquidator of an insolvent company is also obliged to provide to the Director a report on matters relating to the liquidation.[5] Following the presentation of such a report to the Director the liquidator is obliged to apply to the court for a restriction order under section 150 of the Companies Act 1990 of each of the directors of the insolvent company, unless the Director relieves the liquidator of such an obligation.[6] Failure to provide a report to the Director or to apply for a restriction order (unless relieved of his obligation) is an offence;[7]

(j) to co-operate with the Director of Corporate Enforcement.

These duties are considered further later in this chapter and in Chapter 26.

Types of Liquidation

There are essentially two types of liquidation — a voluntary winding up and a compulsory winding up. The objective of both is the same, namely the realisation and distribution of the company's assets. However, there are fundamental differences between the two types, the most notable being that the court has little or no role to play in a voluntary liquidation whereas a compulsory liquidation is carried out by the court itself, which appoints an official liquidator to act on its behalf. Both types of liquidation are now considered further.

---

4 Section 57(1) Company Law Enforcement Act, 2001.
5 Section 56(1) ibid.
6 Section 56(2) ibid.
7 Section 56(3) ibid.

Compulsory Liquidations

A compulsory liquidation begins with the presentation of a petition to the High Court. Section 215 of the Principal Act provides that any of the following may present such a petition.

(a) The company — an authorising resolution must be approved by the shareholders. A general resolution will suffice if the company is insolvent; otherwise a special resolution is required.
(b) A creditor — this category also includes contingent or prospective creditors who must establish to the satisfaction of the court a *prima facie* case and provide such security for costs as the court may direct.
(c) A contributory — this category of applicant can only present a petition where they have satisfied the requirements of section 215(a) of the Principal Act. This section provides that a contributory shall not present a petition to wind up the company unless the number of members is reduced below the legal minimum or he has been a registered member of the company or has held shares which have devolved through the death of a shareholder, for at least six months in the previous eighteen months.
(d) Any person entitled to bring an action under section 205 of the Principal Act.
(e) The Director on foot of a report by an inspector appointed by either the court or the Director.[8]

Other parties may also petition the court to have the company wound up,[9] and the court itself may make an order to wind up the company in certain circumstances.[10]

1. *The Grounds for Presenting the Petition*

The grounds for presenting a petition are specified in section 213 of the Principal Act and include the following:

(a) the company has by special resolution resolved that the company be wound up by the court;
(b) the company does not commence its business within a year from its incorporation or suspends its business for a whole year;
(c) the number of members is reduced below the legal requirement for a company of its type;[11]

---

8 Sections 8 and 14 of the Companies Act 1990.
9 Including the Registrar of Companies and a company receiver.
10 The court may order the winding up of a company without being requested to do so following a report by an inspector appointed under the Companies Act 1990 or by an examiner appointed under the Companies (Amendment) Act 1990.
11 Regulation 11 of the European Communities (Single-Member Private Limited Companies) Regulations 1994 (SI 275/1994) removes private companies limited by shares or by guarantee from the ambit of this subsection.

(d) the company is unable to pay its debts;

(e) the court is of the opinion that it is just and equitable to wind up the company;

(f) the court is satisfied that the company's affairs are being conducted, or the powers of the directors are being exercised, in a manner oppressive to any member or in disregard of his interests as a member, and that despite the existence of an alternative remedy, the circumstances warrant the winding up of the company.

The last three grounds have been the subject of most petitions, and are considered further below.

The Company Is Unable to Pay Its Debts

Section 214 of the Principal Act deems a company to have been unable to pay its debts if any of the following circumstances exist.

(a) A creditor is indebted in a sum exceeding £1,000 (€1,269) and that amount is unpaid after three weeks from the time a demand in writing has been made to the company. It should be observed that a creditor may not use the petition as a debt-collecting process, nor will the petition be successful if the claim against the company is bona fide disputed on reasonable grounds. This was made clear in *Re Pageboy Couriers Ltd*,[12] where the court rejected a petition because the petitioner's claim for unpaid director's fees was vehemently disputed by the company. The court accepted the view that until a person is established as a creditor he has no *locus standi* to present the petition, and to use the procedure as a means of deciding a disputed debt is an abuse of the court process.

(b) An execution or other process issued on a judgment, decree or order of any court in favour of a creditor is unsatisfied. When the petitioner is relying on this ground he must be careful that a genuine attempt was made to obtain satisfaction of the judgment.[13]

(c) It is proved to the satisfaction of the court that the company is unable to pay its debts and the court in its determinations has taken into account the contingent and prospective liabilities of the company. In this instance the creditor must demonstrate either that the company is unable the pay its debts as they fall due (the commercial insolvency test) or that the company's assets are less than its liabilities (the balance sheet insolvency test). If a creditor cannot satisfy either of these tests, any other evidence of actual or prospective insolvency may be produced.

The Just and Equitable Ground

The legislative provisions do not prescribe any preconditions which must be fulfilled before this ground can be invoked. The courts are loath to set any

---

12 [1983] ILRM 510.

13 In *Re a Debtor* (No. 340 of 1992) [1994] 2 BCLC 171.

guidelines in this regard because to do so would have the effect of limiting their broad discretionary power. However, it is clear that the petitioner, to invoke the remedy, must come to court with clean hands.[14] Although each case will turn on its own facts, the following are examples of the circumstances in which the court has wound up a company on this ground.

(a) The Substratum of the Company Has Failed

A company is used as a vehicle for obtaining certain objectives. Once these are achieved, and the *raison d'être* no longer exists, the company is usually liquidated voluntarily. Where the objectives have not or cannot be achieved and the company is not voluntarily liquidated it is open to an applicant, which will usually be a shareholder, to petition the court for the winding up of that company on the just and equitable ground. In *Re German Date Coffee Co.*,[15] the company had been formed for the sole purpose of manufacturing coffee from dates under a German patent. When this patent proved impossible to obtain, the company manufactured under a Swedish patent. A contributory successfully petitioned for a winding up order because the sole purpose of the company could not be achieved. It is important to note that where a company has several objects, failure to achieve one will not be a sufficient ground for a petition of this type. Furthermore, a company may always alter its objects by special resolution.[16]

(b) The Company was Formed for an Illegal or Fraudulent Purpose

A company cannot be formed to achieve an illegal purpose. In the unlikely event of such a company being registered, a petition for its winding up could be presented on the just and equitable ground. The same would apply where a company was set up for reasons which, although not illegal, were motivated by fraud. In *Re Shrinkpak Ltd*[17] a liquidator succeeded in having a company wound up on the ground that it was being used for the fraudulent purpose of diverting funds from another insolvent company.

(c) Deadlock in Management

Where it appears to the court that the relationship between the shareholders and directors has irretrievably broken down, it may order the winding up of a company however profitable it appears to be. Such was the case in *Re Yenidje Tobacco Co.*,[18] where two sole traders had merged their businesses to form a company, of which they were the only shareholders and directors. The relationship between the two subsequently broke down and communications

---

14 *Re Vehicle Buildings and Insulations Ltd* [1986] ILRM 239.
15 (1882) 2 Ch D 169.
16 See Chapter 5.
17 High Court, 20 December 1989, noted in Courtney, *The Law of Private Companies*, 1994.
18 [1916] 2 Ch 426.

were non-existent except through the medium of the company secretary. Despite the fact that the company was successful, it was held that a winding up was justified. Similarly, in *Re Vehicle Buildings and Insulations Ltd*,[19] when the relationship between the only two shareholders and directors irreparably broke down, an order was made to have the company wound up.

(d) The 'Quasi-partnership' Relationship has Failed

Where the company is being operated in a manner similar to a partnership, and the relationship of trust and mutual confidence has broken down, the court may also make an order on the just and equitable ground.[20]

The Oppression of Minority Shareholders

Where the company's affairs are being conducted or the director's powers are being exercised in a manner oppressive to the applicant or to any other member, he can apply to court for an order under section 205 of the Principal Act which deals with oppression of shareholders. Alternatively, a shareholder can apply under section 213(g) of the Principal Act for an order that the company be wound up. The court will usually only grant an order of this type where no other remedies are appropriate. This area of the law is considered in greater detail in Chapter 15.

2. The Hearing

When considering a petition the court may consider the views of other parties, particularly creditors.[21] At any time after the petition has been presented and before a winding up order has been made the court may, on the application of the company or any creditor or contributory, stay or restrain proceedings pending against the company.[22]

The court may also make an interim order appointing a provisional liquidator whose powers will be determined by the court.[23] A provisional liquidator will usually be appointed where it is necessary to protect the rights and interests of the company and its creditors. Once a provisional liquidator has been appointed, no action or proceeding can be taken against the company without the leave of the court.[24] The initial role of the provisional liquidator mirrors that of an official liquidator in that he must take into his custody or under his control all the property and things in action of which the company is or appears to be entitled.[25]

---

19 [1986] ILRM 239.
20 *Re Westbourne Galleries Ltd* [1973] AC 360 and *Re Murph's Restaurant Ltd* [1979] ILRM 141. See Chapter 15, Minority Protection.
21 *Re R.W. Sharman* [1957] 1 All ER 737, *Re Bula Mines Limited*, High Court, 18 July 1986 (Costello J.) and Supreme Court 13 May 1988.
22 Section 217 of the Principal Act.
23 Section 226 of the Principal Act.
24 Section 222 of the Principal Act.
25 Section 229 of the Principal Act.

Having heard the petition the court may dismiss it, adjourn it or make any other order as it sees fit, including a winding up order. A winding up order, if made, operates in favour of all the creditors and of all the contributories of the company in the same manner as if they had presented a joint petition.[26]

3. Notification and Filing Requirements

A copy of the winding up order must be delivered by the company, or by such other person as the court may direct, to the Registrar of Companies within twenty-one days.[27] The liquidator must also cause to have published in *Iris Oifigiúil* a notice of his appointment and deliver to the Registrar of Companies a copy of the court order appointing him.[28] The directors and secretary of the company, or such other person as the court may direct, must also, unless otherwise agreed by the court, file a statement of affairs of the company with the court. The statement must be filed within twenty-one days of the appointment of a provisional liquidator or the making of a winding up order, or such longer period as the court may agree.[29] Where any person defaults in complying with this requirement he shall be liable to a fine not exceeding £500 (€635). The statement of affairs must be presented in the prescribed form, be verified by affidavit and show the following particulars:

(a) the company's assets, debts and liabilities;
(b) the names, residences and occupations of its creditors and the securities held by them respectively;
(c) the dates when the securities were respectively given; and
(d) such other information as may be prescribed or as the court may require.

4. Effect of the winding up Order

Once the court makes the order to wind up the company, the following takes effect:

(a) An official liquidator is appointed to wind up the company. The official liquidator shall receive such salary or remuneration as the court may direct.[30] The acts of the liquidator will be valid notwithstanding any defect later discovered in his appointment.[31]
(b) The order will take effect from the date the petition is presented. If a voluntary liquidation was already under way, the order takes effect from the date the authorising resolution for the voluntary liquidation was passed.[32]

---

26 Section 223 of the Principal Act.
27 Section 221 of the Principal Act.
28 Section 227(1) of the Principal Act.
29 Section 224 of the Principal Act.
30 Section 228(d) of the Principal Act.
31 Section 228(g) of the Principal Act.
32 Section 220 of the Principal Act. The significance of this is considered further in the next chapter.

(c) No proceedings may be continued or instituted against the company without the consent of the court.[33]

(d) Any disposition of the company's property and any transfer of its shares , subsequent to the commencement of liquidation are void unless the court otherwise directs.[34]

(e) Any attachment, sequestration, distress or execution put in force against the property of the company after the commencement of the winding up shall be void.[35]

(f) Every invoice, business letter and order for goods which bears the name of the company must state that the company is in liquidation.[36]

(g) The employees of the company are automatically dismissed, but the liquidator may re-hire them if he so wishes.

(h) The directors' powers are assumed by the liquidator.

(i) Any floating charges crystallise.

(j) If a receiver has already been appointed he can no longer bind the company as its agent.

5. Committee of Inspection

If the court so orders, the liquidator shall summon a meeting of the creditors and contributories to decide whether or not to apply to the court for the appointment of a committee of inspection to assist him in carrying on the business.[37] The committee of inspection will be composed of creditors and contributories in such proportions as they agree or, failing agreement, in such proportion as the court will decide. The committee will meet on its own initiative or when called upon to do so by the liquidator. Decisions are made by a majority of the committee members, but the members cannot make a decision unless a majority is present at the meeting. A member of the committee of inspection may resign by notice to the liquidator and in specified circumstances his office becomes vacant.[38] Furthermore, a member of the committee may be removed by an ordinary resolution of the creditors or contributories, depending on which category he represents.

6. Powers of the Liquidator in a Compulsory Liquidation

Once appointed, the liquidator is obliged to take under his control all the property and things in action to which the liquidator is or appears to be entitled.[39] The court

33 Section 222 of the Principal Act.
34 Section 218 of the Principal Act.
35 Section 219 of the Principal Act.
36 Section 303 of the Principal Act.
37 Section 232 of the Principal Act.
38 If a member becomes bankrupt or makes an arrangement with his creditors or is absent from five consecutive meetings of the committee without consent.
39 Section 229 of the Principal Act.

260

may also direct that the company's property shall vest in the liquidator by his official name.[40] In order to fulfil his duties, section 231 of the Principal Act confers on the liquidator a number of powers, some exercisable at his discretion and others qualified in that they can only be exercised with the sanction of the court or the committee of inspection. The general powers of the liquidator are as follows:

(a) to sell any of the company's property — the liquidator shall not sell by private contract a non-cash asset to anyone who is, or was, in the three years prior to the date of the liquidator's appointment, an officer of the company, unless he has given at least fourteen days notice of his intention to do so to all the creditors of the company;

(b) to execute all necessary documents on the company's behalf;

(c) to prove in bankruptcy against any contributory;

(d) to draw, accept, make and endorse any bill of exchange or promissory note on behalf of the company;

(e) to mortgage the company's assets;

(f) to take out letters of administration on any deceased contributory for the purpose of obtaining payment of any monies due by that contributory to the company;

(g) to give security for costs in the name of the company;

(h) to appoint agents to do such work as the liquidator is unable to do himself; and

(i) to do all other things necessary for the winding up.

The qualified powers include the following:

(a) to bring or defend any action in the company's name;

(b) to carry on the business of the company, if necessary for a beneficial winding up;

(c) to appoint a solicitor to assist him in his duties;

(d) to pay any class of creditors in full;

(e) to make any compromise or arrangement with creditors;

(f) to compromise claims against debtors.

7. Court Powers

The legislative provisions also empower the court to do any of the following.

(a) On the application of the liquidator or any creditor or contributory, annul the winding up order or stay any proceedings in relation to the winding up, on such terms and for such period as the court may deem fit.[41] Where such an application is made the court may, before making an order, require the liquidator to furnish to the court a report relating to any matters which are relevant. An office copy of any order to annul the winding up order or stay proceedings in relation to the winding up must be forwarded by the company,

---

40 Section 230 of the Principal Act.
41 Section 234(1) of the Principal Act.

or such other person as the court may direct, to the Registrar of Companies.[42]

(b) Settle a list of contributories and cause the assets of the company to be collected and applied in discharge of the company's liabilities.[43]

(c) Direct any contributory, trustee, receiver, banker, agent or officer of the company to pay such monies and deliver such property, books and papers, to which the company is prima facie entitled, to the liquidator.[44]

(d) Make calls on contributories.[45]

(e) Exclude claims by creditors not fixed within the period fixed by the court.[46]

(f) Make an order allowing for inspection of the company's books and papers following an application by a creditor or contributory or Director of Corporate Enforcement.[47]

(g) In the event that the assets of the company are insufficient to satisfy its liabilities, make an order that the costs, charges and expenses of the winding up be paid out of the assets of the company in such order of priority as the court thinks just.[48]

(h) Summon before it and examine, where necessary under oath, officers and any other person known or suspected to have in his possession any property of the company or supposed to be indebted to the company or any person whom the court deems capable of giving information relating to the affairs of the company and order them where appropriate to pay any indebtedness owed by them to the company or to deliver any money, property or books or papers in their possession which belong to the company.[49]

(i) Require the attendance of any officer at a meeting of creditors or contributories or at a meeting of the committee of inspection for the purpose of giving information in relation to the affairs of the company.[50]

(j) Order the arrest of, and the seizure of assets belonging to, any contributory director, shadow director, secretary or other officer of the company where there is evidence that such a person is about to quit the State or remove any of his property from the State.[51]

(k) Order the return of certain property or assets fraudulently transferred;

(l) Order that the company be dissolved where its affairs have been completely wound up.[52]

---

42 Section 234(4) of the Principal Act.
43 Section 235 of the Principal Act.
44 Section 236 of the Principal Act.
45 Section 238 of the Principal Act.
46 Section 241 of the Principal Act.
47 Section 243 of the Principal Act.
48 Section 244 of the Principal Act.
49 Sections 245 and 245A of the Principal Act.
50 Section 246 of the Principal Act.
51 Section 247 of the Principal Act.
52 Section 249 of the Principal Act.

8. *Resignation and Removal of the Official Liquidator*

A liquidator appointed by the court may resign or, on cause shown, be removed by the court.[53] A vacancy which arises as a result of the resignation or removal of an official liquidator shall be filled by the court.

Voluntary Liquidations

Section 251(1) of the Principal Act provides that a company may be wound up voluntarily in any of the following circumstances:

(a) when the period, if any, fixed by the articles of association for the duration of the company has expired;
(b) when the members resolve by special resolution that the company be wound up voluntarily;
(c) if the company in general meeting resolves that it cannot by reason of its liabilities continue in business and that it should be wound up voluntarily.

There are two types of voluntary liquidations; a members' voluntary winding up and a creditors' voluntary winding up. The most notable difference between the two is one of solvency. In a members' voluntary winding up the company must be solvent, while this is not the case in a creditors' voluntary winding up. Therefore where the company resolves that it cannot by reason of its liabilities continue in business and should therefore be wound up, the liquidation must proceed as a creditors' voluntray winding-up liquidation. The differences between the two types of liquidation are now considered further.

1. *Members' Voluntary Winding Up*

Before a members' voluntary winding up proceeds the directors must, at a properly convened directors' meeting, make a statutory declaration of solvency.[54] In essence, this declaration is a sworn statement by the directors that in their opinion, following a full enquiry into the company's affairs, the company will be able to pay its debts within twelve months of the commencement of the winding up. Before the declaration of solvency will have effect it must comply with the following:

(a) it must be made within the twenty-eight days immediately preceding the date of the passing of the resolution to wind the company up;[55]
(b) it is to be delivered to the Registrar of Companies within fifteen days of the delivery to the Registrar of a copy of the resolution to wind the company up;[56]

---

53 Section 228(c) of the Principal Act.
54 Section 256(1) of the Principal Act.
55 Section 256(2)(a) of the Principal Act.
56 Ibid.

(c) it must embody a statement of the company's assets and liabilities at the latest date that is practicable and in any event at a date not more than three months before the making of the declaration;[57]

(d) it must have attached to it a report, from an independent person who is qualified to be an auditor of the company, which must state that in his opinion and to the best of his information the opinions of the directors in the declaration of solvency and the statement of the company's assets and liabilities are reasonable;

(e) a statement from the independent person is attached to the effect that he has given his written consent to the issue of the declaration with the report attached; and

(f) a copy of the declaration is attached to every notice of the general meeting at which it is intended to propose a resolution for voluntary winding up.

If, having made the declaration of solvency, it transpires that the company is not solvent the court may, on the application of the liquidator or any creditor or contributory of the company, declare that any director who was a party to the declaration without having reasonable grounds for his opinion shall be personally liable for any or all of the debts as the court may specify.[58] If the company's debts are not paid within twelve months after the commencement of the winding up, there is a presumption that the directors did not have reasonable grounds for their opinion.[59] This latter provision is intended to deter a director from making a declaration unless circumstances clearly suggest that the company is solvent. Once the declaration has been made, and the resolution of the company passed, notice of the resolution must be published in *Iris Oifigiúil* within fourteen days of its being passed.[60]

Once the company has completed the statutory formalities, it may appoint a liquidator to wind up the company. The liquidator must consent, in writing, to the appointment.[61] The company in general meeting will determine his remuneration.

2. Creditors' Voluntary Winding Up

Notwithstanding the fact that a members' voluntary winding up has commenced, it may still be converted into a creditors' winding up. Section 256(5) of the Principal Act provides that the court may make an order converting the liquidation into a creditors' winding up if, on the application of a creditor or creditors representing at least one-fifth in value and number of the creditors of the company, the court is of the opinion that the company is unlikely to pay its debts within twelve months. An application must be made within twenty-eight days after the authorising resolution to wind up the company has been

---

57 Section 256(2)(b) of the Principal Act.
58 Section 256(8) of the Principal Act.
59 Section 256(9) of the Principal Act.
60 Section 252(1) of the Principal Act.
61 Section 276A of the Principal Act.

advertised. In the event that the court makes such an order, a copy of the court order must be delivered to the Registrar of Companies by either the liquidator or the company itself.

Section 261 of the Principal Act provides that a liquidator is obliged to call a meeting of the creditors where, in a members' voluntary winding up, he is of the opinion that the company will not be able to pay its debts within the twelve months. The meeting must be called within fourteen days from the day he formed the opinion and it must be notified to the creditors and advertised in *Iris Oifigiúil* and two daily newspapers. At this creditors' meeting the liquidator must attend, preside and present a statement of affairs of the company. From this time onward the liquidation becomes a creditors' liquidation and the creditors can replace the liquidator with their own appointee.

Liquidations can also commence as a creditors' voluntary winding up, where the company has resolved that because of its liabilities it cannot continue and should be wound up voluntarily. Where this occurs the company must call a meeting of the creditors for the day or the day after the resolution for the voluntary winding up is to be proposed, with at least ten days' notice of meeting having been given to creditors.[62] The directors must present to the meeting a full statement of the company's affairs together with a list of creditors and the amounts owing to them. The creditors and the company at their respective meetings may nominate a person to be liquidator and if they nominate different persons, the person nominated by the creditors will be the liquidator, although an appeal can be made to the court to have this changed.[63] If the proposed liquidator has any connections with a creditor, that connection must be made known to the creditors' meeting. The court can appoint a voluntary liquidator where there is no other liquidator acting, and it can replace or remove one on cause shown.[64]

Where a liquidator has been appointed by the company and the creditors' meeting has not yet been held, the liquidator cannot exercise certain powers without the sanction of the court.[65] This provision is designed to prevent a 'friendly' liquidator from exercising his powers in a manner which might not be to the benefit of the company's creditors.

The creditors of a company have the power to appoint a committee of inspection which will consist of not more than five persons nominated by the creditors.[66] The company may also appoint three persons to the committee. However, the creditors may object to these appointees and the court may, on an application by the creditors, disqualify them from so acting.[67] The committee of

---

62 Section 266(1) of the Principal Act.
63 Section 267 of the Principal Act.
64 Section 277 of the Principal Act.
65 Section 131 of the Companies Act 1990.
66 Section 268 of the Principal Act.
67 Section 268(2) of the Principal Act.

inspection has considerably more powers than in a compulsory liquidation in that it may determine the remuneration of the liquidator, determine whether the liquidator should continue the business of the company, sanction the exercise of certain of the liquidator's powers and determine whether the powers of the directors should continue.[68]

3. Effects of the Appointment of a Voluntary Liquidator

The effects of the appointment of a voluntary liquidator are essentially the same as in a compulsory winding up. However, there are notable differences in that:

(a) while the directors' powers are assumed in a compulsory liquidation, the committee of inspection or the creditors can sanction the continuance of some or all of the directors' powers in a creditor's voluntary liquidation or the general meeting can sanction those powers in a members' voluntary winding-up;

(b) a voluntary liquidation commences on the day the resolution is passed — it is not retrospective;

(c) the liquidator is not an officer of the court;

(d) there is no automatic stay of legal proceedings against the company;

(e) there is no automatic dismissal of the employees. However, the liquidator is unlikely to retain employees unless he is given the power to carry on the company's business;

(f) the company shall, from the commencement of the winding-up, cease to carry on business except where it is necessary for the beneficial winding-up of the company;

(g) any transfer of shares made after the commencement of the winding-up without the sanction of the liquidator is void;

(h) any alteration in the status of the members of the company made after the commencement of the winding-up is void.

4. Powers of Voluntary Liquidators

Section 276(1) of the Principal Act sets out the powers which can be exercised by a voluntary liquidator, which are similar to those of an official liquidator. However, unlike the official liquidator, he may exercise the following powers without the sanction of the court or committee of inspection:

(a) bring or defend any action or other legal proceedings in the name of and on behalf of the company;

(b) carry on the business of the company for the benefit of the winding up;

(c) appoint a solicitor to assist him in the performance of his duties;

---

68 Section 269 of the Principal Act.

(d) exercise the powers of the court in relation to settling lists of contributories, making calls and summoning general meetings;

(e) pay the debts of the company and adjust the list of contributories.

All other powers exercisable by the sanction of the court or the committee of inspection in relation to a compulsory liquidation must only be exercised by a liquidator in a member's voluntary winding up, with the sanction of the special resolution and, in the case of a creditors' voluntary winding up, with the sanction of the court or the committee of inspection.

5. *Duties of the Liquidator*

In addition to the normal duties of a liquidator, he is obliged to hold annual meetings of the company and creditors (in a creditors voluntary winding-up) until such time as the winding-up is complete. He must lay before each meeting an account of his acts and dealings during the preceding year. He must send a copy of this report to the Registrar of companies within seven days.

6. *Court Powers in Voluntary Winding-up*

The court may, on the application of the Director of Corporate Enforcement, make an order for the inspection by the Director of any books and papers in the possession of a company, and the company and every officer and the liquidator shall co-operate with the Director in this regard.[69] The court may summon before it, for examination, any officer or person known or suspected to have in his possession any property of the company or supposed to be indebted to the company, or any person whom the court deems capable of giving information relating to the promotion, formation, trade, dealings, affairs or property of the company,[70] and order them where appropriate to pay any indebtedness owed by them to the company or to deliver any money, property books or papers in their possession which belong to the company.[71] The court may order the arrest of, and seizure of assets belonging to, any contributory, director, shadow director, secretary or other officer of the company where there is evidence that the person is about to quit the State or remove any of his property from the State.[72]

7. *Converting from Voluntary to Compulsory Liquidation*

At any stage during the course of a voluntary winding up the court may be petitioned to wind up the company compulsorily. In such a case the petitioner must demonstrate that one of the grounds for such a winding up exists. It must also give good reason to the court as to why an order should be made converting

---

69 Section 282A Principal Act.

70 Section 282B of the Principal Act.

71 Section 282C of the Principal Act.

72 Section 282D of the Principal Act.

the liquidation from a voluntary to a compulsory one. Of particular concern to the court will be the added costs involved where the liquidation is carried out by the court. This is of particular concern if the company's assets are already inadequate to cover the liabilities. In *Re Gilt Construction Ltd*,[73] a two-member company had agreed to be wound up. The members' choice of liquidator differed and the non-petitioning shareholder's choice was supported by the creditors. The petitioner argued that the other shareholder was manipulating the assets of the company for his own personal benefit. In considering the liquidator's skills, honesty and integrity, and the additional costs involved in a court-appointed liquidator, the court refused the order sought.

8. Completion of Voluntary Winding-Up

When the affairs of the company are fully wound up, the liquidator must present an account of the winding-up — showing how the winding-up has been conducted and how the assets of the company have been disposed of — to a general meeting of the company and a meeting of the creditors (in the case of a creditors' voluntary winding-up). The liquidator must also send the Registrar notification of his final report and three months after receipt by the Registrar, the company is deemed to be dissolved.

---

73 [1994] 2 ILRM 456.

CHAPTER TWENTY-SIX

ASSETS REALISATION AND DISTRIBUTION

Introduction

As mentioned in the previous chapter, the liquidator's primary function is to gather in and realise the assets of the company and apply the proceeds in a manner prescribed by law. A liquidator is also obliged to investigate the affairs of the company, which may lead to the imposition of criminal and civil liability on the directors and other officers of the company. Where civil liability is imposed the liquidator may be in a position to 'swell the assets' available for distribution to the company's creditors and members. The liquidator's functions will be considered under the following headings:

1. asset realisation;
2. application of assets;

Asset Realisation

Once appointed, the liquidator will establish the extent of the company's assets and liabilities. He must take the company's property into his possession and he may apply to the court to have the title of the property vested in his name.[1] The liquidator may, subject to providing such indemnity as the court may direct, bring or defend in his name any action or legal proceedings relating to that property. The general rule is that from the commencement of the liquidation a disposition of the company's property cannot be made unless approved either by the court in a compulsory winding up or by the debenture holder or committee of inspection in a voluntary winding up.[2] The difficulty in the case of a compulsory winding up is that the liquidation date is fixed at the date the petition was made. As it would be unusual for an order to wind up the company being granted on the same day that the petition was presented, the liquidation will have retrospective effect. Accordingly, the directors and other officers of the company should take great care in dealing with the company's assets from the date the petition is presented in case the petition proves successful and a liquidator retrospectively invalidates any dispositions.

In carrying out his function, the liquidator will attempt to maximise the assets available for distribution and reduce the liabilities. Where a liquidator is selling property he must generally try to obtain the best possible price.[3] In any case the liquidator can apply to the court under section 280 of the Principal Act for

---

1 Section 230 of the Principal Act.
2 Section 218 of the Principal Act.
3 *Van Hool McArdle Ltd v. Rohan Industrial Estates Ltd & Anon* [1980] IR 137.

directions in relation to any matters which may arise during the course of the liquidation. Where the liquidator has any doubt he would be advised to exercise his options under section 280, particularly as a liquidator may be liable for misfeasance.[4] As part of his asset realisation functions, the liquidator is conferred with what are often referred to as 'asset-swelling' powers which have their origin in bankruptcy rules. The primary 'asset-swelling' measures are:

1. disclaimer of onerous contracts under section 290 of the Principal Act;
2. fraudulent preference transactions under section 286 of the Principal Act;
3. avoidance of floating charges under section 288 of the Principal Act;
4. pooling and contributions orders under section 140 of the 1990 Act;
5. the return of assets which have been improperly transferred under section 139 of the 1990 Act;
6. applications to hold directors civilly liable for breach of their statutory duties or for any other wrong done to the company.

1. Disclaimer of Onerous Contracts — Section 290 of the Principal Act

Section 290 of the Principal Act applies an age-old bankruptcy rule to companies by allowing a liquidator to disclaim any of the company's property which has onerous obligations attaching to it. The object of the power is not to deny creditors their legal rights but rather to enable the liquidator to carry out his functions expeditiously without dragging out the liquidation process. The effect of the section is that a liquidator may discriminate against some creditors by disclaiming the company's obligations to them on the grounds that the performance would be unduly burdensome to the company. The liquidator has twelve months from the commencement of a liquidation to disclaim, and the court must approve all disclaimers. However, a creditor can force the liquidator to make a decision within a shorter period of time by making an application in writing to the liquidator asking him whether or not he intends to disclaim.[5] The liquidator must then respond within twenty-eight days, or such longer period as the court may allow. Failure to respond within this time frame has the effect of denying the liquidator the power to disclaim.

Practically speaking, almost any contract may be disclaimed, giving the liquidator wide scope. This is because section 290(1) of the Principal Act defines the property and interests which are capable of being disclaimed as that which consists of:

> land of any tenure burdened with onerous covenants, of shares or stock in companies, of unprofitable contracts or any other property which is unsaleable or not readily saleable by reason of its binding the possessor thereof to the performance of any onerous act or to the repayment of any sum of money.

---

4 Section 298 of the Principal Act.
5 Section 290(5) of the Principal Act.

The principal issue that arises in relation to the disclaimer of onerous property is the position of creditors and third parties affected by the disclaimer. The effect of a disclaimer on a third party can be seen in *Tempany v. Royal Liver Trustees Ltd.*[6] There the liquidator disclaimed a lease because the rental was far in excess of the current market value and was therefore a drain on the company's resources. The defendant was the guarantor of the company's obligations under the lease and naturally opposed the application. The High Court held that it was not necessary to disclaim the guarantee to effect the disclaimer of the lease and, furthermore, the concern of the court was not the effect the disclaimer had on third parties but rather the effect it had on the interests of the company.

Under section 290 any individual suffering loss as a result of the disclaimer shall be deemed to be a creditor of the company and may prove the amount as a debt in the winding up.[7] The extent of a creditor's entitlement under a disclaimed contract has been the subject of much litigation. However, most cases have concerned bankruptcy rules, and as there are subtle distinctions between those and the insolvency rules of disclaimers, great care should be taken when such cases are being considered. In *Re Ranks Ireland Ltd*,[8] the contracts being disclaimed were telephone equipment leases. The terms of the lease provided that in the event of its repudiation a specified amount would become payable as damages. Murphy J. held that this was not the correct measure of damages in these circumstances, as that amount was only appropriate where the hirer had repudiated his contract. A repudiation, he said, was not the same as a disclaimer. Accordingly, the appropriate measure of damages was held to be the difference between the rent the company would have paid the lessor and the rent the lessor is likely to earn during the unexpired residue of the lease.

If a liquidator uses property which is later the subject of a 'disclaimer', that portion of the contractual amount payable during the period of usage must be paid by the liquidator. This principle has been established by case-law and is reflected in the rules of the Superior Court. In *Re GWI Ltd*,[9] Murphy J. held that:

> where a liquidator takes possession or remains in possession of leasehold property for the purposes of winding up, the rent of the premises ought to be regarded as a debt contracted for the purpose of winding up the company and ought therefore to be paid in full like any other debt or expense properly incurred by the liquidator for the same purpose.

In that case, the lessor had claimed the full amount of the lease for the period of liquidation on the basis that the liquidator enjoyed possession. In fact the liquidator was not in physical possession, but he had sublet it for an amount of £4,000. Murphy J. rejected the lessor's claim on the basis that he could have

---

6 [1984] ILRM 273.
7 Section 290(9) of the Principal Act.
8 [1988] ILRM 751.
9 High Court, 10 November 1987.

ordered the liquidator out for not paying the rent. He substituted the lessor's claim of £17,000 for the lesser amount of £4,000, representing what had been paid to the liquidator under the sub-lease.

2. Fraudulent Preference under Section 286

A number of statutory provisions exist to prevent a company, knowing that its financial situation is terminal, from dissipating company assets which would otherwise be available for the general body of creditors. The reason for such provisions is to protect one of the core principles of insolvency law — that creditors of the same class should be treated on a *pari passu* basis. Reference has already been made to the fact that post winding up dispositions are invalid without the consent of the court or the committee of inspection. In addition, transactions which took place while the company was insolvent but before the commencement of the winding up can also be avoided.

Under the Principal Act, any transaction by a company which is intended to favour a creditor, and was entered into in the six months prior to a company going into liquidation at a time when the company was unable to pay its debts as they fell due, can be set aside for fraudulent preference.[10] Since the introduction of the 1990 Act, the time frame has been extended to twenty-four months in the case of a transaction concerning connected persons. Furthermore, the statutory provisions now raise a presumption of fraudulent preference where transactions involve connected persons, related companies or a trustee or surety of any debt due to a connected person or a related company.[11] The section has a potentially wide application because the nature of the transactions likely to be impugned are not specified. It would seem that liquidators can challenge any transaction provided it meets the criteria of the section. In *Peat v. Gresham Trust*[12] it was held that the failure of a company to oppose an application to the court to extend the time for registering a charge was an action that could come within section 286.

Essentially, under section 286 the liquidator must prove that there was a dominant intention to prefer on the part of the company. This raises three difficulties. First, it is the 'intent' of the company itself that must be proven. As the company has no mind of its own, a liquidator must impute the intent of its agents to the whole company and this is difficult to do. In *Corran Construction v. Bank of Ireland Finance Ltd*,[13] the question arose as to whether the intention of a director could be imputed to the entire company. There the defendant bank had taken a mortgage over certain of the company's land and some time later the bank discovered that the mortgage had not been registered in accordance with

---

10 Section 286 of the Principal Act.
11 Section 286(3) of the Principal Act as inserted by section 135 of the Companies Act 1990.
12 [1934] AC 252.
13 [1976–7] ILRM 175.

the Companies Act. The bank persuaded the director, who at that time was quite ill, to give a fresh charge. The evidence showed that the director appreciated the fact that the defendant would be secured in the event that the company did not repay its debt and that there was every chance, given the company's insolvency, that it could not meet the repayments. Despite this, the court held that the evidence was not sufficient to infer an intention on behalf of the company to prefer a creditor.[14]

The second difficulty lies in the fact that there will rarely be direct evidence of an intention to prefer. Therefore the court will be obliged to look at the surrounding circumstances in order to infer an intention. In *Station Motors v. AIB*,[15] the company had a large overdraft with the defendant bank which was guaranteed by the member-directors of the company, a husband and wife. The company became insolvent and the couple resolved that it should be wound up. Before this happened they caused certain payments to be made to the overdraft account which had the effect of reducing their exposure under the guarantee. The court held that the payments were a fraudulent preference designed to benefit the bank directly and the couple indirectly. In doing so Carroll J. considered the following points.

(a) Just because there is a preference, one cannot infer an intention to prefer. The liquidator has to positively prove that an intention to prefer existed at the time of the transaction and the onus rests on the liquidator to so prove.
(b) Where there is no evidence of an intention to prefer there is no legal principle precluding the court from drawing an inference of such an intention from the circumstances.
(c) The circumstances must demonstrate that the intention was a dominant one. It is not enough to say that a person benefited from an action which was motivated by another reason.
(d) Where the case involves directors and where they obtain an advantage from the transaction, the court may draw an inference from those transactions which must involve at the very least the taint of dishonesty.

As the payments were made to the company's current account after it was resolved to wind up the company, and those payments had the effect of reducing an overdraft which was personally secured by the directors, Carroll J. held that there was sufficient evidence to infer a fraudulent preference within the meaning of section 286.

The third difficulty arises because even when an intention to prefer is established it is further necessary to demonstrate that the intention was a 'dominant' one. In *Re FLE Holdings Ltd*,[16] a defective charge was registered. At

---

14 See also *Kelleher v. Continental Irish Meats*, High Court, 9 May 1978.
15 [1985] IR 756.
16 [1967] 1 WLR 1409.

the bank's request, the company executed a new charge and had it registered. The contention that the bank had been preferred was rejected on the grounds that the dominant intention was not to confer a preference on the bank, but to benefit the company by keeping on good terms with the bank.

3. Avoidance of a Floating Charge under Section 288

Another statutory provision designed to protect the general body of creditors by preventing a reduction of an insolvent company's assets is section 288 of the Principal Act, as amended.[17] It provides that where a company is being wound up, a floating charge created in the twelve months prior to the commencement of the winding up shall, unless the company was solvent immediately after the time the charge was created, be invalid. Where a charge is created in favour of a connected person the relevant period has been extended from twelve months to two years. Section 288 provides for exceptions where money was paid, or the price or value of goods or services sold or supplied, to the company at the time of or subsequently to the creation of and in consideration for the charge. As section 288 only applies in a winding up situation, if a chargee moves quickly to enforce his security before the company goes into liquidation he can retain the entire proceeds of realisation.[18]

Section 288 does not apply to fixed charges. However, in an appropriate case a fixed charge could be avoided under section 286 as a fraudulent preference.

A floating charge can only be invalidated if the company was at the time of giving the charge insolvent. The test of solvency to be applied was set out in *Re Creation Printing Co. Ltd*.[19] There, McWilliam J. held that where a company is unable to pay its debts as they fall due, it is insolvent irrespective of its balance sheet position.[20]

Section 288 will not apply to a charge that is given in consideration for *inter alia* money actually advanced or paid to the company either at the time the charge was created or later. The question of what constitutes 'at the time' the charge was created has given rise to litigation. In *Re Daniel Murphy Ltd*,[21] it was held that provided there was no delay in executing the charge and the transaction was not intended to deceive the creditors, a difference of thirty-five days between the time of advancing the cash and the taking of the charge could not be said to be unreasonable. The court will be concerned with the substance of any transaction that took place, and not simply its form. The test to be applied is whether the company indeed received funds in exchange for the security and

---

17 Section 136 of the Companies Act 1990.
18 *Mace Builders (Glasgow) Ltd v. Lunn* [1987] BCLC 55.
19 [1978] ILRM 219.
20 This test was accepted by the Supreme Court [1981] IR 353.
21 [1964] IR 1.

whether the transaction benefited the company.[22] As Barron J. observed in *Smurfit Paribas Bank Ltd v. AAB Export Finance Ltd*.

> in order to treat payments made to the company before the execution of the charge as payments made at the time of the charge, the necessary elements to be established are; that an honest transaction has been put in place and there was a reasonable expedition in and about the preparation and execution of the charge.[23]

In that particular case, although the monies advanced were advanced on the basis that a company would grant a charge over its assets, the charge was not in fact duly executed until two years later. In Barron J.'s view such a protracted delay could not be justified and accordingly the floating charge was invalid.[24]

Section 289 of the Principal Act provides for additional circumstances whereby a floating charge may be avoided. Where a company is being wound up and it was within the previous twelve months indebted to an officer of the company and that debt was discharged wholly or partly by the company or any other person and the company had created a floating charge in favour of that officer within the twelve month period, that charge is invalid to the extent of the repayment unless it can be shown that the company was solvent immediately after the creation of the charge. This provision prevents the avoidance of section 288 by the directors who arrange to have their loans repaid and then on the basis of fresh advances to the company obtain a floating charge.

4. Pooling and Contribution Orders

Section 140 of the 1990 Companies Act has the effect of cutting across the veil of incorporation, as it applies to groups of companies, by empowering the liquidator to apply to the court for an order directing that a related company contribute to the assets of the company being wound up.

By virtue of Section 141 of the Companies Act 1990, the liquidator may apply to the court for an order directing that the assets of a related company which is also being wound up be pooled between the creditors of both companies. (See Chapter 2 for definition of related company.)

The main criterion for determining whether a contribution or pooling order should be made is that the court is of the opinion that it is 'just and equitable' to do so. The court in deciding this question must consider specific criteria regarding the relationship between the companies, the conduct of the related company towards the creditors of the company being wound up, and the extent to which the conduct of the related company contributed to the winding up of the other company. Furthermore, the court must, when considering making a

---

22 *Re Destone Fabrics Ltd* [1941] Ch 319.
23 [1991] 2 IR 19 at 30.
24 In the UK it has been held that the value must be provided contemporaneously with the creation of the charge: *Power v. Sharpe Investments Ltd* [1994] 1 BCLC 111.

contribution order, have regard to the effect of such an order on the creditors of the related company. When considering whether to make a pooling order the court must also have regard to the extent to which the businesses of both companies were intermingled.

5. *Return of Improperly Transferred Assets*

If on the application of the liquidator the court is satisfied that:

(a) any property of the company was disposed of by act or omission; and
(b) the effect of such disposal was to perpetrate a fraud on the company, its creditors or members;

the court may, if it considers it just and equitable to do so, order any person who appears to have the use, control or possession of the property or the proceeds of sale of that property to deliver the property or the proceeds to the liquidator on such terms as it sees fit.[25]

6. *Application to have Officers Held Personally Liable for Debts of Company*

Where a liquidator in the course of the winding up discovers evidence suggesting that either the directors' duties have been breached or a wrong has been done to the company, he may apply to the court for the appropriate declarations or orders. Many of these declarations can hold the directors responsible, in whole or part, for the debts of the company or order that the director account to the company for any loss suffered by the company or for any gain made by the directors. Many of these duties have been considered at length in previous chapters, including the following:

(a) the fiduciary duties of directors;[26]
(b) the duty of care and competence;[27]
(c) the duty to act *intra vires* the company;[28]
(d) the duty to maintain proper books of accounts;[29]
(e) the duty to take care when making a declaration of solvency in connection with the giving of financial assistance for the purchase of shares in the company;[30]
(f) statutory duties owed to the company's creditors under the fraudulent and reckless trading provisions of the Principal Act.

---

25 Section 139 of the Principal Act.
26 See Chapter 18.
27 Ibid.
28 Ibid.
29 Section 202 of the Companies Act 1990: see Chapter 19.
30 Section 60(5) of the Principal Act: see Chapter 10.

The Application of Assets

Once the assets have been realised the liquidator must then apply the proceeds among the creditors of the company in accordance with the provisions of the Companies Acts. If any surplus is available after these debts have been discharged, it will be distributed among the company's shareholders. Before any distributions will be made to creditors their claims must be proved.

1. Proving Claims

Section 283(1) of the Principal Act sets out those debts which may be proved in a winding up. All debts payable on a contingency, and all claims for damages against the company, whether present or future, certain or contingent, are admissible to proof against the company. The liquidator will advise the creditors of the company, in the form of an advertisement, as to where they should send their claims. When the claims are submitted the liquidator must then ascertain their validity. He will notify all claims to the High Court examiner who will adjudicate upon them. Irrespective of whether a claim is allowed or requires further proof, the liquidator must notify the relevant creditors. Where claims require further proof the examiner will fix a time for the creditors to attend and where necessary provide such information as the examiner or liquidator may require by way of affidavit. Any final adjudication must be certified by the examiner.

2. Order of Distribution of the Assets

Once the liquidator has established the valid claims he must apply the assets. There are detailed rules in the Companies Acts as well as the Bankruptcy Acts which determine the manner and priority in which the assets must be applied. If the company has sufficient assets to meet its liabilities there is unlikely to be a dispute regarding the application of assets. It is where the assets are insufficient that a jostling for pole position among creditors, attempting to maximise their recovery, will occur. As already mentioned, creditors must be treated equally on a *pari passu* basis.[31] However, there are a number of exceptions to the *pari passu* principle and in practice its application is more appropriate to classes of creditors. Accordingly, if there is any shortfall in the assets, which will usually be the situation in an insolvent winding up, all creditors in the same class must have the amount owing to them reduced on a *pro rata* basis. Class creditors may, for example, each receive fifty cent for every euro owing to them. While the amount may vary depending on the availability of assets the principle of equality remains, so that a class creditor cannot receive a greater amount than another creditor from a distribution to a particular class. Of course, a creditor may belong to a number of different classes with the result that his consolidated position,

---

31 See section 275 of the Principal Act.

following a distribution to all classes, appears superior to that of other creditors. Once the classes of creditors and members have been established, the following rules generally apply regarding the distribution of assets.

Expenses of an Examiner

Where a company is wound up following a period of court protection, section 29(3) of the Companies (Amendment) Act 1990 provide that the remuneration, costs and expenses of the examiner shall be paid before any other claim, whether secured or unsecured.

Costs of the Winding Up

When a liquidator is appointed he will require remuneration and will always incur expenses. A liquidation may necessarily be dragged out over a long period of time, and some have been known to last for years. Obviously a liquidator is not going to invest his time, energy and resources into a winding up if there is a risk that he will not get paid. It is for this reason that a priority position is given to the costs of a winding up. In the case of a voluntary winding up, section 281 of the Principal Act provides that all costs, charges and expenses properly incurred in the winding up, including the remuneration of the liquidator, shall be payable out of the assets of the company in priority to all other claims.

In the case of a compulsory winding up, section 244 of the Principal Act provides that the court may, where the assets are insufficient to satisfy the liabilities, make an order as to the payment from the assets of the costs, charges and expenses incurred in such order of priority as the court thinks just. This section is supplemented by the Rules of the Superior Court 1986[32] which provides for a priority for the fees and expenses incurred in preserving and realising the assets of the company, which includes the remuneration, costs and expenses the court may allow to a liquidator where the company had previously commenced to be wound up voluntarily. Furthermore, the remaining assets must then be applied to meet the costs of the petition, the costs incurred in making a statement of affairs, any remaining disbursements of the official liquidator, the costs of the solicitor for the official liquidator, the remuneration of the official liquidator and the out-of-pocket expenses, if any, of the committee of inspection.

Secured Creditors

Generally speaking, secured creditors[33] may opt out of the insolvency queue because they have the right to realise or otherwise deal with their security.[34]

---

32 Order 74, rule 128.
33 Defined by section 3 of the Bankruptcy Act 1988 as 'any creditor holding any mortgage, charge or lien on the debtor's estate or any part thereof as security for a debt due to him'.
34 Section 136(20) of the Bankruptcy Act 1988.

However, a secured creditor has a number of other options open to him. These are set out in paragraph 24 of the First Schedule to the Bankruptcy Act 1988, which provides that he may:

(a) realise the security and claim any shortfall;
(b) value the security and claim any shortfall;
(c) surrender the security and claim for the full debt.

It should be noted that not all secured creditors are entitled to realise their security in priority to other creditors. Holders of fixed charges over book debts may be subordinated to the claims of certain preferential creditors, namely VAT and PAYE.[35] Furthermore, all holders of floating charges are subordinated to the claims of preferential creditors.

Preferential Creditors

Legislation has ordained that certain creditors should obtain a priority position in the insolvency queue. Section 285 of the Principal Act confers preferential status on the following:

(a) all local rates and taxes due and payable within twelve months before the relevant date;
(b) taxes, including income tax and corporation taxes, assessed on the company up to the preceding 5 April, provided it does not exceed one year's liability;
(c) sums due in respect of PAYE deductions in the twelve months prior to the relevant date;
(d) wages and salaries of employees in respect of services rendered to the company during the four months preceding the relevant date up to a maximum of £2,500 (€3,174) in each case;
(e) accrued holiday remuneration for employees;
(f) except where the company is being wound up for the purposes of reconstruction or amalgamation –
   (i) national insurance and social welfare contributions for the twelve months before the relevant date;
   (ii) amounts due under workmen's compensation legislation and damages for injuries to employees except where covered by insurance;
(g) sums due under any scheme to employees absent owing to sickness and any sums due from the company under any superannuation scheme.

Where payments in respect of employees' wages, salaries and holiday pay are funded by another party such as a bank, it has the right of subrogation under section 285(6) of the Principal Act. Accordingly, it may step into the shoes of the preferential creditors to obtain a priority position.

---

35 Section 115 of the Principal Act as amended by section 174 of the Finance Act 1995, now section 1001 Taxes Consolidated Act 1997: see Chapter 11.

In addition to the above mentioned categories, employment legislation elevates the following payments to preferential status in a winding up situation:

(a) any compensation payable by the company under the Unfair Dismissals Act 1977;[36]
(b) payments under the Redundancy Payments Act 1967;[37]
(c) amounts payable under the Minimum Notice and Terms of Employment Act 1973;[38]
(d) payments made by the Minister in respect of the company's obligations under any of the above.[39]

In the event that there are insufficient assets to meet the preferential payments, all preferential creditors will rank equally among themselves.[40] Preferential status will apply only to those debts which have been notified or have become known to the liquidator within six months of his advertisement for claims.

Floating Charges

Once the preferential creditors have been satisfied, the floating charge-holders are next in the insolvency queue. Where more than one floating charge is created over the same property and each is properly registered under section 99 of the Principal Act, the charge that was created first will rank first in terms of priority.

Unsecured Creditors

If and when the floating charge-holders have been paid in full, the next in line are the ordinary unsecured creditors. Unfortunately, in the case of most insolvent liquidations the unsecured creditors will not recover the full amount owing to them. Where there are insufficient assets available, the unsecured creditors must be treated on a *pari passu* basis. As mentioned earlier, section 283 of the Principal Act sets out the types of claims which may be proved but the section specifically excludes, unless the articles provide otherwise, dividends declared more than six years previously which have not been claimed.[41] The difficulty that arises in relation to applying assets among this class of creditors is that some of the claims may be contingent and therefore difficult to value. The usual practice is for the court to make an estimate of the value of the claim subject to a right to amend the claim at a later date, provided the amended claim does not interfere with distributions already made.[42]

---

36 Section 12.
37 Section 42.
38 Section 13.
39 Protection of Employees (Employer's Insolvency) Act 1984.
40 Section 285(7)(a) of the Principal Act.
41 Section 283(2) of the Principal Act.
42 For a detailed discussion of the rights of contingent creditors, see Lynch, Marshall and O'Ferrall, *Corporate Insolvency and Rescue* (Butterworths) 1996.

Members and Contributories

In the event that having satisfied all the creditors' claims assets are still available, they will be distributed among the members of the company according to their rights and interests in the company.[43] These rights and interests will usually be determined by the articles of association.[44]

Where members are also contributories of the company, adjustments of their rights may be necessary. In the case of a compulsory liquidation, the court has the power to settle the list of contributories and adjust their rights taking into account any sums due to them.[45] In the case of a voluntary liquidation, it is the liquidator that carries out this task.[46] Having made the appropriate adjustments, the court or the liquidator, as the case may be, will distribute any surplus among the contributories.

---

43 Section 275(1)(b) of the Principal Act.
44 See Chapter 5.
45 Section 242 of the Principal Act.
46 Section 276(2) of the Principal Act.

CHAPTER TWENTY-SEVEN

COURT PROTECTION

Introduction

Companies unable to pay their debts have traditionally been at the mercy of creditors who can appoint a receiver or cause a liquidator to be appointed. Such actions, however justifiable from the creditors' point of view, usually bring about the demise of the company. This situation was recognised as far back as 1897 when Lord McNaughten in *Salomon v. Salomon* exclaimed, 'Everybody knows that when there is a winding-up, debenture-holders generally step in and sweep off everything. And a great scandal that is.'[1]

For a number of years preceding 1990, demand existed in Ireland for a system to protect companies in financial difficulties from the predatory grasp of creditors whose actions could bring about the company's demise, sometimes prematurely. A new procedure was introduced by the Companies (Amendment) Act 1990 (The 1990 Act) designed to meet this need.

A company which is, *inter alia*, unable to pay its debts may be placed under the protection of the court for a period of time generally not exceeding seventy days. The object of such protection is twofold. First, the company is 'immunised' from actions by creditors, and second, an examiner is appointed to investigate its affairs and make proposals for its survival through a compromise or scheme of arrangement (if possible), so as to keep the company, or part of it, alive as a going concern. McCarthy J. in *Re Atlantic Magnetics Ltd*[2] summarised the intention behind the legislation:

> ... its purpose is protection — protection of the company and consequently of its shareholders workforce and creditors. It is clear that parliament intended that the fate of the company and those who depend upon it should not lie solely in the hands of one or more large creditors who can by appointing a receiver pursuant to a debenture effectively terminate its operation and secure as best they may the discharge of the monies due to them to the inevitable disadvantage of those less protected, the Act is to provide a breathing space albeit at the expense of some creditor or creditors.

The 1990 Act had been hurried into law to prevent the collapse of the Goodman Group of companies and the negative impact that such a collapse would have had on the Irish economy. The Act was fraught with difficulties and was perceived by lending institutions as anti-creditor in its approach. Indeed, the survival of a company under court protection usually had a disadvantageous

---

1 (1897) App Cas 22 HL.
2 [1993] 2 IR 561.

effect on those creditors who would have had superior priority status in a receivership or liquidation scenario. A further criticism of the Act was that it did not give sufficient focus to viable companies.[3] Indeed, many of the companies that used the court protection procedure ultimately failed.

To deal with the perceived weaknesses of the court protection procedure, the Companies (Amendment) (No.2) Act 1999 introduced a number of amendments to the 1990 Act. Many of these amendments reflect the recommendations made in the First Report of the Company Law Review Group.

The Petition

The process of applying for court protection commences with the petition. All petitions are presented to the High Court, which may, if the liabilities of the company are less than IR£250,000 (€317,436), remit the matter to the relevant Circuit Court.

Section 3(1) of the Act lists those persons who may petition the court, and they are as follows:

Directors

In *Re Don Bluth Entertainment Ltd (No. 1)*,[4] Murphy J. held that three of the five directors were entitled to present a petition on behalf of the directors, despite an objection from the other two directors.

The Company

The Act does not specify whether an ordinary or special resolution is required. However, in the above case Murphy J. accepted that, as the decision of the directors to petition for the appointment of an examiner was made pursuant to a properly convened board meeting, the directors were in fact acting on behalf of the company even though the petition was presented in the names of the directors.

The Creditors

Creditors include contingent and prospective creditors, and employees. Where an application is made by any one of these three categories, they are required to put up such security for costs as the court considers reasonable until such time as a prima facie case for the appointment of an examiner has been established to the satisfaction of the court.

The Members

The legislation permits members to petition for the appointment where they hold at least one-tenth of the fully paid-up voting capital.

---

3 Report of the Company Law Review Group 1994.
4 High Court, 27 August 1992 (Murphy J.).

In the case of insurance companies, banks and companies supervised by the Central Bank, the petitioning parties vary from the Section 3(1) list.[5] In the case of insurance companies, only the Minister may present a petition. In the case of banks, only the Central Bank may do so and, in the case of all non-banks supervised by the Central Bank, only the Central Bank and those parties listed in section 3(1) may petition the court. However, where the company, its directors, creditors or members petition the court in such circumstances, they must give notice to the Central Bank which will be entitled to be heard at any hearing relating to the petition.

Contents of the Petition

The petition, when presented, must nominate a person to be appointed as examiner[6] and it must be accompanied by a consent signed by the person nominated.[7] A person is only qualified to be an examiner if he is qualified to be a liquidator of the company. The report must also be accompanied by a report of an 'Independent Accountant' who is either the auditor of the company or who is qualified to be the auditor of the company.[8] The petition may be accompanied by a copy of the proposals for a compromise or scheme of arrangement (if they have been prepared) for submission to interested parties.

The Independent Accountant's Report

The report of the Independent Accountant shall comprise the following:

(a) details of the identity of the company directors, other officers and shadow directors;
(b) details of other companies of which the directors are also directors;
(c) a statement of affairs of the company setting out the debts, assets, liabilities, and identity of all creditors and details of all securities held by them;
(d) a statement of opinion by the independent accountant as to whether any deficiency between the assets and liabilities of the company have been satisfactorily accounted for or, if not, whether there is evidence of a substantial disappearance of property that is not adequately accounted for;
(e) a statement of opinion by the independent accountant as to whether the company, and the whole or any part of its undertaking, would have a reasonable prospect of survival as a going concern and a statement of the conditions which he feels are essential to ensure such survival, whether as regards the internal management and controls of the company or otherwise;

---

5 Section 3(2) of the 1990 Act.
6 Section 3(3) ibid.
7 Section 3(4) ibid.
8 Section 3(3A) ibid.

(f) a statement of opinion as to whether the formulation, acceptance and confirmation of proposals for a compromise or scheme of arrangement with the company's creditors and members would offer a reasonable prospect of the survival of the company, and the whole or any part if its undertaking, as a going concern;

(g) his opinion as to whether an attempt to continue the whole or part of the undertaking of the company would be likely to be more advantageous to the members as a whole, and the creditors as a whole, than a winding-up;

(h) his recommendations as to the course he thinks should be taken in relation to the company, including, if warranted, draft proposals for a compromise or scheme of arrangement;

(i) his opinion as whether the facts disclosed would warrant further inquiries with a view to proceedings under the fraudulent and reckless trading provisions of the Principal Act;

(j) details of the extent of the funding required to enable the company to continue trading during the period of protection and the sources of that funding;

(k) his recommendations as to which pre-petition liabilities should be paid;

(l) his opinion as to whether the work of the examiner would be assisted by a direction of the court extending the role and membership of the creditors committee; and

(m) any other matters he considers relevant.[9]

The requirement to present an independent accountant's report is a new measure introduced by the 1999 Act and meets some of the criticisms levelled against the 1990 Act. Firstly, prior the 1999 Act, the High Court had very little to go on in terms of gleaning the financial position of the company and its future prospects. Secondly, before 1999, the examinership process had proven in many cases to be expensive in terms of those 'certified expenses' which would allow the company to continue trading. Such expense would not necessarily have been anticipated at the petition stage. The courts are now in a better position to judge the overall financial state of the company, the funding required to allow it trade while under the court protection and the source of that funding.

Interim Protection Pending Independent Accountant's Report

Where there are exceptional circumstances outside the control of the petitioner that could not have been reasonably anticipated by him, the court may appoint an interim examiner for a period of ten days pending submission of the independent accountant's report.[10] What will constitute 'exceptional circumstances' remains to be seen, however, the legislation is clear about the fact that the mere appointment of a receiver will not itself constitute 'exceptional circumstances'.

---

9 Section 3(3B) ibid.
10 Section 3A.

Where the court makes an interim order of this nature and the petition has been presented by the members or the creditors of the company, then the company directors must co-operate in the preparation of the independent accountant's report.

If the independent accountant's report is not presented within ten days, the company ceases to be under the protection of the court although a new petition may be presented under section 2.

Uberrima Fides

The Court, on numerous occasions, has stated that all petitions must be made in the utmost good faith. In *Re Seluckwe Ltd*,[11] Costello J. held that there was evidence of a considerable lack of good faith on behalf of the petitioning directors and a lack of candour throughout the examination process. Nevertheless, he confirmed the proposals, subject to modification, on the grounds *inter alia* that the jobs of thirty employees were at stake. In *Re Wogan's Drogheda Ltd*[12] Costello J. said that the utmost good faith is required because the court must depend, to a considerable extent, on the truth of what it is told by the company. If such information is misleading, a potential injustice could arise in the making of a protection order, when the proper course is to wind up the company. He went onto say that in certain circumstances a serious lack of good faith could ultimately result in the examiner being discharged and the examiner's proposals being rejected.

This requirement of 'good faith' has now been codified into legislation. Section 4A provides that the court may decline to hear a petition if it appears that the petitioner, or the independent accountant, has failed to disclose information material to the court in exercising its powers or has in any other way failed to exercise the utmost good faith. The amendment does not impose a statutory duty of good faith on the examiner himself. Presumably, under the authority of the High Court decision in the case of *Re Wogan's Drogheda*, such a requirement remains.

The Hearing

The court will not make an order dismissing a petition or appointing an examiner without allowing each creditor an opportunity to be heard, if so desired.[13] All proceedings under the Act, whether at the hearing stage or later, may be held *in camera* if the court, in the interests of justice, considers that the interests of the company concerned, or its creditors as a whole, so require.

Section 3(6) provides that the court will not give hearing to a petition if a receiver stands appointed to the company for more than three days.

---

11 High Court, 20 December 1991 (Costello J.).

12 High Court, 7 May 1992 (Costello J.).

13 Section 3B, Companies (Amendment) Act 1990.

Appointing an Examiner

Although discretion is given to the court to decide whether or not to appoint the examiner, section 2(1) does lay down one positive and two negative criteria which must exist before the court has the power to use its discretion, namely that:

(a) a company is, or is likely, to be unable to pay its debts; and
(b) no resolution subsists for the winding up of the company; and
(c) no order has been made for the winding up of the company.

A company is deemed to be unable to pay its debts in any of the following circumstances:

(a) if it is unable to pay them as they fall due (the commercial solvency test);
(b) where the value of its liabilities exceeds its assets (the balance sheet solvency test); or
(c) where section 214(a) or (b) of the Principal Act applies to the company.

In determining the company's insolvency, the court may also have regard to negotiations between the company and its creditors for the re-scheduling of the company's debts, from which it can be reasonably inferred that the company is likely to be unable to pay its debts.

Assuming that these conditions are satisfied, the Court is guided further by the legislation. Section 2(2) provides that the court may make an order appointing an examiner if it considers that there is a 'reasonable prospect' of survival of the company, and the whole or any part of it, as a going concern. The requirement of a 'reasonable prospect' of survival was introduced by the 1999 Act and gives statutory support to the test laid down by Lardner J. in *Re Atlantic Magnetic Ltd.*[14]

The availability of the independent accountant's report, together with the onus of establishing a 'reasonable prospect' of survival, suggest that the onus on the petitioner will be more burdensome than heretofore. As McCracken J. stated in *Re Tuskar Resources*:[15]

> ... the new [requirement] prohibits the court from making an order unless it is satisfied there is a reasonable prospect of survival. If the court is to be 'satisfied' it must be satisfied on the evidence before it, which is in the first instance the evidence of the Petitioner. If that evidence does not satisfy the Court, the order cannot be made and in my view this is tantamount to saying that there is an onus of proof on the Petitioner at the initial stage to satisfy the court that there is a reasonable prospect of survival. For this reason the Court has to view the evidence in a different manner to that applicable prior to the 1999 Act.

---

14 [1993] 2 IR 561. The Company Law Review Group also recommended the adoption of the 'reasonable prospect' test.
15 [2001] 1 IR 668.

The court will not appoint an examiner if the company cannot survive as a 'going concern'. In *Re Tuskar Resources*, a petition was made to appoint an examiner to a holding company whose main asset was shares in a Nigerian company. The court held that such a holding could not constitute a 'going concern' and refused to allow an examiner to be appointed. Furthermore, the proposal to transfer the business of another company into the holding company was deemed to be outside the scope of the Act as it was introducing a new 'undertaking' to the company. This, said McCracken J., was more the job of a liquidator than that of an examiner whose purpose is to rescue an existing undertaking.

Notification Requirements

The petitioner must deliver a notice of the petition to the Registrar of Companies within three days of its presentation.[16]

Within three days of his appointment, the examiner must deliver to the Registrar of Companies a certified copy of the court order appointing him. He must also advertise the fact of his appointment in two daily newspapers within the same time frame. Within twenty-one days, he must put similar notices in *Iris Oifigiúil*.

Every invoice, order for goods or business letter issued by or on behalf of the company, being a document on, or in which, the name of the company appears, must immediately after the name, include the words: 'in examination (under the Companies (Amendment) Act 1990)'.

Effects of Court Protection

If the Court appoints an examiner, the period of protection commences from the date of the presentation of the petition and ends on the expiry of seventy days, or such earlier date as the court may terminate the protection. However, under section 18(3), the time period may be extended by the court for a further thirty days, if the court is satisfied that the examiner can not report to the court within the initial seventy-day period. Under section18(4), the court may grant a further extension to allow it consider the examiner's report. It has usually been only in the rarest circumstance that the court has had to invoke the latter sub-section. In the Goodman and Kentz examinerships, which involved a number of companies and complex negotiations with domestic and overseas creditors and investors, such extensions were permitted.

Section 5, as amended, lists many of the consequences of court protection which effectively suspend all actions by members and creditors (including contingent and prospective creditors) against the company. These consequences are as follows:

---

16 Section 12(1) ibid.

(a) a winding-up of the company can not be initiated;

(b) a receiver can not be appointed, and if appointed within the three days prior to the appointment of an examiner, he must cease to act unless directed otherwise by the court;

(c) no attachment, execution, distress or sequestration can be enforced against the company's property or effects without the consent of the examiner;

(d) secured creditors cannot take steps to realise their security without the consent of the examiner. In *Re Holdair Ltd*[17], instructions from a lending institution to the company to lodge fixed charge receivables into a designated bank account during the court protection period was held to be an action prohibited by this section;

(e) no steps can be taken to repossess goods in the company's possession under any hire–purchase agreement, including conditional sale and retention of title agreements;

(f) no relief under section 205 of the Principal Act can be granted by the court to members against the company concerning the conduct of the affairs of the company or the exercise of the powers of the director prior to the presentation of the petition;

(g) no guarantees by third parties on behalf of the company can be enforced; and

(h) no other proceedings can be commenced against the company except by leave of the court.

In addition to the above, no pre-petition debts can be paid by the company unless the report of the independent accountant contains a recommendation stating that such debts be paid and the court considers that a failure to do so would considerably reduce the prospects of the company, or the whole or any part of its undertaking, surviving as a going concern.[18]

The position of guarantors has now been clarified by the 1999 Act. As mentioned above, a guarantor of a company's debts is protected during the period of court protection. However, under the new section 25A of the 1990 Act, a company creditor can take legal action against the guarantor after the court protection has ended.

Creditor's Committee

An examiner may, and if directed by the Court shall, appoint a Committee of Creditors to assist him in the performance of his functions.[19] Except as otherwise directed by the Court, a committee appointed shall consist of not more than five members and shall include, where they are willing to serve, the holders of the three largest unsecured claims. The examiner should provide the committee with

17 [1994] I IR 416.
18 Section 5A, Companies (Amendment) Act 1990.
19 Section 21, ibid.

a copy of any proposals for a compromise or scheme of arrangement and the committee may express an opinion on the proposals on its own behalf, or on behalf of the creditors or classes of creditors represented thereon.

Receiver and Provisional Liquidator

If a receiver has been appointed not less than three days prior to the successful petition, the court may make any such order as it sees fit including that the receiver shall cease to act, or act only in respect of certain assets, or that he must deliver all books, papers and other records which relate to the goods or possessions in his control to the examiner, or to give the examiner full particulars of all his dealings with the property or undertaking of the company. If a provisional liquidator is already appointed, the court may make similar orders including an order that the provisional liquidator is appointed the examiner. The court will only make an order in relation to a receiver or provisional liquidator if it is satisfied that there is a reasonable prospect of the survival of the company, and the whole or any part of its undertaking, as a going concern.

Related Companies

Under section 4, the examiner may apply to the court for protection of any related company even when that company is not insolvent or near insolvent. The application must be grounded on the examiner's belief that court protection would facilitate the survival of the original company as a going concern. The protection period for related companies only commences from the date of the court order.

Powers of the Examiner

In order to carry out his statutory duties and functions, the examiner has extensive powers. Some of these are automatic from the date of his appointment and others are only available on application to the court. The examiner's discretionary powers are detailed to a large extent in sections 7 and 8, and include the following:

(a) all the powers and rights of an auditor;
(b) the power to convene, set the agenda for, and preside over meetings of the board of directors and general meetings;
(c) the right to be given reasonable notice of, to attend and be heard at, all board meetings and general meetings;
(d) the power to take whatever steps are necessary to halt, prevent or rectify the effects of any act, omission, course of conduct, decision or contract by any party in relation to the assets or liabilities of the company which, in the examiner's opinion, is or is likely to be detrimental to the company or any interested party. This power does not enable the examiner to repudiate a

contract entered into prior to court protection. A provision in any contract preventing the company from borrowing or giving security can not be enforced if the examiner is under the opinion that, were it enforced, it would be likely to prejudice the survival of the company as a going concern. The examiner must serve notice on the parties concerned informing him of his opinion in this regard;

(e) to apply to the court to determine any question arising in the course of his office;

(f) in ascertaining the affairs of the company, an examiner has extensive investigative powers. These powers are supported by a corresponding statutory duty imposed on officers and agents of the company to produce, on the examiner's request, such books and documents including those relating to bank accounts held by directors or officers of the company.

Specific Powers

The Act also provides the examiner with specific powers which are subject to court approval. While each power in its own right appears necessary to enable the examiner to carry out his functions, when they are used together they can have a serious effect on secured creditors.

Directors' Powers

The appointment of an examiner does not affect directors' powers. They will continue to manage the business of the company unless the examiner applies to the court, under section 9, to have all or any of the directors' powers vested in him. One such power granted frequently to examiners is the directors' power to borrow on behalf of the company. In one case, the question arose as to whether the examiner's power of borrowing is subject to the same restrictions that apply to the directors' power. *In Re Holdair Ltd* [20] the examiner had applied for and obtained orders authorising him to borrow monies in order to facilitate the survival of the company as a going concern. Under the terms of a debenture, the directors of the company had been restricted from borrowing without the prior consent of the debenture holders. The court held that the examiner was not so restricted. Although Finlay C.J. felt that the examiner's borrowing was permitted under section 9, he decided the matter by reference to section 7(5) of the Act which enables an examiner to halt, prevent, or rectify, the effects of, *inter alia*, any contract which in his opinion is likely to be detrimental to the company.

Dealing with Property

Under section 11 of the Act, the examiner may apply to the court for leave to dispose of the company's property where he is of the opinion that such action

---

20 [1994] 1 IR 416.

would facilitate the survival of the company. Such property includes that which is subject to a floating or fixed charge, or goods that are in the possession of the company but are subject to a hire-purchase, conditional sale or retention of title agreement. However, the section provides for the proceeds of the sale of such property or goods to be applied towards discharging the amounts owed under the security. In addition, holders of fixed charges are in an even stronger position than the holders of other interests described above, because the court can ascertain the market value of the property subject to the charge and order that the difference between that amount and the actual proceeds will be paid to the fixed-charge holder.

The court will not permit the sale of the company's business and assets where the effect would be such that the company could no longer trade. In *Re Clare Textiles Ltd*,[21] the examiner had entered into conditional contracts for the sale of the company's premises, business, stock and machinery, which he stated would cause the company to cease trading and go into liquidation. Costello J. made it clear that the function of the examinership was to facilitate (if possible) the survival of the company, or the whole or part of its undertaking, as a going concern and not act as liquidator, and on this basis the examiner had no power to enter into such contracts.

Certification of Expenses

One of the most controversial sections in the Act is section 10 which gives the examiner power to certify expenditure incurred during the period of court protection. Such expenditure must have been incurred in circumstances where, in the opinion of the examiner, the survival of the company would otherwise be seriously prejudiced. In addition, those liabilities of the company certified under section 10 will be treated as expenses incurred by the examiner for the purposes of section 29 of the Act. In the event that a company is wound up, this section gives priority to the payment of the examiner's expenses over all other claims including secured (with the exception of fixed charges) and preferential creditors.

Section 10 does not require the examiner's certification to be approved by the court in advance. In *Re Don Bluth Entertainment Ltd*[22] it was contended by the examiner that section 10 conferred upon him a discretion that could not be reviewed by the court. He also argued that if it was reviewable, then this could only be done on the grounds that certification was carried out in bad faith, for an improper purpose, or that it was manifestly unreasonable. He went on to argue that if the court declined to sanction the expenses that arose, it would render null and void a decision properly made by the examiner and defeat the reasonable expectations of the creditors who dealt with the company in reliance of the

---

21 [1993] 2 IR 213.
22 [1994] 3 IR 141.

statutory powers which the examiner purported to exercise. Murphy J. rejected this argument and went on to say:

> As the combined operation of ss. 10 and 29 of the Act of 1990 will frequently result in some creditors of a company being paid in full at the expense of the creditors who hold securities over the assets of the company or creditors who have enjoyed a statutory preference under section 285 of the Act of 1963 if the insolvency of the company in question had resulted in a liquidation rather than an Examinership, it is important that an Examiner should exercise great care and professional expertise in issuing certificates under section 10 aforesaid.

He went on to hold that expenses certified by the examiner in relation to the pre-petition and petition costs of the company were not expenses properly so called within the meaning of section 10. That provision, he said, did not confer any priority on the costs of petitioners and he added that it would seem to him: 'to be inappropriate to alter the scheme of the Act by the fortuitous event that a provisional or interim Examiner might be appointed.' For similar reasons the High Court also rejected pre-petition costs as certifiable expenses of the examiner in *Re Edenpark Construction Ltd.*[23]

Combined Powers

In *Re Atlantic Magnetics Ltd*, the Court considered for the first time the combined effect of the above powers. The issue before the court was whether the examiner could use certain receivables — the subject of an existing fixed charge — to discharge the expenses of examination, including the borrowings of the examiner, during the protection process. The court was essentially asked to reconcile section 29 of the Act with section 11. Reading the sections together the court held that the examiner could apply the assets — the subject matter of a fixed charge — to pay his borrowings, effectively ignoring the charge. This position was reaffirmed by the Supreme Court in *Re Holdair Limited.*[24] The implications of this judgment for secured creditors were severe. A lender who had provided borrowings on a 'back-to-back' basis — in other words secured by cash balances — would traditionally have been in the strongest position in the event of the company's insolvency. In the event of an examiner being appointed, such cash balances would be the most attractive as they are readily available to meet the examiner's costs. This would put the secured creditor in an untenable situation as his security would become ineffective. Even if there are no readily available assets such as cash, the examiner could borrow monies, as he did in the Atlantic Magnetics case, and certify the borrowings as expenses within the meaning of section 29. The lender to the examiner would therefore be paid before all other creditors including those holding fixed charges.

---

23 [1994] 3 IR 126.
24 [1994] I IR 416.

The 1999 Act has rectified this position somewhat. Now, the remuneration costs and expenses of the examiner where sanctioned by the court, take priority over all other claims, whether secured or unsecured. However, expenses 'certified' by the examiner under section 10, while still maintaining a priority status in terms of other claims including floating charges, do not have a priority over fixed charges or pledges.

Hearing Concerning Irregularities

Under section 13A of the 1990 Act, the court may hold a hearing if irregularities in the report of the independent accountant are discovered. Creditors are entitled to attend and be heard at such sittings. Following a hearing of this kind, the court may make such orders as it deems fit, including, where appropriate, an order for the trial of any issue relating to the matter concerned.

Proposals for a Compromise or Scheme of Arrangement.

The examiner's primary duty is to formulate proposals for a compromise or scheme of arrangement.[25] In this regard, he has the power to convene and preside at meetings of members and creditors, to consider the proposals and report to the court within thirty-five days of his appointment or such longer period as the court may allow. At plenary meetings of members and creditors the examiner's proposals can be modified, but only with his consent.

The contents of the proposals for a compromise or scheme of arrangement are set out in section 22(1) of the Act. The proposals must:

(a) specify each class of the company's members and creditors;
(b) specify those classes of members and creditors whose interests or claims will not be impaired by the proposals together with those who will be impaired by the proposals;
(c) provide equal treatment for each claim or interest of a particular class unless the holder of a particular class or interest agrees to less favourable treatment;
(d) provide for the implementation of the proposals;
(e) specify whatever changes should be made in relation to the management or direction of the company where the examiner considers it necessary or desirable to do so in order to facilitate the survival of the company;
(f) specify any changes the examiner considers should be made to the memorandum or articles of the company with regard to the management or direction of the company;
(g) contain any other matters which the examiner considers appropriate;
(h) contain any such other matters as the court may direct.

A statement of the assets and liabilities of the company at the date of the proposals must be attached. There should also be attached a description of the

---

25 Section 18(1).

estimated financial outcome of a winding-up for each class of members and creditors.

Proposals will be deemed to be accepted by a meeting of members if a majority of the votes cast are in favour of the resolution for the proposals. The proposals are deemed to have been accepted by the creditors when a majority in number, representing a majority in value of the claims represented at the meeting, have voted in favour of the resolution for the proposals.[26]

If the proposals cannot be agreed by at least one class of creditors, the matter will return for consideration to the court which may direct that the company be wound up.

The Examiner's Report

The examiner is required to report back to the court within thirty-five days of his appointment. The contents of the report are set out in section 19 and include:

(a) the proposals, if any;
(b) any adopted modifications of the proposals;
(c) the outcome of each meeting;
(d) the committee of creditors' recommendations, if any;
(e) a statement of the company's assets and liabilities (including contingent and prospective creditors);
(f) a list of the officers of the company;
(g) the company's creditors, the amount owed to each of them and their priority status in an insolvency context (see Chapter 26, Assets Realisation and Distribution);
(h) a list of the company's officers;
(i) the examiner's recommendations; and
(j) any such other matters as the examiner deems appropriate or the Court directs.

The examiner must deliver a copy of his report to the company on the same day as he delivers it to the court. Furthermore, the examiner must provide a copy of his report to any interested party upon a written application being made to him. The court may direct that the supply of such a report be the subject of an omission particularly, if otherwise, it would prejudice the survival of the company, or the whole or any part of it, as a going concern.

The report shall be set down for consideration by the court as soon as possible thereafter. The company and any creditor or member whose claim or interest will be impaired if the proposals were implemented may appear at the hearing to consider the report. Section 22(5) defines an impaired creditor as one who receives less in payment of his claim than the full amount due at the date of

---

26 Section 23.

presentation of the petition. In *Re Jetmara Teo Ltd*[27] Costello J. rejected a contention by the examiner that a lending institution which was to be repaid in full, although over a longer period of time than had been contractually agreed and without interest, was not an impaired creditor. At such court hearings, any member or creditor whose rights are impaired may object to the proposals on the following grounds:[28]

1. That irregularities existed in, or at, the plenary meetings of the creditors or members.
2. That acceptance of the proposals was obtained by improper means.
3. That the proposals were put forward for an improper purpose.
4. That the proposals were unfairly prejudicial to the interests of the objector.

If any such objection is upheld, the court may order that the decision be set aside and that another plenary meeting be held. As a rule, the court may as it thinks fit, confirm the proposals unconditionally, confirm them subject to modifications or reject them entirely.[29] However, it will not accept them in the following circumstances:

(a) unless at least one class of creditors whose interests or claims would be impaired by the implementation of the proposals has accepted the proposals; or
(b) where the sole or primary purpose of the proposals is the avoidance of the payment of taxes;[30] or
(c) where the court is not satisfied that the proposals are fair and equitable in relation to any class of impaired creditors which has not accepted the proposals; or
(d) where the proposals are not unfairly prejudicial to any other interested party. In *Re Seluckwe Ltd*[31] Costello J. modified proposals which involved the release of two directors' personal guarantees. However, in *Re Antigen Holdings Ltd*[32] the court approved a scheme of arrangement where shareholders benefited from the scheme before all creditors had been paid off. Confirming the scheme where there was a high prospect of success, McCracken J. declared: 'disproportionately disadvantaged does not constitute unfairly prejudicial.'

Where the court confirms proposals, whether modified or not, they are binding on all members and creditors affected by the proposals, and also on the company. The court may make such orders as it deems fit for the implementation of the compromise or scheme of arrangement. The compromise or scheme of arrangement shall come into effect from a date fixed by the court which must be

---

27 [1992] I IR 147.
28 Section 25.
29 section 24(3).
30 Section 24(4).
31 High Court, 20 December 1991 (Costello J.)
32 Unreported, High Court, 8 November 2001 (McCracken J.)

within twenty-one days from the date of confirmation. A copy of the confirmation order must be given to the Registrar of Companies and published in *Iris Oifigiúil* by the examiner within fourteen days of the order being granted.

If the company and any other interested party can show that the confirmation was procured by fraud, they can apply to the court within 180 days of the confirmation to have the decision revoked. If the court is satisfied that there was fraud, section 27 of the Act empowers it to revoke its confirmation or make such orders as it thinks fit. The court is directed by the Act to have regard for the interests of any bona fide purchaser for value of property who relied on the confirmation.

If the examiner's report is unfavourable to the extent that he does not believe that the company is capable of survival, he may apply to the court which may make such order as it deems fit including an order for the winding-up of the company.

Examiner's Costs Remuneration and Expenses

As already discussed, section 29 of the Act provides for the payment of the examiner's costs, remuneration and expenses before all other claims in the event of the liquidation of the company. We have seen where the court disapproved of certain certified expenses and a number of cases suggest that the court will do the same in relation to the examiner's costs and remuneration. In *Re Wogan's Drogheda Ltd* (No.3),[33] Costello J. refused to sanction the payment of the examiner's remuneration costs and expenses because he felt that the activities of the examiner were such as to abuse the court process. In *Re Clare Textiles Ltd*, Murphy J. held that the examiner's remuneration and costs would only be paid up to the point when he ought to have ceased acting as an examiner. In addition, he refused to allow the examiner his remuneration for completion of his statutory report as it did not comply with the requirements of the legislation. In *Re Coombe Importers Ltd*,[34] Hamilton C.J. refused to sanction expenses that had been certified by the examiner, on the grounds that they were not a necessary expense of the examinership. In *Re Edenpark Construction Ltd*,[35] Murphy J. appproved only 80 per cent of the examiner's fee because it was clear from the information provided that the court protection ought to have been terminated some time prior to when it did.

Termination of Court Protection

The protection granted to a company ends either:

(a) on the coming into effect of the compromise or scheme of arrangement under the Act, or

(b) on such earlier date as the Court may direct.

---

33 High Court, 9 February 1993 (Costello J.)
34 [1999] 1 IR 492.
35 [1994] 3 IR 126.

Index